DATE DUE

Don't
Never
Forget

Brigid Brophy

Don't
Never
Forget

Collected views and reviews

Holt, Rinehart
and Winston
New York   Chicago
San Francisco

81113—0117
Printed in the United States of America

Contents

I am certain of nothing but of the
holiness of the Heart's affections
and the truth of Imagination

JOHN KEATS

To
Anne Graham Bell

Note

People (even those who do not mean to be rude) often ask me whether my journalism interferes with my serious writing. As a matter of fact, my journalism *is* serious writing.

With one exception, which is explained on p. 50, all these pieces have been published or broadcast. I have in each case noted when and where—and have occasionally restored sentences which editors cut. I am (all the same) very grateful to all the editors concerned for permission to reprint.

BRIGID BROPHY

Morals
and Manners

The Rights of Animals

Sunday Times, October 1965

Were it announced tomorrow that anyone who fancied it might, without risk of reprisals or recriminations, stand at a fourth-storey window, dangle out of it a length of string with a meal (labelled 'Free') on the end, wait till a chance passer-by took a bite and then, having entangled his cheek or gullet on a hook hidden in the food, haul him up to the fourth floor and there batter him to death with a knobkerry, I do not think there would be many takers.

Most sane adults would, I imagine, sicken at the mere thought. Yet sane adults do the equivalent to fish every day: not in panic, sexual jealousy, ideological frenzy or even greed — many of our freshwater fish are virtually inedible, and not one of them constitutes a threat to the life, love or ideology of a human on the bank — but for amusement. Civilisation is not outraged at their behaviour. On the contrary: that a person's hobby is fishing is often read as a guarantee of his sterling and innocent character.

The relationship of *homo sapiens* to the other animals is one of unremitting exploitation. We employ their work; we eat and wear them. We exploit them to serve our superstitions: whereas we used to sacrifice them to our gods and tear out their entrails in order to foresee the future, we now sacrifice them to Science and experiment on their entrails in the hope — or on the mere off-chance — that we might thereby see a little more clearly into the present. When we can think of no pretext for causing their death and no profit to turn it to, we often cause it nonetheless, wantonly, the only gain being a brief pleasure for ourselves, which is usually only marginally bigger than the pleasure we could have had without killing anything; we could quite well enjoy our marksmanship or crosscountry galloping without requiring a real dead wild animal to shew for it at the end.

It is rare for us to leave wild animals alive; when we do, we often do not leave them wild. Some we put on display in a prison

15

just large enough for them to survive, but not in any full sense to live, in. Others we trundle about the country in their prisons, pausing every now and then to put them on public exhibition performing, like clockwork, 'tricks' we have 'trained' into them. However, animals are not clockwork but instinctual beings. Circus 'tricks' are spectacular or risible as the case may be precisely *because* they violate the animals' instinctual nature—which is precisely why they ought to violate both our moral and our aesthetic sense.

But where animals are concerned humanity seems to have switched off its morals and aesthetics—indeed, its very imagination. Goodness knows those faculties function erratically enough in our dealings with one another. But at least we recognise their faultiness. We spend an increasing number of our cooler moments trying to forestall the moral and aesthetic breakdowns which are liable, in a crisis, to precipitate us into atrocities against each other. We have bitter demarcation disputes about where the rights of one man end and those of the next man begin, but most men now acknowledge that there are such things as the rights of the next man. Only in relation to the next animal can civilised humans persuade themselves that they have absolute and arbitrary rights —that they may do anything whatever that they can get away with.

The reader will have guessed in some detail by now what sort of person he confronts in me: a sentimentalist; probably a killjoy; a person with no grasp on economic realities; a twee anthropomorphist, who attributes human feelings (and no doubt human names and clothes as well) to animals, and yet actually prefers animals to humans and would sooner succour a stray cat than an orphan child; a latter-day version of those folklore English spinsters who in the nineteenth century excited the ridicule of the natives by walking round Florence requesting them not to ill-treat their donkeys; and *par excellence*, of course, a crank.

Well. To take the last item first: if by 'crank' you mean 'abnormal', yes. My views are shared by only a smallish (but probably not so small as you think) part of the citizenry—as yet. Still, that proves nothing either way about the validity of our views. It is abnormal to be a lunatic convinced you are Napoleon, but equally (indeed, numerically considered, probably even more) abnormal to be a genius. The test of a view is its rationality, not the number of people who endorse it. It would have been cranky indeed in the ancient world to raise the question of the rights of slaves — so cranky that scarcely a voice went on record as doing so. To us it seems incredible that the Greek philosophers should have scanned so deep into right and wrong and yet never *noticed* the immorality of slavery. Perhaps three thousand years from now it will seem equally incredible that we do not notice the immorality of our oppression of animals.

Slavery was the ancient world's patch of moral and aesthetic insensitivity. Indeed, it was not until the eighteenth and nineteenth centuries of our own era that the human conscience was effectively and universally switched on in that respect. Even then, we went on with economic and social exploitations which stopped short of slavery only in constitutional status, and people were found to justify them. But by then the exploiters had at least been forced onto the defensive and felt obliged to produce the feeble arguments that had never even been called for in the ancient world. Perhaps it is a sign that our conscience is about to be switched on in relation to animals that some animal-exploiters are now seeking to justify themselves. When factory farmers tell us that animals kept in 'intensive' (i.e. concentration) camps are being kindly spared the inclemency of a winter outdoors, and that calves do not mind being tethered for life on slats because they have never known anything else, an echo should start in our historical consciousness: do you remember how the childlike blackamoors were kindly spared the harsh responsibilities of freedom, how the skivvy didn't feel the hardship of scrubbing all day because she was used to it, how the poor didn't mind their slums because they had never known anything else?

The first of the factory farmers' arguments is, of course, an argument for ordinary farms to make better provision for animals in winter, not for ordinary farms to be replaced by torture chambers. As for the one about the animals' never having known anything else, I still shan't believe it valid but I shall accept that the factory farmers genuinely believe it themselves when they follow out its logic by using their profits to finance the repatriation of every circus and zoo animal that was caught in the wild, on the grounds that those *have* known something else.

Undismayed by being a crank, I will make you a free gift of another stick to beat me with, by informing you that I am a vegetarian. Now, surely, you have me. Not only am I a more extreme crank, a member of an even smaller minority, than you had realised; surely I *must*, now, be a killjoy. Yet which, in fact, kills more joy: the killjoy who would deprive you of your joy in eating steak, which is just one of the joys open to you, or the kill-animal who puts an end to all the animal's joys along with its life?

Beware, however (if we may now take up the first item in your Identikit portrait of me), how you call me a sentimentalist in this matter. I may be less of one than you are. I won't kill an animal in order to eat it, but I am no respecter of dead bodies as such. If our chemists discovered (as I'm sure they quickly would were there a demand) how to give tenderness and hygiene to the body of an animal which had died of old age, I would willingly eat it; and in principle that goes for human animals, too. In practice I suspect I should choke on a rissole which I knew might contain bits of Great-Aunt Emily (whether through love for or repulsion from her I am not quite sure), and I admit I might have to leave rational cannibalism to future generations brought up without my irrational prejudice (which is equally irrational whether prompted by love or by repulsion for the old lady). But you were accusing me, weren't you, of sentimentality and ignorance of economic realities. Have you thought how much of the world's potential food supply *you* unrealistically let go waste because of your sentimental compunction about eating your fellow citizens after they have lived out their natural lives?

If we are going to rear and kill animals for our food, I think we have a moral obligation to spare them pain and terror in both processes, simply because they are sentient. I can't *prove* they are sentient; but then I have no proof *you* are. Even though you are articulate, whereas an animal can only scream or struggle, I have

no assurance that your 'It hurts' expresses anything like the intolerable sensations I experience in pain. I know, however, that
when I visit my dentist and say 'It hurts', I am grateful that he
gives me the benefit of the doubt.

I don't myself believe that, even when we fulfil our minimum
obligation not to cause pain, we have the right to kill animals. I
know I would have no right to kill you, however painlessly, just
because I liked your flavour, and I am not in a position to judge
that your life is worth more to you than the animal's to it. If
anything, you probably value yours less; unlike the animal, you
are capable of acting on an impulse to suicide. Christian tradition
would permit me to kill the animal but not you, on the grounds
that you have, and it hasn't, an immortal soul. I am not a
Christian and do not avail myself of this licence; but if I were, I
should in elementary justice see the soul theory as all the more
reason to let the animal live out the one mortal life it has.

The only genuine moral problem is where there is a direct
clash between an animal's life and a human one. Our diet proposes no such clash, meat not being essential to a human life; I
have sustained a very healthy one for ten years without. And in
fact such clashes are much rarer in reality than in exam papers,
where we are always being asked to rescue either our grandmother
or a Rubens from a blazing house. Human fantasy often fabricates
a dilemma (yours did when you suggested I love animals in preference to people—there is no psychological law which prevents
me from loving both) as an excuse for inertia. It is a principle of
'divide and do nothing'. In reality, your own preference for
humans over animals will not justify you in resisting my hint that
you should send a cheque to the Performing Animals' Defence
League (11, Buckingham Street, Adelphi, wc2, by the way)
unless you really and actually *do* get round to sending it instead
to Oxfam (c/o Barclays Bank, Oxford).

The most genuine and painful clash is, of course, on the subject
of vivisection. To hold vivisection never justified is a hard belief.
But so is its opposite. I believe it is never justified because I can see
nothing (except our being able to get away with it) which lets us
pick on animals that would not equally let us pick on idiot humans

(who would be more useful) or, for the matter of that, on a few humans of any sort whom we might sacrifice for the good of the many. If we do permit vivisection, here if anywhere we are under the most stringent minimum obligations. The very least we must make sure of is that no experiment is ever duplicated, or careless, or done for mere teaching's sake or as a substitute for thinking. Knowing how often, in every other sphere, pseudo-work proliferates in order to fill time and jobs, and how often activity substitutes for thought, and then reading the official statistics about vivisection, do you truly believe we *do* make sure? (The National Anti-Vivisection Society is at 51, Harley Street, w1.)

Our whole relation to animals is tinted by a fantasy — and a fallacy — about our toughness. We feel obliged to demonstrate we can take it; in fact, it is the animals who take it. So shy are we of seeming sentimental that we often disguise our humane impulses under 'realistic' arguments: foxhunting is snobbish: factory-farmed food doesn't taste so nice. But foxhunting would still be an atrocity if it were done by authenticated, pedigreed proletarians, and so would factory-farming even if a way were found of making its corpses tasty. So, incidentally, would slavery, even if it were proved a hundred times more economically realistic than freedom.

The saddest and silliest of the superstitions to which we sacrifice animals is our belief that by killing them we ourselves somehow live more fully. We might live more fully by entering imaginatively into their lives. But shedding their blood makes us no more full-blooded. It is a mere myth, often connected with our myth about the *savoir vivre* and sexiness of the sunny south (which is how you managed to transform me into a frustrated British virgin in Florence). There is no law of nature which makes *savoir vivre* incompatible with 'live and let live'. The bullfighter who torments a bull to death and then castrates it of an ear has neither proved nor increased his own virility; he has merely demonstrated that he is a butcher with balletic tendencies.

Superstition and dread of sentimentality weight all our questions against the animals. We *don't* scrutinise vivisection rigorously — we somehow think it would be soft of us to do so, which we apparently think a worse thing to be than cruel. When, in February of this year, the House of Lords voted against a Bill banning animal acts from circuses, it was pointed out that animal-trainers would lose their jobs. (Come to think of it, many human-trainers must have lost theirs when it was decided to ban gladiator acts from circuses.) No one pointed out how many unemployed acrobats and jugglers would *get* jobs to replace the animals. (I'm not, you see by the way, the sort of killjoy who wants to abolish the circus as such.) Similarly with the anthropomorphism argument, which works in both directions but is always wielded in one only. In the same House of Lords debate, Lady Summerskill, who had taken the humane side, was mocked by a noble lord on the grounds that were *she* shut up in a cage she would indeed suffer from mortification and the loss of her freedom, but an animal, not being human, wouldn't. Why did no one point out that a human, in such circumstances, dreadful as they are, would have every consolation of the human intellect and imagination, from reading books to analysing his circumstances and writing to the Home Secretary about them, whereas the animal suffers the raw terror of not comprehending what is being done to it?

In point of fact, I am the very opposite of an anthropomorphist. I don't hold animals superior or even equal to humans. The whole case for behaving decently to animals rests on the fact that we are the superior species. We are the species uniquely capable of imagination, rationality and moral choice—and that is precisely why we are under the obligation to recognise and respect the rights of animals.

The Immorality of Marriage

Sunday Times Magazine, March 1965

Traditionally, marriage has been regarded as the price men had to pay for sexual intercourse, and sexual intercourse as the price women had to pay for marriage.

During the twentieth century this rather vulgar-minded tradition has been shattered—by two items of observation, and two of technology. It has been more and more widely observed that women are capable of enjoying sex, and men of enjoying domesticity. And meanwhile industrialisation has made more and more widely available two cardinal inventions: contraceptives, and babies' feeding bottles.

The result of these four items, each of which inter-reacts with all the others, is a new psychological freedom for both sexes. Women are free to admit to themselves that they have a taste for sexual intercourse—precisely because they can now indulge that taste without risking pregnancy unless they choose to. Men need no longer pretend that looking after babies is a mysterious and exclusive instinctual endowment of the female sex (as though no mother of a first-born had ever been frightened out of her wits to find that instinct provides, in fact, no instructions whatever). The belief that women somehow just *knew* about babies was a superstition, and men have been able to free themselves from it because a man who picks up a baby is no longer a hamfisted incompetent, mentally apologising to the baby for the dryness of his breasts; given an affectionate character and average dexterity, a man can now suckle a baby as adequately as a woman can.

Our new freedom amounts to this: a man can now be a mother if he wants to, and a woman needn't if she doesn't.

In any other sphere this increase in our power to choose would be accepted by every one as progress. So long as 'nature' means tornadoes and epidemics, or waterfalls whose force can be turned into electricity, everyone agrees that the task of civilisation is to conquer nature and set human beings free from the restrictions of circumstance. Only on the subject of the relation between the sexes do reactionaries start citing 'nature' as an ideal. They are to be heard nowadays complaining that our psychological and technological advances have produced an 'unnatural' state where it is increasingly hard to distinguish men from women. Many reactionaries shew strange misapprehensions about the distinction nature does make between men and women: they speak, for instance, as though it were natural for a woman's hair to grow long but for a man's to stop short at two and a half inches: and no doubt they would all be horrified if we adopted what is unquestionably the most 'natural' state, and at the same time the one where it would be quite impossible to mistake which of us are women and which men, by going naked.

To a rational view, any increase in the *voluntariness* of our behaviour is an advance in civilisation. It is the mark of a peasant that he is tied to the land, of a civilised man that he chooses — and he may, of course, choose to go 'back to the land'. Equally, modern married people are free to choose to go back to the 'natural' division of rôles between the sexes — provided they can discern what on earth that is; for what distinguishes the human from other species is that our instincts impose no single pattern on our marriages or our societies, and the one thing which is consistently natural for humans is to try by intelligence and imagination to improve on nature.

In any marriage, as in any society (and indeed, a couple in love *is*, as John Donne pointed out, a sovereign state of two), there will be some division of labour, some implied social contract. In the feudal state, who was lord and who was villein was decided by hereditary circumstance; in feudal marriage, the circumstance of sex decided that it must be the woman who stayed with the children, and usually that there must be a great many children to stay with. Modern marriage, like modern society, is able to attempt social justice. The rôles can now be allotted according to talent and inclination, and marriage has the advantage over society that, if two people cannot agree beforehand on its constitution, there is — or should be — no reason for them to enter on a marriage at all.

One of the greatest social triumphs of our century is to have abolished that branch of class warfare which was known as 'the sex war'. I am thankful that to my readers under twenty-five the sex war will be an archaism whose conventions need footnoting like those of visiting-card procedure in Edwardian novels. For those readers let me explain that the sex war was a guerilla scuffle in which women tried to trap men into marriage, and men tried to ambush women into bed. At its mildest, it made inevitable an armed suspicion in which one irresistible question ('if he really loves me, why doesn't he marry me?') was pitted against another ('if she really loves me, why doesn't she go to bed with me?'), to the slow-poisoning of love; in its violent form, it produced terrible social casualties in the shape of 'ruined' or 'fallen' women and men whose personalities were malformed by addiction to compulsive Don Juanism.

Only now that the war is over has marriage of true minds become feasible. The 'merging' of the sexes lamented by the reactionaries really has taken place in one realm, where it is the opposite of lamentable—in the imagination. Men and women are no longer unimaginable beings to one another. Husband and wife need no longer suspect, because they are now perfectly capable of imagining, one another's motives. They can achieve imaginative identification, in which there can be no question of rivalry or a conflict of self-interests; the self-interest, ambitions and ideals—the very Ego—of each *are* those of the other. It would be thoroughly awkward and disappointing if husband and wife were really one flesh; for them to be one mind is, as those who have experienced it can testify, the highest happiness.

Marriage as a social institution is, naturally, inadequate to this marriage of true minds. An institution cannot be asked to be more than a framework; love being almost wholly involuntary, parliaments cannot legislate it into existence and lovers cannot honourbly promise (though thousands do promise) to keep it in existence. On scrutiny, however, certain parts of the social framework of marriage turn out to be not merely inadequate to true marriage but actually inimical.

It goes without saying (like most atheists, I am a fanatic for religious tolerance) that religious people must be left at complete liberty to follow their own rules about what they promise at marriage and how, if ever, a marriage may be dissolved in the eyes of their church. Those matters, like their promises at baptism and confirmation, are their own concern — though only theirs; they have, of course, no more right to seek to impose their marriage rules on the rest of the community than they would to try to impose baptism or confirmation on us all. Most of us, however, are irreligious, and most of us who are irreligious and married became married for reasons of social convenience: perhaps to appease 'respectable' relatives; and almost certainly because it is easier to rear children if they are not technical bastards, and easier for two people to sleep together under the roof of a landlady or an *hôtelier* if they are married.

Even in taking this elementary social cover, we irreligious married people have probably done wrong. My husband and I do not believe that bastards are wickeder than other children, or that unmarried matings are necessarily (though of course they, just like married ones, may be) immoral, but we have tacitly endorsed a spurious 'respectability' which we do not believe has anything to do with genuine morals. We have withheld three people, ourselves and our child, from the group which 'respectability' unjustly outlaws: yet only when headmasters and landladies are confronted with such quantities of bastards and unmarried couples that they must either take them in or go without customers will the superstition of 'respectability' give way.

By the same token, the irreligious married take for themselves an unjust privilege when they accept for their own marriages of true minds a social convenience and approbation which are denied to marriages of true minds which happen to be between people of the same sex.

The most virulent immorality of marriage lies in our divorce laws. Like any other contract, marriage can be known by the conditions on which it may be terminated: you give implicit consent to those when you enter the contract. There is only one clearcut circumstance in which it is always moral for a marriage to be dissolved, and that is when both parties wish it. That is the one circumstance in which English law absolutely declines to consider doing so. The very vocabulary of the law betrays that the law *expects* there to be a conflict of self-interest between husband and wife. The term 'matrimonial offence' is itself an offence to anyone who has experienced a marriage of identification; the concept of 'conjugal rights' turns the act of love into legalised rape.

No doubt the introduction of marriage into primitive communities worked towards social stability: it gave a man some assurance that his property would not be inherited by children who might not be his, and that a rival would not oust him from his wife's bed by force. But our civilised community should be growing out of its concern with personal property and seeing to it that all children, no matter whose they are, are well provided for; and when civilised lovers fall victim to that most natural but most despicable and ungenerous of emotions, jealousy, they struggle not with the persons they love but with themselves to overcome it. Civilised married people want one another's happiness, not the right to hang a 'No Trespassers' notice on one another's sexual organs.

Marriage has long been a respectable and is just at the moment a highly fashionable institution: but morally it is on the rocks. To rescue it we shall have to make reasonable divorce laws, extend marriage to homosexual people and recognise that social marriage, which probably ante-dates all the extant religions, has now no connexion with or obligation to religion of any kind.

Secular marriage is still slightly ashamed of not taking place in a church. Its drab ceremony skulks in a drab cubicle, usually next door to the public baths. The rest will take time, but the ceremony at least could be instantly set to rights and made worthy of the concept of a marriage of true minds. All that is needed is a simple act of nationalisation — and one which, moreover, would displease nobody. The Book of Common Prayer is part of the inheritance of all English-speaking people, and the passage I propose the secular state should appropriate from it is, through its notably un-Christian nature, only an embarrassment to the Christians. In one of the most beautiful phallic metaphors (a metaphor mimed as well as spoken) and one of the most beautiful pieces of solemn prose ever created, it gives an exact description of the ceremonialising of a marriage of true minds: 'With this ring, I thee wed, with my body I thee worship ... '

Monogamy

Queen, April 1965

There is a belief, widely held among both sexes, that whereas men are irked by monogamy women are suited to it by nature.

Even on the face of it, this seems fishy. After all, monogamy is what we actually have; and the social, religious and legal systems which gave it us were all invented, and until recently run, by men. I can well believe men were masochistic enough to impose monogamy on themselves as a hairshirt, but I find it a touch implausible that the hairshirt designed for the husband just happened to be a comfortable and perfectly fitting garment for the wife.

And indeed I suspect that, if you scrutinize the notion that women are naturally monogamous, it turns out to be based on no sounder authority than that rhyme which begins 'higamus hogamus, woman is monogamous', and no more cogent evidence than a one-eyed view of biology which is in fact about as good science as 'higamus hogamus' is good Latin.

The 'biological' argument goes like this. A man can, if pressed for time, beget a child in twenty-five seconds flat, but a woman can't bring it to birth in less than nine months (seven if it's premature). A woman can therefore, the argument proceeds, be set up in the reproductive business and kept fully occupied at it by the expenditure of only a tiny fraction of a man's time and sexual capacity; he, on the other hand, will have so much of both those to spare that a natural impulse will drive him to distribute them among several other women. Thus, the argument concludes, a woman is so constituted by nature that she can be made happy and 'fulfilled' by the part-time attentions of one man, but if a man is not allowed to pay his attentions to several women he will be frustrated and unhappy.

What is one-eyed about this view is that it sees nothing in biology but reproduction. It is also remarkably ignorant of women. In point of fact, biology endows women not only with the ability and an instinct to bear children but also with the ability to experience pleasure and an instinct to seek it. Close the eye which sees nothing but reproduction and open instead the eye which sees the over-riding biological instinct towards pleasure, and you get a very different biological argument. A man is sexually excited on small provocation, satisfied quickly, and often so exhausted by the process that he falls straight asleep. A woman, on the other hand, requires long and skilled wooing if she is to be satisfied at all; when she is, she is often ready to start being wooed again within half a minute. The needs of a man can, therefore, be satisfied to exhaustion point by one woman, but she will still retain capacities and desires which will be frustrated unless she has further men to go on to. Indeed, what her biology really requires is a large number of lovers, from whom she will discard those whose love-making doesn't suit her, and will pick out and keep not one—who would be too quickly exhausted—but three or four permanent husbands. Thus, higamus hogamus, it is man who is monogamous and, hogamus higamus, woman who is, by her biological nature, polygamous.

There is of course no reason why we should be bound by nature and biology at all. Much of civilization consists of overcoming them and setting ourselves free to choose. Many people of both sexes choose monogamy, overcoming their biological tendency to polygamy. But it is unreasonable of society to—without good cause—impose monogamy on the ones who have not chosen it. Above all, there is no reason why, human relationships being almost infinitely various, we should impose any one pattern on all marriages—especially when it so often doesn't work.

At present, monogamy is the corset into which we try to fit every married couple—a process which has on so many occasions split the seams that we have had to modify the corset. There used to be a social modification which, excused by the erroneous belief that men were naturally more polygamous than women, gave the sort of glancing blow that is really an approving pat to men who broke out of monogamy but seriously and cruelly disapproved of women who did. The injustice of this 'double standard' is now pretty clear to everyone, and in its place we have introduced a legal modification of monogamy. Divorce is a device which makes polygamy permissible, but only non-simultaneous polygamy. In practice, even this is modified. The law sometimes insists that a divorcée remain a man's wife economically though she is no longer so in name or in bed. The result is that, just as in Mohammedan countries the number of wives a man may legally have simultaneously is often whittled down in practice to the number he can support, so in Europe and the United States, under our modified monogamy, the number of ex-wives a man may legally have simultaneously is often limited to the number of *those* he can support.

Apart from this economic bias against men, divorce is much fairer than the double standard, since it is equally available, on the same grounds, to men and women. Its unfairness starts with the grounds. Divorce is an excellent solution when both married people want to say goodbye. But let them admit that that's what they both want, and English law refuses them a divorce. Often they have to pretend an adultery — which is, legally considered, the best and, rationally considered, the worst conceivable grounds for divorce. Nothing could be more wasteful of that rare and rarely beautiful quality, married love, than that a marriage should break simply because one of the partners would like to enlarge it by co-opting a third.

To be sure, the whole business of love and people's behaviour under its stress is irrational in itself; but that is all the more reason to be as rational as we can in coping with our most irrational area. Sexual jealousy is one of the most painful emotions on earth. But in coping with it society licenses us to indulge in a two-year-old's tantrum. To divorce your mate because he has mated with someone else is to cut off your nose to spite the face you suddenly feel holds less attraction for him; it is to act on the principle that no bread is better than half a loaf. In some countries an un-written law even permits the slighted spouse to kill the adulterous one. Here you may merely make him dead as far as you are con-cerned, by cutting him out of your life by divorce. This is probably the most perverse approach you could make to what, if you love him, you want, which is to have him living, and with you.

The obvious remedy is at least respectabilised and for preference legalised polygamy. No one in his senses could suppose it would be easy or painless to work. But it would give less pain than either of the other courses: to stand on your full monogamous rights and insist that the person you love forgo the company of someone he loves; or to avail yourself of the legal modification to monogamy and insist on yourself forgoing the company of the person you love.

Where our schooling does *not* succeed is in developing understanding or respect for either imagination or reason. We do not
care twopence if the other people in the theatre-party think us
deaf to a dramatic subtlety or impervious to the point of an
argument. We want only to demonstrate that we can see the point
of a joke. Therefore when the opera producer interrupts a Mozart
aria by comic business, we drown out the music with our laughter,
lest our host, six stalls and three chocolate boxes along, should
think us stuck-up enough to want to listen to Mozart; the cabaret-
performer has only to name a real-life politician and we will
upset the wine on the table in laughing at the topicality; the judge
has only to enquire 'What *is* television?' and we, the audience,
titter like obsequious Victorian schoolboys when the master turns
sarcastic; and in the English theatre, fifty years after Eliza
Doolittle, an actor can still raise a long, dwelling laugh by saying
'bloody', because every member of the audience is afraid his
neighbours would mistake his silence for shock.

It is on the question of shock that we most grotesquely betray
our belief that humour is a contest in taking it. Put five British
men convivially together, and they will start competing about the
bawdiness of the contrived situations in which they can assemble
an Englishman, an Irishman and a Scotsman: instantly, their five
British wives will start competing to see who can say first and
most often that she can take a dirty joke providing it's really
funny. (My experience is that I can take *almost* any amount of
funniness providing it's really dirty.) The trouble with our national
sense of humour is that, though we are immensely conceited about
having it, we don't take a proper pride in it—don't, that is, take
it seriously. If we did, we would see that there is no future for the
British dirty joke unless we recognise that, like sex itself, it demands
finesse and imagination and that to leave it to well-meaning high
spirits is to invite it to flounder into fiasco; no future for the
British theatre and cinema until, taking them too seriously to use
them as less taxing versions of the dinner party, we nerve ourselves
to venture into them alone or with someone we know intimately
enough to ignore; and no future for the British sense of humour
until we admit humour is a twist in the aesthetic faculty. (You

can't have a sense of humour unless you have a sense of art: but you can have a sense of art without any sense at all of humour. It is a British habit to over-rate humour and assume that any artist who lacks it would be a better artist for it. Some — D. H. Lawrence, for example — would. Other and greater ones wouldn't. Wagner with a sense of humour would be intolerable.) While we're about it, we might as well admit humour is an art.

That is just what our traditional humour is concerned to deny. Rather than submit to the canons, which are ruthless, of artistic elegance and economy, it insists on weltering in laboured gestures and overweight facetious diction. Then it asks to be judged not by whether it's funny but by whether it's in good taste. The result is that when it does escape genteelism, it's hardly more than vulgar; a British film could never have taken off, as *Some Like It Hot* takes off, into the poetic — the dizzy rococo — heights of real bad taste.

Not only the practice but the very content of British humour is anti-art. Here again it shews its Victorian genesis. When, in 1880, the Victorians made education compulsory, they convinced the British public that the exercise of intellect and imagination, which is what education is about, was something which had to be enforced or actually inflicted and could therefore have nothing to do with pleasant experiences like being interested or amused. Nine years after getting compulsory education, the British public got *Three Men In A Boat*, whose success confirmed the belief that the only way to be funny was to be facetious, unthinking, unsubtle and insensitive to the verge of being cruel. The national philistinism had achieved a national monument second only to the Albert Memorial, and apparently as lasting. So firmly did Jerome K. Jerome set the pattern — the great tin jelly-mould — for British humour that his manner had a success all over again and was actually welcomed as something entirely new when, in 1954, *Lucky Jim* resurrected Jerome's half-literate belief that long words are automatically funny ('There was a small golden emblem on his tie ... proving on closer scrutiny to be congealed egg-yolk. Substantial traces of the same nutritive were to be seen round his mouth') and carried Jerome's crypto-philistinism to an open culmination when Jim thinks to himself 'filthy Mozart'.

The British public has made it crystal-clear that it wants neither wit nor comedy; but it will at a pinch take comedy because it thinks it less clever, less malicious and more likely to be basically tragic. It is in every case mistaken. Wit carries as many tears in its train as clowning does, but its tragedies are those of irony. A comic inspiration is as relentlessly logical and intellectual as an aphorism: the only difference is that comedy works out the logic of a personal poetical idea, which no one but the artist could have seen, whereas a witticism works out the logic of the external world, which anyone could have seen had he been as quick-witted as the wit. That the shortest distance between two points is a straight line is not only a brilliant but a witty observation. Many of Oscar Wilde's observations anticipate psycho-analysis. Wit is always some form of analysis — which is why the Englishman, who is still receiving the analysis of water into H_2O as an assault on the natural beauty of Windermere, believes wit to be malicious and destructive. His own preferred humour is simply seeking to destroy art and thought. That leaves him free to assert that British humour is essentially genial and kind-hearted.

Since he has refused all along even to try to be a clever chap, in the same spirit that he would refuse even to try to be a murderer, he is not disconcerted by his own inconsistency when the objection he brings against the latter-day satirists is that they fail to damage their target. As a rule, he has misunderstood their target. To call a Minister of the Crown a bloody fool is not very pointed satire on the Minister. It is passably good satire on the holy Dimbleby hush wherein none of us would dream of expressing such an opinion though we're all — how can we help it? — thinking it.

Although our libel laws are a step towards it, we have not yet legislated against either clowns or wits. Occasionally we are given the chance, as we were with Wilde, to trap a wit and break his heart on other grounds, much as the Americans get their gangsters for tax evasion if they can't get them for gangsterism. Usually, we punish our clowns and wits by laughing at them and not taking them seriously. We never take their advice. Wilde's epigrams have not yet persuaded us to abolish social injustice, any more than his tragedy has to abolish sexual injustice. We are not particularly proud of our comic geniuses: nationally we make no attempt to live on our wits. Go into the park and observe what we give the foreign *au pair* girls to read: seldom Wilde or Shaw; never Gibbon, Swift, Jane Austen or Pope; nearly always *Three Men In A Boat*. Pressed, we will admit that our national monuments of humour are not always as old as they pretend to be, but at least they're built, we insist, on the *site* of something old — Merrie England. When will someone have the bad taste to proclaim our heritage of Wittie England?

Women

Saturday Evening Post, November 1963

All right, nobody's disputing it. Women are free. At least, they *look* free. They even feel free. But in reality women in the western, industrialised world today are like the animals in a modern zoo. There are no bars. It appears that cages have been abolished. Yet in practice women are still kept in their place just as firmly as the animals are kept in their enclosures. The barriers which keep them in now are invisible.

It is about forty years since the pioneer feminists, several of whom were men, raised such a rumpus by rattling the cage bars — or created such a conspicuous nuisance by chaining themselves to them — that society was at last obliged to pay attention. The result was that the bars were uprooted, the cage thrown open: whereupon the majority of the women who had been held captive decided they would rather stay inside anyway.

To be more precise, they *thought* they decided; and society, which can with perfect truth point out 'Look, no bars', *thought* it was giving them the choice. There are no laws and very little discrimination to prevent western, industrialised women from voting, being voted for or entering the professions. If there are still comparatively few women lawyers and engineers, let alone women presidents of the United States, what are women to conclude except that this is the result either of their own free choice or of something inherent in female nature?

Many of them do draw just this conclusion. They have come back to the old argument of the anti-feminists, many of whom were women, that women are unfit by nature for life outside the cage. And in letting this old wheel come full cycle women have fallen victim to one of the most insidious and ingenious confidence tricks ever perpetrated.

In point of fact, neither female nature nor women's individual free choice has been put to the test. As American Negroes have discovered, to be officially free is by no means the same as being

38

actually and psychologically free. A society as adept as ours has become at propaganda — whether political or commercial — should know that 'persuasion', which means the art of launching myths and artificially inducing inhibitions, is every bit as effective as force of law. No doubt the reason society eventually agreed to abolish its anti-women laws was that it had become confident of commanding a battery of hidden dissuaders which would do the job just as well. Cage bars are clumsy methods of control, which excite the more rebellious personalities inside to rattle them. Modern society, like the modern zoo, has contrived to get rid of the bars without altering the fact of imprisonment. All the zoo architect needs to do is run a zone of hot or cold air, whichever the animal concerned cannot tolerate, round the cage where the bars used to be. Human animals are not less sensitive to social climate.

The ingenious point about the new-model zoo is that it deceives both sides of the invisible barrier. Not only can the animal not see how it is imprisoned; the visitor's conscience is relieved of the unkindness of keeping animals shut up. He can say 'Look, no bars round the animals', just as society can say 'Look, no laws restricting women' even while it keeps women rigidly in place by zones of fierce social pressure.

There is, however, one great difference. A woman, being a thinking animal, may actually be more distressed because the bars of her cage cannot be seen. What relieves society's conscience may afflict hers. Unable to perceive what is holding her back, she may accuse herself and her whole sex of craven timidity because women have not jumped at what has the appearance of an offer of freedom. Evidently quite a lot of women have succumbed to guilt of this sort, since in recent years quite an industry has arisen to assuage it. Comforting voices make the air as thick and reassuring as cotton wool while they explain that there is nothing shameful in not wanting a career, that to be intellectually unadventurous is no sin, that taking care of home and family may be personally 'fulfilling' and socially valuable.

This is an argument without a flaw: except that it is addressed exclusively to women. Address it to both sexes and instantly it becomes progressive and humane. As it stands, it is merely anti-woman prejudice revamped.

That many women would be happier not pursuing careers or intellectual adventures is only part of the truth. The whole truth is that many *people* would be. If society had the clear sight to assure men as well as women that there is no shame in preferring to stay non-competitively and non-aggressively at home, many masculine neuroses and ulcers would be avoided, and many children would enjoy the benefit of being brought up by a father with a talent for the job instead of by a mother with no talent for it but a sense of guilt about the lack.

But society does nothing so sensible. Blindly it goes on insisting on the tradition that men are the ones who go out to work and adventure — an arrangement which simply throws talent away. All the home-making talent which happens to be born inside male bodies is wasted; and our businesses and governments are staffed quite largely by people whose aptitude for the work consists solely of their being what is, by tradition, the right sex for it.

The pressures society exerts to drive men out of the house are very nearly as irrational and unjust as those by which it keeps women in. The mistake of the early reformers was to assume that men were emancipated already and that therefore reform need ask only for the emancipation of women. What we ought to do now is go right back to scratch and demand the emancipation of both sexes. It is only because men are not free themselves that they have found it necessary to cheat women by the deception which makes them appear free when they are not.

The zones of hot and cold air which society uses to perpetuate its uneconomic and unreasonable state of affairs are the simplest and most effective conceivable. Society is playing on our sexual vanity. Just as the sexual regions are the most vulnerable part of the body, sexuality is the most vulnerable part of the Ego. Tell a man that he is not a real man, or a woman that she is not one hundred per cent woman, and you are threatening both with not being attractive to the opposite sex. No one can bear not to be attractive to the opposite sex. That is the climate which the human animal cannot tolerate.

So society has us all at its mercy. It has only to murmur to the
man that staying at home is a feminine characteristic, and he will
be out of the house like a bullet. It has only to suggest to the
woman that logic and reason are the province of the masculine
mind, whereas 'intuition' and 'feeling' are the female *forte*, and
she will throw her physics textbooks out of the window, barricade
herself into the house and give herself up to having wishy-washy
poetical feelings while she arranges the flowers.

She will, incidentally, take care that her feelings *are* wishy-
washy. She has been persuaded that to have cogent feelings, of the
kind which really do go into great poems (most of which are by
men), would make her an unfeminine woman, a woman who
imitates men. In point of fact, she would not be imitating men as
such, most of whom have never written a line of great poetry, but
poets, most of whom so far happen to be men. But the bad logic
passes muster with her because part of the mythology she has
swallowed ingeniously informs her that logic is not her *forte*.

Should a woman's talent or intelligence be so irrepressible that
she insists on producing cogent works of art or watertight meshes
of argument, she will be said to have 'a mind like a man's'. This
is simply current idiom; translated, it means 'a good mind'. The
use of the idiom contributes to an apparently watertight proof
that all good minds are masculine, since whenever they occur in
women they are described as 'like a man's'.

What is more, this habit of thought actually contributes to
perpetuating a state of affairs where most good minds really do
belong to men. It is difficult for a woman to *want* to be intelligent
when she has been told that to be so will make her like a man. She
inclines to think an intelligence would be as unbecoming to her
as a moustache; and many women have tried in furtive privacy
to disembarrass themselves of intellect as though it were facial
hair.

Discouraged from growing 'a mind like a man's', women are
encouraged to have thoughts and feelings of a specifically
feminine tone. For society is cunning enough not to place its whole
reliance on threatening women with blasts of icy air. It also
flatters them with a zone of hot air. The most deceptive and

cynical of its blandishments is the notion that women have some specifically feminine contribution to make to culture. Unfortunately, as culture had already been shaped and largely built up by men before the invitation was issued, this leaves women little to do. Culture consists of reasoned thought and works of art composed of cogent feeling and imagination. There is only one way to be reasonable, and that is to reason correctly; and the only kind of art which is any good is good art. If women are to eschew reason and artistic imagination in favour of 'intuition' and 'feeling', it is pretty clear what is meant. 'Intuition' is just a polite name for bad reasoning, and 'feeling' for bad art.

In reality, the whole idea of a specifically feminine — or, for the matter of that, masculine — contribution to culture is a contradiction of culture. A contribution to culture is not something which could not have been made by the other sex — it is something which could not have been made by any other *person*. Equally, the notion that anyone, of either sex, can create good art out of simple feeling, untempered by discipline, is a philistine one. The arts are a sphere where women seem to have done well; but really they have done *too* well — too well for the good of the arts. Instead of women sharing the esteem which ought to belong to artists, art is becoming smeared with femininity. We are approaching a philistine state of affairs where the arts are something which it is nice for women to take up in their spare time — men having slammed out of the house to get on with society's 'serious' business, like making money, administering the country and running the professions.

In that 'serious' sphere it is still rare to encounter a woman. A man sentenced to prison would probably feel his punishment was redoubled by indignity if he were to be sentenced by a woman judge under a law drafted by a woman legislator — and if, on admission, he were to be examined by a woman prison doctor. If such a thing happened every day, it would be no indignity but the natural course of events. It has never been given the chance to become the natural course of events and never will be so long as women remain persuaded it would be unnatural of them to want it.

So brilliantly has society contrived to terrorise women with this threat that certain behaviour is unnatural and unwomanly that it has left them no time to consider — or even sheerly observe — what womanly nature really is. For centuries arrant superstitions were accepted as natural law. The physiological fact that only women can secrete milk for feeding babies was extended into the pure myth that it was women's business to cook for and wait on the entire family. The kitchen became woman's 'natural' place because, for the first few months of her baby's life, the nursery really was. To this day a woman may suspect that she is unfeminine if she can discover in herself no aptitude or liking for cooking. Fright has thrown her into such a muddle that she confuses having no taste for cookery with having no breasts, and conversely assumes that nature has endowed the human female with a special handiness with frying pans.

Even psycho-analysis, which in general has been the greatest benefactor of civilisation since the wheel, has unwittingly reinforced the terrorisation campaign. The trouble was that it brought with it from its origin in medical therapy a criterion of normality instead of rationality. On sheer statistics every pioneer, genius and social reformer, including the first woman who demanded to be let out of the kitchen and into the polling booth, is abnormal, along with every lunatic and eccentric. What distinguishes the genius from the lunatic is that the genius's abnormality is justifiable by reason or aesthetics. If a woman who is irked by confinement to the kitchen merely looks round to see what other women are doing and finds they are accepting their kitchens, she may well conclude that she is abnormal and had better enlist her psycho-analyst's help towards 'living with' her kitchen. What she ought to ask is whether it is rational for women to be kept to the kitchen, and whether nature really does insist on that in the way it insists women have breasts. And in a far-reaching sense to ask that question is much more normal and natural than learning to 'live with' the handicap of women's inferior social status. The normal and natural thing for human beings is not to tolerate handicaps but to reform society and to circumvent or supplement nature. We don't learn to live minus a leg; we devise an artificial limb.

That, indeed, is the crux of the matter. Not only are the distinctions we draw between male nature and female nature largely arbitrary and often pure superstition: they are completely beside the point. They ignore the essence of *human* nature. The important question is not whether women are or are not less logical by nature than men, but whether education, effort and the abolition of our illogical social pressures can improve on nature and make them (and, incidentally, men as well) *more* logical. What distinguishes human from any other animal nature is its ability to be unnatural. Logic and art are not natural or instinctive activities; but our nature includes a propensity to acquire them. It is not natural for the human body to orbit the earth; but the human mind has a natural adventurousness which enables it to invent machines whereby the body can do so. There is, in sober fact, no such creature as a natural man. Go as far back as they will, the archaeologists cannot come on a wild man in his natural habitat. At his most primitive, he has already constructed himself an artificial habitat, and decorated it not by a standardised instinctual method, as birds build nests, but by individualised — that is, abnormal — works of art or magic. And in doing so he is not limited by the fingers nature gave him; he has extended their versatility by making tools.

Civilisation consists not necessarily in defying nature but in making it possible for us to do so if we judge it desirable. The higher we can lift our noses from the grindstone of nature, the wider the area we have of choice; and the more choices we have freely made, the more individualised we are. We are at our most civilised when nature does not dictate to us, as it does to animals and peasants, but when we can opt to fall in with it or better it. If modern civilisation has invented methods of education which make it possible for men to feed babies and for women to think logically, we are betraying civilisation itself if we do not set both sexes free to make a free choice.

The Menace of Nature

New Statesman, September 1965

So? Are you just back? Or are you, perhaps, staying on there for the extra week? By 'there' I mean, of course, one of the few spots left where the machine has not yet gained the upper hand; some place as yet unstrangled by motorways and unfouled by concrete mixers; a place where the human spirit can still—but for how much longer?—steep itself in natural beauty and recuperate after the nervous tension, the sheer stress, of modern living.

Well (I assume you're *enough* recuperated to stand this information?): I think you've been piously subscribing to a heresy. It's a heresy I incline offhand to trace, with an almost personally piqued sense of vendetta, to the old heresiarch himself, the sometimes great, often bathetic but never cogently thoughtful poet, William Wordsworth. Since the day he let the seeds of heresy fall (on, no doubt, the Braes of the Yarrow or the Banks of Nith), the thing has spread and enlarged itself into one of the great parroted, meaningless (but slightly paranoid) untruths of our age.

I am not trying to abolish the countryside. (I *state* this because it is true; I emphasise it because I don't want the lynch mob outside my window.) I'm not such a pig as to want the country built on or littered up with bottles and plastic bags merely because it doesn't appeal to *me*. As it happens, my own taste for countryside, though small, is existent. I've found the country very pleasant to be driven through in a tolerably fast car by someone whose driving I trust and whose company I like. But I admit that landscape as such bores me—to the extent that I have noticed myself in picture galleries automatically pausing to look at 'Landscape with Ruins' or 'Bandits in a Landscape' but walking straight past the pure landscapes at a speed which is obviously trying to simulate the effect of being driven past in a car.

I'm not, however, out to dissuade *you* from spending your holiday as a sort of legalised bandit in the landscape. Neither am

I anti-holiday. Holidays have been sniped at lately as things everyone feels an obligation to enjoy but no one really does. Yet I suspect there would be fewer dissatisfied holiday-makers if social pressure didn't try to limit our choice to 'Landscape' or 'Landscape with Seascape'. You can be made to feel quite guiltily anti-social in the summer months if you are, like me, constitutionally unable either to relax or to take a suntan. Indeed, relaxation is becoming this decade's social *sine qua non*, like Bridge in the 'thirties. They'll scarcely let you have a *baby* these days if you can't satisfy them beforehand you're adept at relaxing. But on the in some ways more private question of having a holiday, constitutional urbanites are still free, if only they can resist being shamed onto the beaches, to opt out of a rest and settle for the change which even the proverb allows to be as good as it. By simply exchanging their own for a foreign city, they are released from the routine of earning their daily bread and washing up after it, but don't suffer the disorientation, the uncorseted discomfort, which overtakes an urbanite cast up on a beach with no timetable to live by except the tides.

Still, it isn't in the holidays but during the rest of the year that the great rural heresy does its damage. How many, for example, of the middle-class parents who bring up their children in London do so with unease or even apology, with a feeling that they are selfishly depriving the children of some 'natural heritage' and sullying their childhood with urban impurities? Some parents even let this guilt drive them out to the suburbs or further, where they believe they cancel the egocentricity of their own need or desire for the town by undergoing the martyrdom of commuting. This parental masochism may secure the child a rural heritage (though parents should enquire, before moving, whether their child has the rural temperament and *wants* the rural heritage) but it deprives him of the cultural one; he gains the tennis club but is condemned to the tennis club light-opera society's amateur production of *No, No, Nanette* because the trains don't run late enough to bring him home after Sadler's Wells.

The notion that 'nature' and 'nature study' are somehow 'nice' for children, regardless of the children's own temperament, is a sentimental piety—and often a hypocritical one, like the piety which thinks Sunday School nice for *them* though we don't go to church ourselves. (In fact, it is we middle-aged who may need fresh air and exercise; the young are cat-like enough to remain lithe without.) Historically, it is not inept to trace the supposed affinity between children and 'nature' to Wordsworth's time. It was about that time that there settled on England, like a drizzle, the belief that sex is *not* 'nice' for children. Children's sexual curiosity was diverted to 'the birds and the bees' and gooseberry bushes; and birds, bees and bushes—in other words, 'nature'—have remained 'suitable' for children ever since.

If the romantic belief in children's innocence is now exploded, its numinous energy has only gone to strengthen the even more absurd romantic belief in the innocence of landscape's, as opposed to man-created, beauty. But I reject utterly the imputation that a brook is purer than Bach or a breeze more innocent than *As You Like It*. I warn you I shall be suspicious of this aesthetic faculty of yours that renders you so susceptible to the beauty of Snowdon if it leaves you unable to see anything in All Souls', Langham Place; and I shall be downright sceptical of it if (I am making allowance for your sensibility to run exclusively in that landscape groove which mine leaves out) you doat on the Constable country but feel it vaguely impure to take a 74 to the V. & A. to see a Constable.

You'll protest you feel no such impurity. Yet didn't you read the first paragraph of this article without taking so much as a raised eyebrow's worth of exception? Didn't you let the assumption pass that the city is corrupt? Weren't you prepared to accept from me, as you have from a hundred august authorities—sociologists, physicians, psychologists—that *idée reçue* about the nervous tension and stress of modern urban life? But what in heaven's name is this stressful modern urban life being compared with? Life in a medieval hamlet? Will no one take into account the symptoms into which the stress of *that* erupted—the epidemics of dancing madness and flagellation frenzy? Or life in a neolithic cave—whose stress one can only imagine and flinch at?

The truth is that the city is a device for *reducing* stress—by giving humans a freer choice of escapes from the pressure (along with the weather) of their environment. The device doesn't always work perfectly: traffic jams *are* annoying; the motor car does maim and must be prevented from doing so: but the ambulance which arrives so mercifully quickly is also powered by a motor. The city is one of the great indispensable devices of civilisation (itself only a device for centralising beauty and transmitting it as a heritage). It is one of the cardinal simple brilliant inventions, like currency. Like currency, it is a medium of exchange and thereby of choice —whereas the country is a place where one is under the thumb of chance, constrained to love one's neighbour not out of philanthropy but because there's no other company.

What's more, in the eighteenth century the city was suddenly upgraded from a device of civilisation to a manifestation of it. The city became an art form. (The form had been discovered, but not very consciously remarked, earlier. It was discovered, like many art forms, by accident—often, as at Venice and Bruges, an accident of water.) We are in dire danger now of clogging up our cities as devices and at the same time despoiling them as works of art; and one of the biggest villains in this process is our rural heresy.

Most western European beings have to live in cities, and all but the tiny portion of them who are temperamental rustics would do so contentedly, without wasting energy in guilt, and with an appreciative eye for the architecturescapes round them, had they not been told that liking the country is purer and more spiritual. Our cities run to squalor and our machines run amok because our citizens' minds are not on the job of mastering the machines and using them to make the cities efficient and beautiful. Their eyes are blind to the Chirico-esque handsomeness of the M1, because their hearts are set on a rustic Never-Never Land. Rustic sentimentality makes us build our suburban villas to mimic cottages, and then pebble-dash their outside walls in pious memory of the holiday we spent sitting agonised on the shingle. The lovely terraced façades of London are being undermined, as by subsidence, by our yearning, our sickly nostalgia, for a communal country childhood that never existed. We neglect our towns for a fantasy of going 'back' to the land, back to our 'natural' state. But there isn't and never was a natural man. We are a species that doesn't occur wild. No pattern in his genes instructs man on what pattern to build his nest. Instead, if he's fortunate, the Muses whisper to him the ground-plan of an architectural folly. Even in his cave, he frescoed the walls. All that is infallibly natural to our species is to make things that are artificial. We are *homo artifex*, *homo faber*, *homo Fabergé*. Yet we are so ignorant of our own human nature that our cities are falling into disrepair and all we worry about is their encroachment on 'nature'.

For, as I said at the start, the rural fantasy is paranoid. A glance at history shews that it is human life which is frail, and civilisation which flickers in constant danger of being blown out. But the rural fantasy insists that every plant is a delicate plant. The true paranoid situation is on the other foot. I wouldn't wish to do (and if we live at sensibly high densities there's no need to do) either, but were I forced either to pull down a Nash terrace or to build over a meadow, I'd choose the latter. If you don't like what you've put up on the meadow, you can take it away again and the meadow will re-seed itself in a year or two; but human semen is lucky if it engenders an architectural genius a century. The whole Wordsworthian fallacy consists in gravely underestimating the toughness of plants. In fact, no sooner does civilisation admit a crack — no sooner does a temple of Apollo lapse into disuse — than a weed forces its wiry stem through the crack and urges the blocks of stone further apart. During the last war, the bomber engines were hardly out of earshot before the loosestrife* leapt up on the bombed site. Whether we demolish our cities in a third world war or just let them tumble into decay, the seeds of the vegetable kingdom are no doubt waiting to seize on the rubble or sprout through the cracks. *Aux armes, citoyens.* To your trowels and mortar. Man the concrete mixers. The deep mindless silence of the countryside is massing in the Green Belt, ready to move in.

---

* This is what we called it at the time. I'm told by country-lovers that it's not the correct name.

The Nation in the Iron Mask

(This was commissioned and paid for as a talk in the Third Programme, at the time of the Profumo Affair. But the B.B.C. decided not to broadcast it.)

The Profumo-cum-Ward affair has been the most dazzling free entertainment laid before the British public since the trial of Oscar Wilde—another piece of buffoonery that suddenly turned tragic on our hands thanks to the vindictiveness, sanctimoniousness and sheer unthinkingness of our laws and our public opinion.

The Profumo-Ward affair didn't have such a good script as the Wilde trial--naturally, since it didn't have for its central figure one of the universe's great wits. It was more of a spectacular. What it had was girls girls girls, considerable sociological interest, a wide and distinguished cast that recurrently promised to become wider (and, as information about them came out, less distinguished), and the suspense value of being published by instalments. It excited some people to outrage and some to terror, but almost all tastes agreed that it *was* exciting. That is why so many people have come forward to tell us it was boring.

I don't proffer that as a fake Oscar Wilde paradox, but as sober semantic analysis. 'Boring' is one of the many words and forms of words in English which have a technical as well as their everyday meaning. Words are being used in a technical sense whenever the papers report 'Smash and grab raiders made a £5,000 haul last night. Police chased the raiders down the King's Road. Later, three men were arrested in Chelsea.' Anyone who has been brought up in England knows precisely what that means. But a—let's suppose an innocent Polynesian, who has been taught only our language: he would be left to conclude that the sub-editors on English newspapers have a curiously inconsequent turn of mind.

That might pass for what the cliché calls harmless deception, inasmuch as nobody—except the Polynesian who hasn't mastered our idioms—is deceived. However, deception is seldom *quite* harmless. In a case like this we don't deceive, or even hope to deceive, one another; but we do deceive ourselves, communally. The technical forms of words imposed on our newspapers by our far- and often rather capriciously-reaching laws of libel and contempt of court are effective in very little except permitting us to congratulate ourselves. *Our* prisoners get much fairer treatment than they would under the horrid continental system; *our* papers may not irresponsibly print 'The police suspect John So-and-So' but have to put it that the police are anxious to interview Mr So-and-So who they believe may be able to assist them in the enquiries. In point of fact, what our papers print means exactly the same as what the horrid continental papers print, and nobody takes it to mean anything else. The best we really achieve is to wrap our judicial system in a watertight day-dream of its own superiority, so that it neglects to make reforms which, as Louis Blom-Cooper points out in his recent paperback on the A6 murder, it could to its benefit borrow from the horrid continental system.

Doubletalk is so much the tenor of our language that we don't notice when we are talking it. An instance came up recently on the Third Programme. The speaker was discussing this very subject, which he called 'indirect speech' — not in the grammatical sense but in the sense of a roundabout or euphemistic way of putting things. One of the examples he took was that employers speak of 'redundancy' when what they mean is that they are going to sack the workers. Another was — and I'm quoting him word for word — 'the woman of commercial virtues advertises "French lessons".' Evidently he just didn't notice that 'woman of commercial virtues' is every bit as indirect a way of putting it as 'French lessons'.

When public figures pronounce the whole Profumo affair 'a bore', they don't mean it *is* boring. They mean 'You ought to treat it as you would if it *were* boring, namely by averting your eyes.'

This technical use of the word 'boring' began, I think, with book-reviewers, who noticed that if they denounced a book as salacious they were inclined to shoot up its sales. They therefore adopted the formula 'a bit of a bore', which is now accepted reviewers' jargon for 'something so exciting I think it would harm you to read it'.

It is, of course, always *you* who ought to avert your eyes. *I*, of course, have a duty to look—how else would I be able to tell you when not to look? It is a peculiarity of life in Britain that everyone in the country is performing this kindly and parental duty on behalf of someone else. English life, like English film censorship, is inspired by the principle 'Not in front of the children'. In its social extension, this principle becomes 'Not in front of the servants'— those servants who, along with wives, weren't to look at *Lady Chatterley*. And at its ultimate extension, all of us, upper class and lower class, parents and children, are united in one big, imperial conspiracy of silence with the motto 'Not in front of the natives'.

What we often forget is that each of these enclosures of silence sets up a conspiracy on the opposite side of the fence, too. The children are careful not to let their parents know how sexy the conversation is in the school cloakroom. They do this out of pure kindness. They think their parents would be shocked. The same reciprocal hypocrisies go on between the social classes. Oscar Wilde exposed them when he had Algernon Moncrieff say of his manservant, 'Lane's views on marriage seem somewhat lax. Really, if the lower orders don't set us a good example, what is the use of them?' But although this exposure was made sixty-eight years ago, the hypocrisies continue. The ladies and gentlemen still fall silent when the manservant comes into the room; they're afraid he would be shocked by the free and cynical way they talk. But an equal silence falls on the servants' hall when a lady or gentleman penetrates down there. The servants are convinced the soft, gently-nurtured gentlefolk have never seen 'real life' and would be shocked silly if they knew the half of what goes on below stairs and the foul-mouthed way it's spoken of. The posh papers were shocked that the popular press published various life histories connected with the Ward scandal in all the detail they could purchase; the popular press was equally shocked that the posh papers published the Ward trial evidence in full.

Shock is an emotion peculiar to England. It isn't the same as surprise, which other nationalities feel: it's surprise you feel with reference to somebody else. Not many people can have been *surprised* by what we've learnt in the past few months. Not many of us can have been so ill-informed before as not to know that, sometimes, politicians lie, men have mistresses and girls make money out of sex. Anyone who *was* so ignorant had no business to be, and ought to be grateful for the chance to catch up on his education. However, though few of us were surprised, almost all of us were shocked. The cause was not the information itself but the fact that we knew the rest of the world was watching us receive the information—the rest of the world being, by definition, wogs, fuzziwuzzies and *par excellence* the natives. What we haven't noticed is that the natives some time ago carried *their* conspiracy to the practical point of getting rid of us and our leading-reins and blinkers. During the Profumo crisis the English nation comported itself as a dotty old imperial dowager saying, 'Hush dear, not in front of the servants' and refusing to get it into her head that the servants have long since gathered up their insurance cards and left.

We pique ourselves that ours is a country where public opinion counts. And that is perfectly true—in the sense that not only does each of us have his opinions, as people do all over the world, but each of us has also his public opinions. Everyone has his list of things it wouldn't be 'suitable'—another exclusively English conception—to admit in front of his parents or his children, his boss or his employees. We all have a public iron mask for clamping over our faces the instant we notice there are strangers in the room.

Our doubletalk formulae are the vocabulary of this public mask. The really pernicious thing about them is that we don't use them purely as mechanical formulae—which really would be harmless, as though we simply agreed to substitute the symbol X wherever the word 'banana' occurred. Because we don't notice when we are using them, we can at arbitrary moments slip out of their technical meaning and into their everyday meaning without knowing we are doing it. This is most perilous when the words happen to include a moral judgment. The Wilde scandal, for instance, turned on one of our technical formulae—'unnatural

vice'. The Ward scandal turned on another—'immoral earnings'.
These are only forms of words for what we really meant, but
unfortunately, because we didn't employ mere uncoloured
symbols like X and Y, a whole circular argument was, without our
noticing it, implied. *Of course* it's immoral to live on immoral
earnings; nobody could dispute it. Of course it's vicious to practise
unnatural—or any other sort of—vice. We get our heads so deep-
buried in the formula that it becomes impossible to look and see
whether prostitutes really do earn a living in a more immoral way
than all the other people, from pop singers to photographic
models, who raise money on their sex appeal, and whether pimps
really are loathsome on a quite different and much deeper-dyed
scale of depravity than other forms of agent and publicity man.
We become incapable of even asking whether homosexuality really
is a vice—let alone whether we can really call something unnatural
when to such a large fraction of the human race it comes so
naturally that you can't iron it out of them even by threatening
them with prison.

Again, there is that phrase used by the broadcaster, 'woman
of commercial virtues'. This, like the old-fashioned phrase he
modelled it on, 'woman of easy virtue', implies an argument in
a circle. People sometimes complain that modern usage is vulgar
because it says 'morals' in the exclusive sense of sexual morals.
But in fact the vulgarity is a very old one. For centuries a woman's
'virtue' meant one thing only. It couldn't possibly be referring to
the woman's generosity, courage or kindness to animals. And this
expression, too, assumed a conclusion without deigning to prove it.
Of course it's bad, of course it's unvirtuous, to lose your virtue. To
this day, as another recent controversy has shewn, many people
are unwilling to let it be so much as asked whether chastity really
is a virtue. Someone wrote to the *Observer* the other day saying the
value of chastity was 'not controversial' but 'fundamental', and
that anyone who 'queries the need for it is unfit to hold any public
post'.

In this atmosphere of unproven—indeed, unqueried—assump-
tions, it has escaped our notice that chastity is no longer a virtue
but has become a neutral. In a rational view, the one sexual action,

apart from rape, which unquestionably *is* immoral and irrespons-
ible, is to beget or conceive a child without taking care to equip it
with a fastidiously selected heredity and two parents willing and
able to devote love and energy to its upbringing. So long as it
involved the risk of bringing an unequipped child into the world,
promiscuity really and rationally was immoral. On a rational
view, which goodness knows society hasn't always taken, homosexuals and women beyond the age of childbearing have been
exempted all along, but for the rest of us chastity was, until
recently, a virtue. But now we can manufacture reliable contraceptives cheaply and in quantity. This technological advance
has revolutionised sexual ethics, just as the invention of the camera
revolutionised the aesthetics of naturalism in painting. Yet many
people still have not noticed the revolution has happened. They
write to the papers saying contraceptives should be withheld from
young people because possession of them makes it easy for young
people to behave immorally—forgetting that in rational terms the
only thing which *makes* promiscuous sexual intercourse immoral is
the risk of producing a bastard.

I emphasise that this is the rational view. Many people don't
profess to form their moral judgments rationally—they form them
according to taboo, superstition or religious faith. Neither I nor
anyone else suggests that anybody should be obliged—or even
urged by fashion—to be promiscuous against his conscience or his
tastes: rape under pressure from public opinion would still be
rape, and still immoral. But it is only just that freedom from social
pressure should be distributed fairly. Christians have their own
reasons—or, rather, what they hold to be more-than-reasons—for
continuing to maintain that chastity is a virtue. But it is unjust to
suggest that those who don't accept that the Christian faith
transcends reason should go on believing that something is a virtue
when there is no longer reasonable grounds for believing it. Yet this
doesn't prevent people from writing to the papers saying everyone
in England should recognise the virtue of chastity because 'we
are, after all, a Christian country'.

This last statement is untrue. I don't argue this on the lines that
the majority of British citizens are not practising Christians,

though I'm sure it's true they're not. I argue it historically. We *used* to be a Christian country—in the days when the law compelled everyone to go to church. The Roman Empire became a Christian Empire—became, in effect, Christendom—when Justinian pronounced a law headed 'Concerning the most high Trinity and the Catholic Faith and that no one should dare publicly to dispute it'. But the history of England consists to a great extent of a struggle, often involving bitter martyrdoms, to cast off that habit of thought. The upshot of the struggle is that we are not a Christian country. We are a tolerant country. And the whole point of the state of affairs we have achieved is that atheists like myself, Christians like you and Buddhists like him *should* dare to dispute the Trinity—or even the moral standing of chastity. What's more I believe enlightened Christians would support me and agree both that we are and that we're right to be a tolerant country, because they have long ago perceived that a Christianity which goes to church because it will have to pay a fine if it doesn't isn't worth having.

At the Ward-Profumo scandal it was our public mask which got a shock. Privately, we were not shocked. We had no cause to be. Dr Ward had not behaved anti-socially, since he took care not to burden the community with unwanted babies; it was unreasonable to exact from him a public declaration of his immorality when he did not personally subscribe to, and reason does not insist that everyone should obey the rules of, the morality concerned. It was the public mask of Britain which put on its panic grimace and began shrieking that the community's most important values were under attack. A leading article in the *Guardian* made an extraordinary statement. 'Other things', it said, 'have been prostituted in this salacious case than the bodies of a few young girls. One of them, not discussed much because it is so personal, is the idea of genuine and durable human relationships, of the close bond between a man and a woman which includes a physical sex relationship but is not circumscribed by it.'

That statement reminds me of the cries we heard at the time of the Wolfenden recommendations about homosexuality, to the effect that marriage and heterosexual love were under threat.

That could be true only if the heterosexuals of England were heterosexual merely *faute de mieux* and were secretly longing, but did not dare, to be homosexual. Likewise, the only circumstance in which the life led by Stephen Ward can 'prostitute', whatever that means, or can be any sort of threat to 'genuine and durable human relationships' is if, in those relationships, the husband would much prefer to make use of call-girls, but dare not, and the wife would much prefer to *be* a call-girl but lacks either the courage or the talents, which include not only good looks but a facility in bodily relaxation, necessary for the job. But in that case the 'genuine and durable human relationships' are not genuine at all — and barely human. Each partner is cheating the other and employing the other as a second-best outlet for desires he dare not gratify in the way that really appeals to him as first-best; each partner is, in effect, using the other as a thing. Such a transaction would be a good deal more sordid than a transaction with a prostitute, where the market price is openly paid and there's no pretending about love.

As a matter of fact, when the public mask of Britain speaks about love, morality and marriage, it often does utter concealed slanders of this kind and often does distort the things it is intending to praise. There is, for instance, the much quoted complaint made by Lord Denning that public opinion does not frown on adultery as fiercely as it would on 'any other form of stealing'. The implication must be that, from the moment the marriage certificate is signed, a husband or wife becomes an object which can be stolen, a thing without rights or volition of its own, which another person may use and in which he has property rights. Lord Denning's remark has been taken to shew that he is a strict moralist. If this is strict morality, may we all be libertines. But in point of fact it is neither strict morality nor the morality of our country as that has evolved during our history. It is some years now since our country discarded the concept that a person can be a thing — the concept, in other words, of slavery.

Along with it, we discarded intolerance.

An open letter to the Director of Public Prosecutions

(Catalogue of the World Book Fair, 1964; reprinted in *Books And Bookmen*)

Dear new Director,

About the major part of your job I'm sure you feel in no need of advice from me — and even if *I* felt it might profit you, a Book Fair is not the place to offer it. However, one corner of your resplendent office does deal with books, and here I think it only humane to offer you some guidance.

If you are not to be bewildered, you must forget your legal habits of thought. The world you are used to is hard-headed. When the law speaks of loss or injury, it means something concrete: the theft of goods to a certain monetary value, the loss of x pounds' worth of earning capacity for y years. Should I be unlucky enough to lose them, the courts will even value in sterling my good repute, or my husband's love. Dangers the law rarely takes into account until they have come to pass, and then it enquires whether a reasonable person, going on his experience, would have foreseen that the circumstances would cause a disaster. You are, moreover, accustomed to the law's employing words in a way that may not be idiomatic or imaginative but is, to the point of pedantry, precise.

You will, therefore, feel at sea when you find that the literary part of your new job turns on a word that has no ascertainable meaning, and is designed to ward off a disaster no one admits to having experienced. Your department does not use the word 'obscene' in its idiomatic sense of 'disgusting'. Which things are or aren't disgusting is, of course, a matter of opinion — like which books have or haven't 'literary merit'. But at least we all roughly agree what those terms mean, even if we differ about what they apply to. In point of fact, you would probably find considerable agreement if you postulated that murder and torture were disgusting. But your department doesn't consider those 'obscene' subjects. You make no attempt to close down the museums and castles where instruments of torture are displayed to parties of schoolchildren. So far as I know, your department has never prosecuted a book for graphically describing the obscene subject of war. In practice, 'obscene' means to your department something to do with sex or excretion. As a practical novelist I know that I risk prosecution if I publish a detailed account of a motion of the bowels, which happens to most of us daily to the benefit of our health and happiness, whereas I shall be in no danger at all if I merely describe one thug disembowelling another.

Even Latin, ancient prop of English legal jargon, does not disclose a concrete meaning for 'obscene'. The secondary meaning of *obscaenus* is merely 'obscene' all over again. Its basic meaning is 'of adverse omen, inauspicious'. You may begin to wonder if you have had the right training for your job. Would you not have done better to take a course in necromancy? This suspicion will only be aggravated if you look through your department's files and see what it used to consider (since Lady C. was acquitted it's been less sure of itself) 'obscene' words. These weren't prosecuted for being ugly: 'duck', 'bit' and 'punt', which rhyme with them, aroused no objections: and anyway, unless 'obscenity' is in question, your department takes no cognisance of artistic merit or demerit. (If it did, I could shew you filthy postcards — with subjects like 'The Goblins' Spring-Cleaning Day' — that would outface your most hardened employees.) Neither was it the words' meaning that was thought 'obscene'. A laxative advertisement makes, more verbosely, exactly the same injunction as one of the four-letter words. That word is obscene neither in sense nor in sound: it is simply taboo. Let a printer rearrange the alphabetical symbols to form 'tish', and all is well, if nonsensical: let him print them in the forbidden order, and unspecified disaster will ensue without discernible causation.

You are, in short, being asked to administer not a law but a primitive superstition. The crime committed by an 'obscene' book is not that it has corrupted someone: the crime is being likely to corrupt someone likely to lay hands on it: two likelihoods with not a certainty to go by. No person need come into court, give his name and complain he has been corrupted, asking the court to assess in sterling the value of his lost innocence. The court judges merely whether the book infringes a taboo. If it does, the book must be hustled out of sight before the magic consequence—a murrain, perhaps, on our tribal cattle?—follows. No one has ever seen this consequence. I have never met a corrupted person. (Am I one myself? I've read *Fanny Hill*, and commended its spirited metaphors and comely cadences to readers of the *New Statesman*.) Yet the danger is so acute that we have to be protected from it by an absolute ban. No ban protects addicts like me from buying and being publicly enticed to buy cigarettes, though lung cancer is tangible and demonstrable and the causal connexion between smoking and cancer statistically established. *Caveat emptor*—all except the would-be *emptor* of 'obscene' (that is, impregnated with immensely powerful black magic) books.

Does your department perhaps hold that *Fanny Hill* would incite people to copy Fanny? I'm sure it isn't so silly as to suppose a description is automatically an incitement. At least, as it doesn't prosecute those, it plainly doesn't think *The Brothers Karamazov* an incitement to murder, or *Treasure Island* to piracy. And murder and piracy are crimes. Sexual intercourse, even for money, isn't. If Fanny did incite anyone, which I don't believe she could unless the person were already so predisposed, to copy her act by act, the acts would still not be criminal. Usually incitement is a crime only if what people are incited to—breaching the peace, for instance—is a crime. From the 'obscenity' of a book no crime follows, and not even the demonstrable corruption of a single named, known person. The crime is the *being* 'obscene': being taboo.

Did you perhaps enter your office in the noble hope of keeping Britain moral? I must disillusion you. Morality consists of *choosing* the good. Whether it is or isn't immoral to read *Fanny Hill*, your department and the magistrate at Bow Street, by making it impossible for us to choose not to read it, have made it absolutely impossible for us to be moral.

I hope these pointers will help you discharge your new duties according to the traditions of your department. Of course, should you decide instead to discharge them according to common

sense, morality and that supreme public virtue, tolerance, you
will do so by letting the literary part of your office lapse into
desuetude.

Yours sincerely,

BRIGID BROPHY

Rococo Pieces

history, an overseas empire and the brightness of the light. Almost
every surface in the city is patterned. Most house fronts are tiled,
so that they look trellised by some intricate green-and-blue or
green-and-yellow flowering plant. Those not tiled are washed in
colour—often deep, porous-looking terracotta or midnight blue.
Many houses wear curving iron balconies like a flutter of black
lace at the bosom. Lisbon pavements are mosaics (the first requirement of a woman visitor is a pair of flat-heeled shoes), and often
the pavement is patterned with arabesques of black or dark-green
on white. The most splendid of all the patterned pavements is a
promenade down the centre of the grand avenue (one of the most
truly grand in Europe) da Liberdade. In the lay-bys of this broad
path, the mosaic underfoot spells out the names of national
heroes, but down the middle it sticks to the abstract curlicues of
high fantasy, as though some very dotty but very grand grand-
duchess had dipped her train in ink and gone swishing down the
hill.

Extravagance of decoration is matched by extravagance of flora
and, indeed, fauna. The grapes in the shop windows are as big as
plums, the cat that throws itself into your lap when you sit down
in the shoe shop (to buy a pair of flat-heeled shoes) as heavy as a
baby. Lisbon is so used to being fruitful that it treats even bread
as breadfruit: the rolls come to table each wrapped in its own
tissue paper, which is made into a bag by a moustachio-twist at
each end—the way oranges are wrapped in England. Wherever
there is space for it, Lisbon has a park; failing that, a tree: failing
that, a flower shop. Palm trees as well as fantasy duchesses march
down the Avenida da Liberdade, alongside a continuous stretch of
water-garden carried from level to descending level by waterfalls
twelve inches deep—which serve to separate the family of white
swans on one of the upper reaches from the black swan who,
usually from inside his house, exotically rules a lower one. In the
Estrela garden the blossom trees are of deep purple, and the water-
scaping here is subtle, sunken, almost secretive. On the edge of the
pool, two storks preen each other—and the whole garden rustles
with large, unusually tame and unusually bright-coloured peacocks.

All Lisbon seems to play with water. Cars are always being hosed in the streets; the streets themselves are hosed on Sunday mornings and are so steep that the water shoots down them as if down a roof; the stone walls of the very flower shops drip from the repeated hosing of their merchandise.

The water games seem echoed by the sounds of the Portuguese language, which is bolted and shuttered against foreigners. You feel that if you tried to learn it you would gain no Portuguese but lose whatever you might have hard-won of Italian, French or Spanish. To the eye comprehensibly latin (though the eye takes a second or two to work out that a shop calling itself *chique* is claiming to be *chic*), it is in pronunciation inimitably Moorish. The ash and ish endings of its words resemble the curly tails of arabesques or the lapsing plumes of a fountain; and their splashing in conversation round you as you walk through the street creates for the imagination a fairytale Arabian water-garden.

Lisbon's more-than-Vuillard riot of conflicting patterns would be intolerable but for two more-than-saving graces. One is natural: the light. Lisbon's is both a southern and a seaside brilliance. It is a city where you are always either going down to the sea or up to an eminence from which you can see the sea. The whole place is drenched in a brightness thrown off by the sea's crumpled silver-paper surface. Perhaps patterns conflict only when you cannot really see them. In Lisbon the glaze on each tile gleams individually, like the separate scales on a lizard in some meticulous eighteenth-century zoological illustration. At the same time, because you are always going up and down, and from darkness into brightness, the city continually composes theatrical effects. Look up a narrow street, and across the top, in full sun, is the façade of a house or—which in Lisbon is usually plainer—a church, lying flat against a vivid matt blue sky: it is pure backdrop, and the faint sea breeze which is always animating Lisbon seems to send a ripple through the canvas. Look down the same street, and the three-dimensional effect is so exaggerated that it seems it must be created of cardboard. Halfway down, as if placed by the designer to impress the perspective on you, you will usually see one of Lisbon's black-shawled, black-stockinged women balancing a tray on her head while she talks to an invisible interlocutor in a dark doorway. (It is presumably by some Middle-Eastern convention that only the women use their heads for portering: the men put their burdens on their shoulder.) The whole scene is like a blatant demonstration, a figure from a trigonometry textbook.

And mathematics, in a sense, is Lisbon's other redeeming grace. The eighteenth-century genius was for the architecture not just of buildings but of cities as wholes. The Marquês de Pombal, who was Joseph I's Minister at the time of the earthquake, took the opportunity to let in air and light—a deep draught of (in the most literal sense) the Enlightenment, of gracefully reasoned mathematics—to what must have been a medieval-cum-Renaissance fortress town. From the top of a belated monument, an Edwardian, rather ugly but impressive Pombal presides over his grand avenue. The avenue is flanked now at the top by modern buildings, further down by nineteenth-century ones—some of which writhe in the last spasms of the rococo manner; theirs is the statuary and the engraved glass of an *art nouveau* rococo, dedicated in spirit to Sarah Bernhardt. But though its components may degenerate, the structure of an eighteenth-century town plan is as immune to decay as the bone structure of a face. (It can of course be massacred: but that needs a fully capitalised philistinism, such as has destroyed London.) The grand design of the grand avenue marches on to the huge Praça Rossio, now agreeably strident, commercial and neoned. This breaks into a perfectly logical grid of small, fashionable shopping streets planned by Pombal even down to what sort of goods were to be sold in each street. One of them now contains a bank whose name seems to epitomise, charmingly, humanity's attempt to have the best of both worlds —the Banco Espírito Santo e Commercial de Lisboa.

The downward streets—the entire plan proceeds downhill— of this network lead into the Praça do Comércio. This is that rarity in Lisbon, a large flat space—a square of which three sides constitute a commanding eighteenth-century palace, colour-washed in a beautifully melancholy green. The fourth side is the sea. In the centre of the square, as though emphasising that this is one of the few spots in Lisbon where you could exercise a horse, there prances a massively and curvaceously rococo equestrian statue.

In the beautiful arcades of the green palace, the paint peels. Above that, the small, economical political posters—which in Portugal means government exhortations—peel too. When you leave the lee of the palace and approach the sea, the wind hits you, and with it melancholy. The quays are as desolating as a disused railway station. You become aware of the close connexion —and the geographical distance—of Brazil. The wind wafts in a dream of empire and at the same time howls for an empire lost. It is on the quays that Lisbon is most conspicuously an inter-national port and an imperial city—and also a provincial market town. In every Lisbonese café a man hopes to be allowed to polish your shoes: down on the quays five or six such men eagerly run at you, carrying their little footrests-cum-seats. There are trays of depressing doughnuts, and of wiry toys; and a rack of cheap, horribly innocent paper books and magazines.

It is provincial—yet imperial. If you go in spring, before winter clothes are discarded, you see men in coats or half-coats with sheepskin collars. They look as if they had just dismounted after a day's work on a South American ranch. In spring, too, the roast-chestnut barrows are still in the streets, putting you in mind of even older empires. The charcoal fire in the belly of the barrow has for a chimney what looks like half an unglazed earthenware pot. Sometimes the pot has been cracked and then riveted and wired together again. It might be any age, last year's pot or three thousand years old. It is dateless in material and in shape—a vast breast. It might be Cretan, Phoenician, Carthaginian.

Lisbon has not, as a matter of fact, forgotten Carthage. In-scriptions over shops—or, sheerly, the telephone directory—shew that Aníbal is a not uncommon first name.

On both sides of Pombal's design for Lisbon rise cliffs of town-scape on which even the eighteenth century could not impose symmetry. What it did do was crown the most salient height with the Estrela church, which is Lisbon's unacknowledged master-piece, and make over to the baroque style the interior of churches

on other eminent points, like São Roque and São Vicente, whose
fabric dates from the sixteenth century. In São Vicente the
bottom altar on the right takes flight into a brilliant baroque
fantasy of Saint Michael. In São Roque the deep-recessed side
chapel of Saint John the Baptist glows with Portuguese extravagance which was in fact designed, by Vanvitelli, in Italy; the whole
thing was, by another kind of Portuguese extravagance, shipped
bodily in 1710.

It is advisable — and in any case probably inevitable — to get lost
on your way to São Vicente, because that is the one sure method of
penetrating the huddled poor quarter you would never find if you
looked for it. Lisbonese slums teem much more *privately* than
Italian slums. Their hermetic life seems not so much European
as North African. Even the distinguishing marks of a Catholic
culture are not visible. No shrines hang on the corners of houses,
and there is none of that black scurrying of priests across sunlit
squares that one knows from Italy, because the Portuguese constitution separates church and state and priests do not walk
abroad in their *soutanes*.

You can go up Lisbon's inhabited cliffs by cruel long hauls of
shallow steps or by sharp stone staircases as sheer as those in a
ship; by a sort of funicular tram; by ordinary tram — one says
'ordinary', but the tramlines look like the tracks left by virtuoso
skiers. Or you can take a taxi. The steepness of Lisbon defeats
even the Lisbonese. It is one of the few cities where the inhabitants
actually use their taxis themselves, and taxis are not only cheap
but available, since they cruise all over the city.

Lisbon also has buses, and for English visitors these have a
peculiar disconcertingness: they are green-and-cream double-
deckers, of the kind you see in the Home Counties. There is a
comic *bizarrerie* about waiting beside a palm tree for what is to all
appearances the municipal transport of Slough. Indeed, whether
through the proximity of Gibraltar, through being, as the English
are taught to say whenever Portugal is mentioned, 'our oldest
ally' or simply through the sympathy of one bereaved imperialist
power for another, the Portuguese have adopted several appur-
tenances of English life. One of them is the umbrella, much more

freely carried by Portuguese than by most South European men. Even more surprising, if you are used to the continental habit of hiding the public telephones in cafés and letter-boxes in walls, is the sight of red-and-cream telephone boxes like English ones, and free-standing vermilion pillar boxes on the English model but just a touch, I think, slimmer.

The easiest way-in to the idiom of Lisbon's architecture is via the museum. Actually, the Museu Nacional de Arte Antiga has much else to offer: an introduction to the painting personality of Domingos António de Sequeira, a Portuguese and lesser but all the same fascinating Goya, and an international collection containing several fine pictures (an Allori 'Rest on the Flight', two Tiepolo *bozzetti* and a Cranach 'Salome') and two masterpieces. It fits in with the long historical wrangle between on the one hand the two nations of the Iberian peninsula and on the other the states that were to resolve themselves into the two Low Countries that the famous Bosch triptych of the Temptation of Saint Anthony should be in Lisbon. But it seems by the merest act of flotsam that a Piero della Francesca should have fetched up there — until you see the picture, which is of a full-length Saint Augustine: round his cope runs a frieze of biblical scenes, almost of tiles, that one would swear had been designed in the Portuguese taste.

That taste itself the museum sketches in a collection of objects removed from churches: painted wood statues two foot in height and charmingly dumpy in design; weighty black-and-gold altars like dressing-tables for a queen in mourning; an entire chapel rescued bodily from a convent, gleaming with tiles, grilles, marble, and wrought and beaten gold-coloured metals. You have to stand and let yourself, too, be wrought and beaten upon for a minute before you become versed in the idiom. All baroque and rococo are acquired tastes, but in Lisbon particularly so because, compared with the style of Salzburg or Bavaria (or even the delightfully eccentric and localised version of it in which Prague is built), the Lisbon style is provincial. Where they offer a porcelain airiness, Lisbon offers the splendour of a piece of chunky jewellery.

Eighteenth-century Lisbon was provincial even while it was

going up. The earthquake was one of the great news items of eighteenth-century Europe, nutshelling for a sceptical age the whole problem of the benevolence of God. It was a San Luis Rey of the old world. But Portugal's own response to its disaster, as Voltaire shews by the bitter fun he pokes in *Candide*, was considered by the rational rest of Europe to be old-fashioned, superstitious and stupidly cruel.

The cruelty, at least, is no longer part of the atmosphere. I expect a Portuguese bullfight is as vile as any other teasing of animals, but—since Pombal's time—they do not kill the bull. An English visitor can be shamed by the poster in the airline office which allures tourists to Britain by a photograph of a foxhunt. We still do kill the fox. The style of Portuguese art and of Portuguese religion (for whole tracts of history the two are pretty well synonymous) is worlds away from the torments of Spanish art and religion. The two countries are as different in *feel* as in language and landscape. Lisbonese churches are almost without paintings of tortures, deaths and atrocities, without crowns of thorns. Indeed, you could tour them without discovering that the Christian deity is male. Lisbon is ruled over by a baroque madonna.

Remaining provincial, Lisbon itself has not caught up with the revolution in taste which would nowadays make its architecture high fashion if it were known to the rest of Europe. The Victorians never acquired the acquired taste for baroque or rococo. Even in 1913, when *avant garde* spirits were beginning to turn back to the eighteenth century, Baedeker was being bad-temperedly dismissive about Lisbon's churches. Lisbon seems to have got stuck in Baedeker's period. (It has, for example, too few open-air cafés for the number of Lisbonese who would like to sit at them. As though it still thinks the open air perilous to health, its café life is Sickertian, conducted in great rooms with bare floorboards, round, marble-topped tables and billiards upstairs.) Tacitly agreeing with Baedeker, Lisbon thinks its churches not worth mentioning or even recording. You can search the shops in vain for a postcard of the outside—let alone the harder-to-photograph inside—of the Estrela, though you may have a hundred tinted pictures of the

madonna at Fátima, who looks as though she had been produced
by Max Reinhardt, and almost any article you can name executed
in cork. And when you ask the friendly taxi-driver for the Estrela
he will—once he has understood that by 'Estrela' you mean what
is in Portuguese pronounced something on the lines of 'Ishtreller'
—assume you want to visit the garden, not the church.

Although it suppresses the harsh and bloody episodes of the
Christian story, Lisbonese church architecture has not gone soft.
The bright white façade of the Estrela, a dizzying fantasy of
pierced towers which half-masks the marvellously mannered and
elongated dome in the centre of the building, is the apotheosis of
sugar-icing architecture: but it is markedly *hard* icing—wedding
cake, yet with an undertaste of the funeral feast. Most of Lisbon's
churches are sad. Their expected exoticism (in any country where
'kiosk' is spelt *quiosque* and pronounced key-oshk, you would
expect the churches to be half mosques) goes so far as to hint at
the barbaric. Besides the Moorish, there is a touch of another
important influence in Portuguese history—a suspicion, in the
deep-hanging metal lamps or in a banister which rails off part of
the nave into a sort of flat gallery, of the synagogue.

Once your eye is in, it sees that decoration is not used to conceal
or merely cover surfaces, but is put into the service of structure,
defining and emphasising forms. One of the brilliant devices of
the Lisbonese church is to push the heaviest decoration outwards,
into the side chapels, so that each separate jewelled construction
is isolated in its own recess and glows individually like Lisbonese
pineapples on their individual hooks. The shapes of Lisbonese
architecture are themselves the shapes of a baroque madonna; it
is an architecture of heavy bosoms. Lisbon never quite took off into
the elegance of the rococo. Provincially, it stayed behind, weighted
down not just by its provincialism but by sorrow. If Lisbon has
almost expunged Jesus Christ from Christian iconography, it has
thereby isolated the sadness of the bereaved and ageing madonna.
What is truly barbaric about its style is that all its beating of metal
is inspired by the same emotion as the beating of a breast; its
extravagant habit of piling marble with lapis lazuli and then
encrusting it with enamel is equivalent to the behaviour of a

provincial widow who piles one outmoded, slightly absurd but splendid garment on top of another as a gesture of mourning.

Knowing the prejudices of 1913, you might guess from Baedeker's remark — 'the fitting up of the interior is ornate rather than artistic' — that the interior of the Estrela would in fact be the most beautiful of all Lisbon's interiors. But neither acquaintance with Lisbon nor reading Baedeker by contraries could tell you in advance that the interior, tall and almost gaunt, is — for all its lacertine splendour of marble — poignantly austere.

The Estrela (officially the Basílica do Santissimo Coronação de Jesus — the high altarpiece is of the flaming Sacred Heart) was designed, apparently in imitation of an earlier eighteenth-century Portuguese church, by Matheus Vicente and Reynaldo Manuel, and was built between 1779 and 1796 to the orders of Maria I of Portugal, who was fulfilling a vow, her prayers for an heir to the throne having been answered. Her lovely and chilling black-and-white tomb stands to the left of the high altar. 'The Latin inscription', says Baedeker, 'is curious.' He seems to have been being malicious. Perhaps he meant the Latin is curious. The inscription itself, though of almost unreadable length, seems a conventional eulogy of Maria's piety and her zeal in building the church, plus a mention of her residence on the other side of the ocean.

As a matter of fact, she died there; her body, following the Portuguese fashion for shipping things, must have been brought home. The personality of Maria I epitomises the tragi-comedy of Lisbon. I see her as a sub-Goya, a Portuguese-Goya — in fact, a Sequeira — queen: short, rather clumsy, her rouge unequally apportioned between her two cheeks. I see her leading in Brazil a life of Ronald Firbank exoticism and exaggerated Catholicism, being fanned by pious maids with pampas grasses. She was the daughter of Joseph I, the earthquake king, and she married her father's brother. Perhaps it was the superstition that such marriages are infertile that made her feel it necessary to pray for an heir. Baedeker does not bother to mention that an altarpiece on a side altar at the left of her church shews the queen, dumpy and sweetly pie-faced in the bottom right-hand corner, beholding in the top left-hand corner a vision of a madonna almost as dumpy as herself. During the Peninsular War the Portuguese royal family took refuge in Brazil. Maria I died in Rio de Janeiro in 1816. She was eighty-two, and had been mad for the last twenty-four years.

When you leave her church, cross the road and go to the Estrela garden opposite, you seem to catch an echo of her gauche poignancy in the squawking of the splendid peacocks under the palm trees.

Mersey Sound 1750

New Statesman, November 1963

To my mind, the two most fascinating subjects in the universe are sex and the eighteenth century. Anyone who so much as partly shares that persuasion would expect *Fanny Hill*, as a cardinal source-book for both subjects, to be an interesting document. An interesting novel, however, you would not expect, if you judged by the run of minor eighteenth-century fictions or, still less, by the run of famous naughty books. As a rule, if there's anything drearier than smut, it's old smut. When *Fanny Hill* turns out to possess, over and above the interest of its material, literary charm, that seems almost too bonus to be true. It is in fact a highly engaging little erotic tale — perhaps the most engaging to emerge from the entire seventeen centuries of European literature that lie between *Daphnis and Chloe* and *Claudine à l'École.*

Not that there could be an instant's doubt which of the seventeen *Fanny Hill* belongs to. Tone, tenor and preoccupations, to say nothing of the heroine's first name, are all so dead-central to the period that it is by an accident of poetical precision that the book was published slap in the middle of the century, in 1750 itself.* No more can one doubt that John Cleland's (quite legitimate) purpose was to entertain and get paid for doing so. He neither aims at nor achieves a masterpiece. When he touches art, which is quite often, it is of a truly artless kind; he is not even trying, in the fashion established soon afterwards by Greuze and towards the end of the century transplanted into literature by Bernardin de Saint-Pierre, to be artless.

That, given the period's wrongheadedness about art and artlessness alike, is to Cleland's advantage. The literary masterpieces of the eighteenth century were produced against the grain of a philosophy convinced that imagining was less useful than moralis-

---

* The precise date of *Fanny*'s first edition is variously given as 1750, 1751 and (according to the 'Supplement' to Mr Alan Hull Walton's translation of Sade's *Justine*) 1748 or 1749, when copies privately printed in Russia reached London.

ing, and often against the grain of the author himself. The century's greatest poet could actually, looking back in admiration to the primitive Golden Age, count among its glories that it had no arts. Laclos cast *Les Liaisons Dangereuses* in the flippant convention of an erotic novel with a perfunctory punishment of vice appended. The result is that we have only just noticed that it is a great novel, and have still not wholly taken in that it is one which turns its convention upside down — not an erotic but a thanatic novel, whose ending, so far from being an appendage, is the tragic doom towards which the characters unconsciously drive themselves all along. Cleland's talent, quite lacking the stamina of Pope's or Laclos's, could never have stood out against the exceptionally marked and uniform grain of his age. Had he attempted high art, he would have got trapped in the marmoreal toga-folds of the eighteenth-century elevated manner. He is saved because, unlike Laclos, he *is* writing an erotic novel. He can skip the elevation and get on with the erections. 'I skip over', Fanny frankly writes, 'the natural grief and affliction which I felt on this melancholy occasion' — that is, 'the loss of my tender fond parents.' Likewise she will 'skip over all that happened to me on the road' — the road, that is, conducting her to London and prostitution from her poor but respectable birthplace near Liverpool.

Cleland's immediate model was perhaps *Clarissa*, which had appeared piecemeal in 1748 and 1749. Cleland adopts the standard epistolary form, but with no attempt at verisimilitude, let alone at providing a textbook of epistolary etiquette. He simply splits his novel into two 'letters': each is framed in a couple of merely formal, though pretty, colophons in the shape of an introductory 'Madam' and a concluding 'I am, Madam, yours, etc.', which are addressed to an anonymous friend to whom Fanny has promised an account of 'the loose part of my life, wrote with the same liberty that I led it.' Having tidied away the paraphernalia, Cleland is able to get on with a remarkably uncluttered narrative line; indeed, he gets Fanny to London, and places her, penniless and friendless, at the mercy of a brothel-keeper, in about as many pages as it takes Richardson volumes to get Clarissa into the same fix.

In outline, Fanny's story apes Clarissa's; but where Richardson, a proto-Sade but less frank, presides sanctimoniously over his heroine's long-drawn degradation, Cleland and Fanny are cheerful. The opening discloses the end will be happy, and in fact everything between is arranged in a manner thoroughly agreeable to Fanny. Quickly escaping the nasty procuress, she takes up with —indeed, falls more than a touch in love with—one who is kind, deals fair financially, and tenderly suffers her girls to have none but gentle and sexually attractive clients. The most remarkable thing about these 'memoirs of a woman of pleasure' is that the pleasure concerned is Fanny's. She may be bought, but she is no inert bit of goods. Her 'downfall' is really one long delightful swoon into the depths of pleasurable sensation—which Cleland has her describe in vigorous and often beautiful metaphorical language; by her own account, her subject is 'properly the province of poetry, nay, is poetry itself.' The emergence of the eighteenth-century heroine, explaining herself in the novel through letters and in the opera through arias, reflects that women had emerged into social articulateness. No longer mere objects of men's pleasure, they can themselves be pleased and say so. A whole public—including the women themselves—was demanding to be told what *did* please women. Cleland's was perhaps the most explicit answer.

True, the century had 'defloration mania', and Cleland caters for it. The parlour game of Fanny's fellow-prostitutes is to swop accounts of how they lost their virginities; and Fanny's own history is a prolonged defloration. It begins at the hands of a prostitute, and proceeds to the loss of her visual innocence when she spies on sexual encounters; even after her first lover deflowers her, it remains for a lover more ithyphallic to enlarge the result; even then, with the help of stage-property blood, Fanny fakes up a maidenhead to have it destroyed all over again by a client whose particularity that is. She undergoes yet another 'initiation' —into a society of four couples who take turns at coupling in front of the others. There follows Fanny's systematically progressive initiation into variations and perversities; and at the last Cleland still has an ironic conceit up his sleeve whereby Fanny, reunited and about to be married to her first love, comes to bed as blushingly as a virgin, though her blushes are now for her non-virginity.

Yet all these pangs of defloration are in the service of erotic pleasure — Fanny's and the reader's. Postponing the culmination of Fanny's deflowering is equivalent to postponing the point where the reader has a mental orgasm. By fulfilling the requirements of the erotic novel, Cleland produced an article rare in the eighteenth century, a full-length (which Voltaire's are not) prose narrative where the climaxes are cumulative instead of cancelling out. Fanny herself propounds the literary problems: to avoid at once gross language and 'mincing ... affected circumlocutions'; and to introduce variety into subject-matter 'eternally one and the same'. Surmounting these problems, Cleland arrived at the craft of the well-made novel. It is all the same craft, whether the novel is erotic or non-erotic; and to a large extent it is the same craft as that of the well-made erotic daydream. Cleland's narrative, in which all inconveniencies — including the very possibility of pregnancy — are simply swept out of consideration, is purest daydream. Its content could not possibly shock anyone who has ever led a fantasy life.

Eighteenth-century philosophy had, like Fanny herself, recognised pleasure as nature's 'principal end'. Cleland is simply practising what Edward Young preached, that 'Pleasure is nought but virtue's gayer name.' Fanny simply opts for virtue in the form of true and single-minded love, but without, as she rightly claims, hypocrisy: she simply finds love ultimately more pleasurable, and wastes no regret on a past which has only the better equipped her, in experience and money, for love.

Her progress is sprigged with pleasure-motifs of the age. Fanny is Johnsonian in devotion to London, and Evelina-like in contempt for provincials. The story's one excursion out of town echoes *The Rape of the Lock* in being 'a party of pleasure ... up the river Thames'. Cleland imports no realistic exoticism from his life in Bombay or as consul in Smyrna. He uses only the fashionably exotic slang of calling a brothel a seraglio. That and the 'ceremonial of initiation' which Fanny undergoes fore-echo Mozart's

themes—and even his serious social intent. Like *Die Zauberflöte*
itself, *Fanny Hill* sketches an ideally benevolent society, albeit in a
brothel. Jealousy is drowned in a diffused bisexuality: even the
constant voyeurism, practised through an implausible quantity of
cracked panelling, symptomises an attempt to render sex sociable.

Opera is, as a matter of fact, one of the motifs which Cleland's
mind, running so true to the age, leaps at for a metaphor of
sexual 'harmony and concert'. The female body he maps according to the great minor art of the age, landscaping. It is to Watteau's
landscapes that he casts back when Fanny calls sexual intercourse
'our trip to Cythera'. Indeed, Cleland's couples share with
Watteau's a grave elegance and a courteous concern for each
other. Even when the four pairs take turns on the couch, 'good
manners and politeness were inviolably observ'd'. Cleland himself is as decent. Mercifully *not* 'robust' or Rowlandsonian, he is
decorous not merely in vocabulary but down to the last cadence
of his fine, plain prose.

Cleland does not achieve the imaginative world of a Watteau
or a Tiepolo; his is the fantasy world of a decorative painter. The
entire novel might be taking place, like his pleasure-party, in a
pavilion whose 'marquise' is 'figur'd with fluted pilasters ... the
whole having a gay effect upon the eye, wherever you turn'd it.'

Sade

Justine

by the Marquis de Sade
Translated and edited by Alan Hull Walton
[Spearman. 30s.]

New Statesman, December 1964

'Let me begin', begins Mr Alan Hull Walton, 'with a very
necessary warning. The Marquis de Sade's novel, *Justine*, is one
of the most terrifying books ever written.' Let me begin with a
necessary amendment. *Justine* is one of the least terrifying books
ever written. But Mr Walton's long introduction to it scares me
pretty badly.

Justine is to picaresque what *Otranto* is to Gothick: the silliest
example of its genre. It has the conventional frame, whereby
chance throws together two long-separated sisters, one of whom
then supplies the body of the book by relating her adventures to
the other. Justine's first-person narrative is one of those eighteenth-
century ribbon developments: a narrow, flat account, always
taking the shortest distance between two events, of what happened
next. It is as under-realised as a synopsis. It gets a move on;
but where to? It isn't graphic enough to be pornographic.

From the quotations Mr Walton gives in French, Sade's style
seems formal without being thoughtful, and (apart from the bad
grammar of 'gave my companion and I places', where presumably
Mr Walton alone is to blame) the translation seems faithful to it.
I did, however, wonder if Mr Walton knew which language he
was translating when he added a footnote explaining that a

character named Du Harpin is spelt with a capital D in the first edition but that later editions use 'the familiar "du".'

Sade wrote the book in fifteen days (of 1787), in the Bastille. As that might suggest, the story patently consists (patently, that is, to anyone prepared to admit to ever having had any such things himself) of scenes from Sade's masturbation fantasies. They are fitted to the picaresque formula on the basis of one episode to one orgasm, and joined by a thread of plot so perfunctory as to be hardly coherent or, in a mood of post-orgasmic drought, by a metaphysical discussion. The one constant character, Justine, represents Sade's own consciousness. The experience to which she is particularly liable is being tied up and beaten (the beatings in masturbation fantasies are, as Freud discerned, a mirror of the rhythmic act of masturbation itself), and the pattern of her adventures is to escape from one such situation and wander until she chances on a protector, to whom she entrusts herself but who promptly discloses the same predilections as the last. Her protectors do violate her sexually, but many of them have a preference for methods that would work equally well if she were a boy—as, of course, she essentially is. The book's true interest is that it seems to preserve some very early layers of childish fantasy, overlaid by the compromises Sade's Ego had to make with the reality of his not being a girl. An episode about halfway through, where Justine's current protectors amputate two of her toes, may even preserve a castration fantasy in which the very young Sade magically became a girl. Its nature (as well as Sade's ludicrousness) is given away not only by Justine's quick and complete recovery (a week of rest at Sens) but by the fact that later protectors never notice that she lacks two toes.

I call them protectors rather than tormentors because Justine's ingenuousness (she always has to be tricked into the situations where she gets beaten up) is transparently another of Sade's devices for fooling his Ego. Justine's accident-proneness is as easy to see through as the publicity-proneness of professedly publicity-shunning film stars. Her tormentors are in fact her lovers, who pass through the story for no purpose except to minister to the tastes she is ashamed to avow. In this work at least, the eponymous hero of sadism is expressing his masochism. Simone de Beauvoir's book on Sade feels its way (through much uneconomical existentialising about the interchangeability of subject and object) to the perception that the sadist's whole purpose is to feel by sympathy the sensations he inflicts on his victim. She also notices that murder is not essential to Sade's eroticism (as a matter of fact, he is such a bad plot-maker that he is sometimes driven to it to get a character off his hands), whereas narrative, told by one character to another, is. In fact, all these characteristics come from masturbation fantasies—which are narratives, whose origins date from the magical, pre-real world where the child can conceive of assaults without their necessary consequences, and where the person who inflicts and the person who feels are bound to be one and the same.

Sade leads me to speculate whether masturbation is the invisible and unmentionable portion of the literary iceberg. The belief among readers and critics, which has infuriated novelists before, since and including Jane Austen, that a novel is 'only a novel' whereas non-fiction is serious, and also the scarcely less philistine belief that if a novel is serious it must be copied from life and cannot be just made up, may be the price fiction pays for the fact that most people's earliest or only experience of making up a narrative is for their sexual fantasies. I suspect that writers themselves often secretly interpret Coleridge's distinction as being between imagination and masturbation fantasy. In reality, art is just as pleasure-seeking ('aesthetic' is only the Greek for 'via the senses') and just as selfish (the author is the sole judge of what does give artistic pleasure) as fantasy; artistic pleasures can be called 'higher' only as some animals can—they are more complex. Sade fails not through being a *fantaisiste* but through being a *naïf*.

His translator, by contrast, is jejune. He can be priceless (deadpan, he lists as Sade's 'desirable recommendations' contraception, education and 'colour of clothing according to age'); he is garrulous (he somehow drags in Canon Rhymes) and inaccurate (misspelling Genet and Cathy Gale); and he asserts 'there can be no doubt of the influence' of Sade on Hitler. If it were so (but then Mr Walton also holds that Nazism was a black-magic secret society), what is he doing loosing that influence on England? He insists on a rigorously sexual definition of masochism, yet says 'true Sadism' need not be sexual but includes 'cruel and tyrannical domination'. Only by that stretch can Sade's inept fantasising be connected with Hitler's real acts. Profuse as he is with irrelevancies, Mr Walton lists the 'most important' books on Sade without mentioning Simone de Beauvoir's (did he hesitate to use the familiar 'de'?), from which he might have learnt that 'the ultimate irony' of Sade's sad life was not whatever it is he claims but that the Revolution censured Sade as too moderate. There is a world — art — between sadism and cruelty. 'Yes,' says Hesione Hushabye, 'cruelty would be delicious if one could only find some sort of cruelty that didn't really hurt.' That is just what Sade was seeking and good artists find.

La Serva Padrona

(Programme note for the Edinburgh performance of an
Opera da Camera production first given in 1963)

Pergolesi himself would probably have said that his important
work of 1733 was *Il Prigionier (Superbo)*, the full-scale opera into
which *La Serva Padrona* was inserted merely as a contrasting
comic interlude. Yet it was the interlude which pointed out the
route that all opera, comic or serious, was to take.

The *buffa* tradition in which *La Serva* is conceived had the
advantage of being slightly beneath the notice both of high fashion
and of aesthetic theory. This left it free to experiment. The
suppleness with which Pergolesi exploited the freedom can be
measured by comparing *La Serva* with its serious — and great —
contemporaries, the Italianate operas of Handel. Whereas
Serpina has scarcely made her first entrance before she and
Uberto are locked in a dialogue as sharp as a duel, thrusting and
impolitely cutting each other's words short, Handel has difficulty
in bringing his characters to grips at all : their rare direct exchanges
are as formal as the exchange of couplets in Racine, and the
succession of their arias seems to follow the rules of debate in some
grave and courteous parliament, where no orator would dream of
interrupting another. Handel did develop a more flexible manner
— but in oratorio, which is more narrative than drama. In the
theatre, although his operas are far from unstageable, his genius
is imprisoned in the splendid baroque edifice of the serious convention : he is confined to illustrating rather than demonstrating
the action, and limited to the psychology of *moods*. Pergolesi has
already invented a texture which can express the psychology of
personalities, because it can shew them actually in inter-action. His
is no more 'natural', no less a convention, than Handel's, but it is
a flexible convention. By the same token, he has carried opera
forward in style : solid baroque symmetry has dissolved into the
flexible line of the rococo.

Having become versatile, the *buffa* idiom was able to do *opera
seria*'s own job better. By 1787 no valid distinction was left

85

between *buffa* and *seria*: Mozart's *Don Giovanni* is a tragic *opera buffa*. It treats buffoonery and tragedy alike in the *buffa* manner, which from then on served, in a variety of developments, simply as the operatic manner. Incongruous as it seems, a revenant from the early eighteenth century would probably classify the style of Wagner's music-drama as more *buffa* than *seria*.

At its original Neapolitan production, *La Serva* (in this resembling other artistic revolutions) seems to have had neither a marked success nor a marked failure. Its triumph came (again not untypically) after its composer's death—in France, where in a pamphleteering war it defeated the native baroque opera and became one of the most influential works of eighteenth-century art. Its subject was to eighteenth-century taste: domestic (it was in the eighteenth century that the novel, most domestic of literary forms, came of age), ironic and, in its theme of intermarriage between the classes, characteristic of the period's social preoccupations. (The Plautus-like story is a simplified version of the plot which Richardson a few years later embodied in *Pamela*, which via Goldoni's dramatisation passed into innumerable eighteenth-century operas.) Indeed, the very notion of the servant turned boss summarises what in political fact happened in France at the end of the century. Not for nothing was Rousseau the partisan of Italian-type (that is, *La Serva Padrona*-type) opera. *La Serva* is a Revolutionary as well as a revolutionary work. It raises in one the two great eighteenth-century rebellions, of servants against masters, and of women against men.

From this famous opera Mozart borrowed not only the flexible idiom which he developed into a subtle psychological instrument but also, by a free play of invention, many actual motifs. Serpina's soprano 'tippití' echoed by Uberto's bass 'tappatà' prefigures the more sophisticated wit of Figaro's bass but feminine 'din-din' and Susanna's masculine though soprano 'don-don'. The heartbeats which the 'tippití' and 'tappatà' represent are heard again in Zerlina's 'sentilo battere' and Belmonte's 'klopft mein liebevolles Herz'. Serpina's 'Voglio esser rispettata ... come fossi padrona' foreshadows Leporello's 'Voglio far il gentiluomo'. La Serva herself is transfigured into the many Mozartian maidservants who, if they do not become bosses, outwit bosses: Susanna (in whom Mozart's meaning was consciously Revolutionary and feminist), Blonde, and Despina in *Così*. The very idea of calling the maid Despina, which is the Greek for 'padrona', is perhaps a deliberate pun on the title of Pergolesi's opera—just such a pun as one might expect of da Ponte, who was learned enough to have been a teacher in a seminary and Revolutionary enough to have been dismissed for his Rousseauist views.

Quintessentially rococo, Pergolesi's style has the brilliant high spirits of a pleasure party, touched with a feeling of the impermanence of pleasure. As an artistic personality, he resembles the great rococo painter of melancholy pleasure parties, Watteau—not just in the brute fact that both died young of consumption but in the sense they give of thinking of themselves as isolated (which in Pergolesi was perhaps emphasised by his being lame). In *La Serva* it is an irresistible inference that the figure with whom the composer identifies himself is the *commedia dell'arte*-inspired mute. Just so, Watteau (also a musician) paints himself set apart from the rest of the pleasure party, playing a sort of rustic bagpipes to which the others dance, or seems to identify himself with the sad clown figures of the 'comédiens italiens'. Fittingly enough, when (two decades after Pergolesi's death and three after Watteau's) *La Serva Padrona* had its great success in France, it was in the repertory of the 'comédiens italiens'.

Don't Never Forget

Mozart

a documentary biography
by Otto Erich Deutsch
translated by Eric Blom, Peter
Branscombe and Jeremy Noble
[Adam and Charles Black. £5]

Sunday Times, July 1965

Mozart's letters allow one to be, in imagination, Mozart. Professor Deutsch's volume allows one to inhabit an eighteenth-century Europe briefly visited and nonplussed, as in a baroque miracle, by Mozart's angelic genius.

Professor Deutsch's technique of biography-*vérité*, previously exercised on Handel and Schubert, is deadpan. After a section of 'antecedents', he starts straight in on January 1756 and the registration of Mozart's baptism and proceeds to print chronologically (and here in versatile translation) every extant document (except, of course, the Mozart family's letters, though he includes even those when they are official petitions) with a bearing on Mozart's life. Selection has been done only by time and chance. The mortar between documents is minimal and scholarly: the provenance of each and (which is sometimes this volume) its place of first publication, plus bare references and cross-references.

Professor Deutsch notes, after the baptismal entry, that Mozart was born on St John Chrysostom's day, but leaves the reader to notice for himself that, in the continental fashion, it is the later Christian names that count, the two by which Mozart called himself being preceded by the saintly sleeping partners Joannes Chrysostomos, and that the Amadeus (presumably given in com-

88

pliment to the godfather) is registered in its Greco-Latin form Theophilus. The multi-lingual wordplay characteristic of Mozart's mentality (and no small part of his operatic aptitude) seems predicted at his very christening.

This technique is, of course, no substitute for insights into Mozart, though it may provoke new ones (or indeed corroborate old; I, for instance, who have traced the influence of *Hamlet*, which Mozart discusses in a letter, on *Don Giovanni*, am charmed to find a contemporary reviewer of the opera saying 'Mozart seems to have learnt the language of ghosts from Shakespear', and Constanze affirming, after his death, that her husband had been 'well acquainted with Shakespeare in the translation').

But the story, simply as a story, is all the vivider for not being told but left to be observed. So is the external, meetable personality of Mozart: a little man with a pale face, blue (by one account) eyes, a tenor singing voice, a passion for billiards, a childhood dread of the trumpet, an adult dislike of the flute and the harp, a talent for drawing, the habit of 'always playing with something, e.g. his hat, pockets, watch-fob … as if they were a clavier' and a propensity (which reminds us that he belongs to the world of Jane Austen) for exchanging with his friends inscriptions in albums. Indeed, in one album Mozart (perhaps, as Professor Deutsch suggests, because he was then considering another trip to England or perhaps through the sheer anglophilia declared in his letters) chose to write in (foreigner's) English: 'Don't never forget your true and faithfull friend'.

In newspapers, advertisements for sheet music, posters, programmes, title pages of libretti, Professor Deutsch's readers get news of Mozart through much the same media as they would if it were all happening now. They experience the shock of his death at thirty-five ('I was beside myself for some considerable time', wrote Haydn) and, from closer to, the agony of Mozart's knowing that he was dying ('I have the taste of death on my tongue') and dying poor. Professor Deutsch's scholarly note bites all the more ironically deep for correcting the legend: 'It was not a pauper's funeral, but the cheapest available.'

Then follow the wads of officialese through which Constanze

eventually secured a widow's pension, and details of the concerts in which she toured to raise money: sometimes she and her sister Aloysia, whom Mozart had been in love with before his marriage, sang his music; once the six-year-old Wolfgang stood on a table in Prague to sing the *Vogelfänger* song his father had written for Papageno. That was how the world paid the artist whose creative imagination and intelligence are perhaps the best vindication the human species could push forward were the evolutionary process to ask why humanity should not be scrapped and replaced. Don't never forget.

Forms
and Genres

The Novel as a Takeover Bid

(broadcast, Third Programme, August 1963; *Listener*, October 1963)

There are signs that novels provoke in their readers some resentment which other writings don't provoke in theirs. Novels seem to bring out the nanny in people — a nanny who is always slapping the novel down. Many readers were brought up on, and still obey, the Victorian adage that one shouldn't read novels in the morning — a thorough nanny's adage, like not eating between meals. I've never met a novelist who thought one shouldn't *write* novels in the morning, though it's a point on which I'd like, if I dared, to question Miss Compton-Burnett. There seems to have been no prohibition about reading poems in the morning, or history books, or maps — or even palms or fortunes in teacups. Newspapers, letters, non-fiction books — all seem to have counted as 'serious', whereas 'novel' was synonymous with 'frivol'.

That belief dates from well before the Victorians. In one of her noblest passages of satire Jane Austen defended the novel against the affected sigh 'O, it's only a novel!'; and for a century before she defended it the novel had been repeatedly attacked as scandalous or slighted as silly. Indeed, to worry about the state of the novel — either its morals or its intelligence or both — is almost as time-honoured as to worry about the state of the younger generation. As yet, even the foggiest old fogey hasn't pronounced that the younger generation has ceased to exist: but the equivalent has been said about novels. Soon after the last war an extraordinary fashion broke out among literary public figures for pronouncing that the novel was dead. What the pronouncers probably could have said with truth was that they were dead to novels. But they went so far beyond that that I don't think *I'm* going too far if I see in their readiness to pronounce the novel dead a wish that it *should be* dead.

Nowadays the fashion for saying the novel is dead is itself dead. Probably only a novelist would remember it ever happened. The novel is allowed to be alive and said to be kicking. And yet it often seems to kick with only one leg: or, rather, only one of its legs is truly fictitious. It's as though novelists have permitted what was recently said about their art to shake their own faith, and would rather not rest their case wholly on fiction. They feel safer if they can claim some extraneous importance as well—usually a sociological one. Many of the novels which have come into notice in the past fifteen years read like grown-up versions of those fictionalised documentaries for adolescents which are called as a genre 'career books' and have titles like 'Janet Takes Up Refuse Disposal'. The author seems unwilling wholly to rely on what he, too, has evidently come to think of as 'only' fiction—only, that is, the art practised by Dostoievsky and Henry James (both of them too frivolous, of course, to be read in the morning) and by Choderlos de Laclos and Jane Austen—'only', as Jane Austen herself put it, 'some work in which the greatest powers of the mind are displayed' and which has 'only genius, wit, and taste to recommend it'.

If people who are not otherwise philistine feel a special resent-ment towards novels, which some novelists feel a need to guard against, it must be because of some property novels possess which other forms of art don't; and the obvious one is that the novel makes a bid completely to take over your consciousness while you are immersed in it. We give our attention to any work of art: to the novel we give our whole conscious minds, and meanwhile we lose the use of them ourselves for our own egoistic purposes. Even music, which seems so absorbing, doesn't supply imagery—or at least not the sort which occupies the imagination down to the last visual corner. Either you follow music intellectually, following the score or an analysis, and keeping up with the argument as you do in reading a non-fiction book: or you let the music create a mood on which you drift or soar away—in which case it's *you* who supply the imagery; you're daydreaming with accompaniment. I think, incidentally, that opera is an exception—not surprisingly, since opera is half literature. I deliberately say half literature rather than half drama, because the plot in an opera can never be unwound as swiftly as it must be in a play: characterisation through music and singing is always slower, and in a great opera it's more reflective, than characterisation through action: the result is that opera is not so much like a straight play as like Shakespeare's poetry-dramas—or even like a novel. Significantly, if there was one thing the intellectuals of the eighteenth century attacked more regularly than the novel, it was the opera.

With the exception of opera, music occupies the mind in time without quite filling it with images: a painting, on the other hand, supplies images but doesn't occupy the mind for a long continuous stretch of time. A building takes time to explore, to sort out, but the time need not be all at one sitting: architecture lacks any equivalent to the novel's trick of binding you to it by sheer suspense. When I read a novel I simply daren't leave the hero hanging over a cliff; but I've never felt that if I don't quickly work out how the cathedral roof is supported the roof will collapse. Again, buildings may suggest, but they don't supply images. Lyrics do; short stories do; but they invite you to pause, shut your eyes and let the images echo on your eyelids at the end—which comes soon. Films and plays approach the novel's (or narrative poem's) power to pin you down for hours at a stretch, and they even have the advantage of appealing to your very ears and appearing to your very eyes, with a much sharper verisimilitude than novels. But they also have the practical disadvantages that come from being a social form of art. They can't keep going for so long. Even the most unrelenting biblical epic has to let up for an interval so that the cinema proprietor may take his retail profit on the soft drinks and the audience may creep out to the lavatory. Only the novel has the tremendous advantage that you can eat your way through an entire supper without lifting your eyes from the print; you can take it with you to the lavatory.

Still, playwrights and filmwrights, although they have to observe more limitations in using it, do command some of the novelist's power to immerse. Or, rather, they did. Nowadays they seem to be either driven from that power or inclined to abdicate. It's interesting that just at the time when novels are becoming alloyed with non-fiction the drama is becoming gripped by a doctrine of alienation which wantonly throws away the singular power fiction can exert over an audience—which deliberately breaks the audience's communal immersion in the drama and forces the members of the audience back each into his own separate consciousness. Films haven't abdicated the power—it's been taken out of their hands. Much of their audience has simply deserted to television—a medium far more successful at documentary or 'actuality' than at fiction (unless you count the advertisements). In any case, fiction or non-fiction, television insists on being bitty. There's no question of your consciousness being taken over for a whole evening by any *one* continuous thing. For total immersion television substitutes sprinkling. That a large part of the cinema audience deserted *en masse* the moment they were offered television seems to me a mass expression of a resentment that must have been felt in the cinema all along, a resentment against the immersing power of fiction—the same resentment which has been shewing itself, sporadically and obliquely, against the novel for longer still.

The affected young women Jane Austen satirised were being hypocritical. They said 'only a novel' but really they adored novels; and as a matter of fact if novels and operas were the forms most attacked in the eighteenth century they were also the most fashionable and popular forms. But there's no hypocrisy about the present-day intellectual—he may even be intelligent, as well —who pointedly 'doesn't read novels'. He genuinely has put them away as childish things. And obviously to be immersed in a story *is* a childish thing—though that's not to say it may not be a mature one as well. It reminds you of daydreaming; the absence of your own consciousness during the process reminds you of actual sleep. To read a novel in the morning was like going to sleep in the morning: a dereliction of duty. The prohibition even had a practical good sense: novel-reading does, momentarily, unfit you to cope with the telephone or the gas-meter man: knock-knock, and for a second you are genuinely not at home; 'you' have been replaced by the novelist. I think one's own Ego may actually be jealous of the novelist's Ego which drives it out. And certainly I think one's own Ego may feel weak—that is, childish— at letting itself be driven out. One resents any temptation one can't resist: that is the whole basis of puritanism.

Of course, some people can prove their self-control to themselves by reading a novel in small bites, with long intervals between. But then some people can eat a bag of peppermint creams at the rate of one a day. They are not, incidentally, people much approved of by the manufacturers either of peppermint creams or of novels. But I don't think I'm arguing merely from the self-interested position of a manufacturer when I maintain that surrender to a novel is not necessarily weak, any more than falling in love is necessarily weak. That, too, involves not merely surrender but some long-term sinking of one's own consciousness in another person's. One of the symptoms of being in love, which does not mark any other form of love or lust, is that you want to hear everything the other person can or will tell you, not primarily for the information it may give you about life or even about the person concerned, but for the preciousness of seeing the world through his eyes—just as you see *a* world through the novelist's eyes, and want to hear everything he is prepared to tell you. What you could say was weak in the moral sense, if you want to talk in the moral sense, and what I would certainly say was weak in the artistic sense, is the present fashion for compromising on a novel which is partly non-fiction. That is like the sort of agreement some puritanical people make with themselves whereby it's all right to commit adultery providing they don't enjoy it. With the novel, you might as well surrender wholly or not at all. Novel-reading really is a sort of catalepsy. Your personality is taken over; you are possessed.

If I were asked 'What is the *point* of letting your Ego be taken over by someone else's?' I should find it hard to answer except by 'Well, what is the *point* of remaining your own Ego, of continuing your own consciousness?' I refuse to believe that art needs or can have any justification other than that it exists. It has no more point than life: that is, its point is inside, not outside, itself. I think it is a growth *on* life, in the same way that life is a growth on matter.

But although one can't—although one, I feel, *mustn't*—make out a justification for art, one can well make out the sources of some of the pleasure it affords. Most people agree that a good novel creates a cosmos of its own, and that what we are applauding when we judge it a good novel is its internal logic, its logic within its own cosmos, irrespective of whether or not that is consistent with the world of reality outside. As a matter of fact, that in itself *is* a reference to the world outside, but at one remove. The very principles of self-consistency, the axioms of logic, whereby we judge whether a novel is self-consistent, come from reality, not invention. It seems likely that when we enjoy exploring the self-consistency of a work of art we are re-awakening the pleasure we took as small children in exploring the real world and discovering that it made sense—or, more importantly and more basically still, the pleasure we took in discovering there is such a thing as making sense.

All the same, I'm quite sure it's wrong to think that all a good novel does is re-tread the old ground we explored as infants and re-assure us that we can still make sense of a logical pattern. One reason why I'm quite sure is that there are artifacts which do just that and nothing more, and we have no trouble in recognising that they are not works of art. A crossword puzzle is composed of words: but it isn't literature. Neither is a detective story that is strictly all detection and no story. We know what these things are: refreshments: not self-justifying activities but retreats from which we can presently *mieux sauter*. They re-assure us—by being recreations: literally, re-creations of our original discovery of logic and order: if we can make the puzzle work out, we emerge with our sense of mastery over the world reaffirmed. But to think a novel does no more than that is to dismiss it as 'only' a novel. The puzzles are perfectly legitimate; we all need them from time to time, especially when we are ill, when our sense of mastery is most shaken. When you visit an invalid you should take him detective stories and crossword puzzles, but not great novels. Great novels are not re-assuring.

Obviously a novel does provide a certain amount of naked wish-fulfilment: it is related to the daydream. Equally, it does satisfy the Ego's more sophisticated wish that there should be order in the universe: in all works of art, the pleasures of form are related to those of the crossword puzzle. All art may be entertainment as well as art. The novel does what we basically and naïvely require of any entertainment: it 'takes you out of yourself'—so thoroughly that we may resent the usurpation. Other works of art allow us to keep our consciousness more or less intact: it is as our recognizable selves that we creep into the cosmos a great painter has imagined, and as we look round our vision blends with his: we are enlarged, but we remain aware of ourselves as the vessels into which his creation is poured. Only the novelist smashes—temporarily—the vessel. The novel doesn't stop short at taking you out of yourself: it puts the author in your place. It forces you to *become* the author. His awareness permeates the book, and what the reader is aware of—*all* he is aware of—during the reading is the author's awareness. If the reader impersonates the characters, he must do so through the author's impersonation of them. What we as readers are required to do is concur in, endorse, the author's consciousness.

Although we become the author in one sense, there is another sense in which we are not the author of the book: we have no choice about the events which happen in it. We can register dislike or disbelief only by switching off before the end—which addicts find it as hard to do as ceasing to eat the peppermint creams before the bag is empty; it remains hard even if you find yourself being sickened by what you are consuming. Yet although we have no choice about the course the book takes, the author's business is to convince us no choice is needed—it's like one-party government—because no alternative is possible: given the premises he posits, what the author says happens in the book is inevitable. The internal consistency of a novel is its inevitability. A novelist invites us to concur in his novel, to endorse its inevitabilities as we endorse that two and two make four. A really great novel is one which it's no use rebelling against. In its own artistic terms it's just right. When we judge it a great novel, we are passing in artistic terms the judgment Pope believed could be passed in moral terms on the whole—the real, the outside—universe: 'Whatever is, is right.' And Pope was in fact trying to justify the universe as the product of an author.

Within the self-contained universe constituted by a work of art, we are asked to go over each of the author's strokes with our own pencil, concurring in the logic whereby the author made the stroke just so and just there. This tremendous responsibility is in one shape or another laid on us by every work of art: and we may resent or shirk it whatever the medium. But a novel lays it on us particularly stringently because it hardly allows us to retain a self to bear the burden. Among artists, the novelist is the only one who comes in for resentment when the reader's consciousness returns to the self from which the novelist expelled it. The novel-reader, as he goes under, as he becomes immersed in the book, is being re-born into a new identity — the novelist's; and then, when the immersion is over or interrupted by the gas-meter man, he has to be re-born all over again into his own identity. It's not surprising that novel-readers sometimes let out new-born yells of shock and protest.

The British Museum and Solitary Vice

London Magazine, March 1963

Not all the instruction in the British Museum Reading Room is in the books. Some of it is in what the books are in.

The standard B.M. format for lodging its miles of books is miles of open shelving. Some books, however, are kept in glass-fronted bookcases, and the bookcases are kept locked. Books must not be taken from them and served to a reader without a nod from high authority.

The B.M. is not so incautious as to name the category of books it keeps in locked cases: it prefers to classify the books according to their lodging, and calls them 'case books'. Evidently, however, it is not simply locking up the antique and irreplaceable: many of the titles are recent. Here and there a title hints what it is the B.M. has in mind. One title includes the word *erotica*. 'Glamour photographs' is presumably the trade term for nudes. 'Handy Hints for Glamour Photographers' or some such title presumably instructs touchers-up how to put the highlights on the nipples.

Into the same case with these few, however, the B.M. has lumped dozens of books which any *London Magazine* reader might have, un-locked up, at home. I say this expressly: in January, the *London Magazine* published *The New Confession of George Barker*; the B.M. keeps *The True Confession of George Barker* behind glass. Its companions include (besides the expected three old Graiai, *Ulysses, Lady C,* and *The Well of Loneliness*) *Marilyn Monroe* by Maurice Zolotow; *The Gravy Train*; a translation of Catullus; Bruce Marshall's *The Fair Bride* ...

It is quite probable that the nod from high up which will release any of these titles to a B.M. reader is never withheld. And in any case the greatest library in the world can hardly be entertaining a serious hope that it can keep readers away from books which they can buy in the shops or borrow free from less great but more public libraries. But results are often a secondary consideration in censorship. The act seems to be done for its own sake: for

pleasure. In many jobs, censorship is a perk of office; the censor
will no more forgo it, even if it is quite ineffectual, than the man
who is entitled to a second biscuit with his tea will forgo that, even
if he dislikes biscuits. On the whole, however, censors probably do
not dislike censorship, which must, on the evidence, be one of the
most nearly universal of pleasures. Even out of office, people play
shadow cabinets with it: the great non-fading parlour game of
literate (in the literal sense) societies is suggesting books which
'ought to be banned'.

Some of the most fluent players have been censored themselves
— which is surprising only if one forgets the lesson of primitive
Christianity, that victims of persecution are not necessarily against
persecution. D. H. Lawrence is the proto-martyr of the cause of
literary freedom — 'a man', says the blurb to the Penguin selection
of his essays, 'who suffered more persecution by censorship than
almost any other writer of the century.' Yet when you actually
open the essays, 'Even I', you find Lawrence saying, 'would
censor the genuine pornography.'

Of course he would. They all would. Nobody would — or does —
censor anything *except* 'the genuine pornography', by which every-
body, Lawrence included, means what *he* doesn't approve of. And
that, as the B.M. shews, can mean pretty well anything.

In *Lady C*, Lawrence was, strictly speaking, challenging the
definition not of pornography but of obscenity. It wasn't what his
characters did and felt but the words they did and felt it in.
Lawrence was, of course, perfectly right to insist on these words,
if only to disprove the primitive superstition that four alphabetical
symbols, if set up by a printer in one particular sequence but not
in any other, constitute a magic spell which will bring disaster on
the land. He was right also about the need to restore the words to
our language with their meanings, instead of a mere explosive
charge, attached to them: but right — which is not unusual with
Lawrence — for the wrong reasons. It has nothing to do with the
'communion' of 'two eternally different streams' of the blood
which 'is the substance of the soul', and everything to do with
syntax. *The Fallen Idol* shewed up the emotional inadequacy of
police jargon like 'to be intimate with'; and as a matter of fact any

phrase in which the man is or does something *with* the woman is linguistically inadequate—inadequate to the act which, of all acts, is transitive, with a male subject and a direct female object. If this seems to us coarse, if it even seems to hint at brutality imposed on the woman, the fault lies with our obsession with brutality. The act *is* so—and is, actually, not the least bit of good to the woman if it isn't. As a matter of fact the verb *love* is also transitive; it has the same vowel sound as, and is neither coarser nor prettier than, the other four-letter verb which represents one of the acts in which it may take expression.

Lawrence was even right to restore the excretory four-letter words: for the simple—the only valid—reason that the alternatives are horrid: horrid not because we have made them so, as we have arbitrarily done with the four-letter ones, but because of the slithery attitude of mind they betoken. The great humiliation of hospital is that it reduces the patient not only to the bodily dependence but to the vocabulary of the toddler at the pottie. People who are ill already should be spared the nurse's 'Number one or number two?' Indeed, though many nurses would probably opt for it, the nurse should be spared *having* to put the enquiry through coynesses of this kind. In our present state of linguistic manners, she has no choice. If she uses the Latin terms taught in her training, not one patient in ten will understand (and no one can blame them, given that the medical profession pronounces Latin even more perversely than the Church). If she uses the English, everyone will understand, but nine out of ten patients will scream for matron.

(All the same, the verbal taboos are—slowly—melting: even in institutions; even in quite genteel institutions. A night or two ago, a female voice from the telephone exchange told me 'Ai'm sorry, caller, the switchboard is oll bollsed up tonaight.')

When Lawrence wanted to distinguish laudable, *Lady C*-type writing from 'the genuine pornography' (both judgments according to Lawrence, of course), he resorted not to argument but to the straight-from-the-shoulder emotive vocabulary of a padre or scoutmaster of the period. It is 'clean' and 'sound' versus 'depraved' and 'dirty'. (He mounts a quite pathological attack on excrement, which can apparently soil sex if thought of in the same breath.) And on days when Pegasus wasn't rising Lawrence's mind was, in fact, as undistinguished as any scoutmaster's—the penalty of any artist who deliberately renounces rationality. However, Pegasus did carry him to one true and basic perception: the reason why he is against 'the genuine pornography' (according to Lawrence, smoking-room stories and, to some extent at least, *Tristan und Isolde*) is that he believes it leads to masturbation. This is also, incidentally (though, not being as honourable as Lawrence, it won't say so), why the watch committee disapproves of 'the genuine pornography' (which to the watch committee means *Lady C*).

Having carried him so far, Pegasus went away and left Lawrence flat—with the conventional, scoutmasterly opinion that masturbation is a 'vice'. Indeed, Lawrence improves on the conventional view: masturbation is 'certainly the most dangerous sexual vice that a society can be afflicted with'. He has two things against it: it leaves the masturbator ashamed; and it is 'the one thoroughly secret act of the human being'.

If Lawrence had not thrown away rationality, he might have reflected that the sexual act he regards as so dangerous to society is in fact the only one which is absolutely guaranteed to do no harm to a second person. He might have wondered whether the masturbator *would* feel so ashamed afterwards if he had not been told masturbation was shameful by so many padres and scoutmasters—and now he has the identical homily thrown at him by the prophet and liberator, Lawrence. He might have asked just what jealous and aggressive fury against other people's sexuality motivated this universal puritanism on his part—for in attacking masturbation he was attacking what is probably the only universal form of sexual expression. And what sexual pleasure was he leaving permissible for the physically maimed or the people who are simply too ugly to attract other people sexually?

The most frightening item in the attack is, however, that Lawrence assumes masturbation must be bad because it is secret. If there is anything positively good, as distinct from neutral and to-be-tolerated, about masturbation, it is the secrecy, because the secrecy fosters the imagination. The masturbator's fabrications may not be the 'soundest' or 'highest' imaginings; but for people who do not read books they may be the only ones. When Lawrence's intuition carried him to the connection between pornography and masturbation, it was glancing at the assonance between reading and masturbation. They are both solitary activities. Reading can be *done* in full view, but it can even less be shared than masturbation. It is anti-social. The watch committee dare not quite express this opinion about all reading, so it picks out the ten per cent of reading matter which it thinks would give us the sharpest pleasure, because there is a sexual bonus as well, and bans that. But in its heart it holds all reading — all imagining — to be not merely a solitary activity but a solitary vice. Even in the urbane scholar or politician there lurks a scoutmaster, and once you give the scholar or politician powers of censorship it is the scoutmaster who speaks: lock up the books — the boys will be healthier, cleaner, sounder, less introspective (less imaginative) if they get out in the open air. Lawrence is against masturbation because, unlike the love-making of Lady C and her lover, it is unlikely to take place in the open air: 'marriage is no marriage ... that is not linked up with the sun and the earth, the moon and the fixed stars and the plants, in the rhythm of days, in the rhythm of months, in the rhythm of ... ' I can't be bothered to copy out any more of this fake-Swinburne incantation. In fact, marriage is no marriage that is not linked up with human imagination ('the marriage of true minds'), and that's all that matters. To express the value of Lawrence's poetic prose, one will have to take the meaning out again from the four-letter words to which he restored it, and use them as expletives.

A Literary Person's Guide to Opera

A forlorn title, that; for who would confess to being literary?

It is one of the neglected puzzles of comparative aesthetics that the word 'literary' is everyone's outcast. Unlike its counterparts, 'literary' isn't wanted even on home ground. Whereas it is a compliment to call a musician 'musicianly' or a painter 'painterly', you do not call a writer 'literary' — still less 'bookish' — unless you mean to insult him. Yet 'literary' won't transplant, either. A writer is glad to be told that his sentences are melodious, and a painter that his colours — or an architect that his proportions — achieve harmony. But none of the arts aspires to the condition of literature. Let some not very talented Victorian paint a picture which tells a story, and his work is condemned as 'literary'. But let Rubens paint the Judgment of Paris or Tiepolo paint Sophonisba receiving the Poison, and connoisseurs give those Old Master-pieces the more dignified name of history or mythology pictures, though in point of fact they tell a story every bit as much as 'When did you last see your father?'

It seems to me that the position of the literary element in opera is analogous — tolerably strictly — to its position in 'history pictures'. And of course the first point on which the analogy rests is that in both cases the literary element is very, very subordinate indeed. An opera whose music is bad can no more be saved by a superb libretto than the superb story about Paris and the three goddesses can save a painting of it if the painting happens to be by a bad painter instead of Rubens. No one in his senses would claim that the literary part of an opera can stand alone, shore up the music or even make an equal contribution to the total. I want only to urge that it need not be detrimental to the music.

I expect few people would say in so many words that they think the very existence of the libretto a pity, and that it's sad that so many great composers suffered the inexplicably wayward folly of putting so much of their greatest music into operas. Yet I suspect, perhaps unjustly, that there is implicit in some operatic criticism and comment a belief that to pay serious attention to the plot and characters would somehow taint the purity of the music and impugn the critic's musical sensitivity. Puritanisms of this sort do arise in some temperaments, and sometimes get taken up and made into a fashion. When as an adolescent during the 'forties I was becoming acquainted with the orchestral repertory through the help of my (slightly) elders and musical betters, it was definitely implied to me that no person of the smallest musical acumen would ever listen to the cadenza in a concerto—especially not in a violin concerto. If one was following the score, one usually *had* to stop at that point anyway, since the cadenza wasn't printed, but even if one was listening with one's ears alone one was meant to switch off one's attention and gaze ostentatiously round the concert hall in order to signal that one had switched off: cadenze were 'impure', virtuoso confections of the nineteenth century (even when they in fact dated from the eighteenth or the twentieth), designed for the flashy and unmusical tastes of fashionable audiences. Not till I was quite grown-up did it occur to me that this was a merely wanton puritanism. If the cadenza *was* horrible, it really would not corrupt me to listen to it for three-quarters of a minute—there was no need to treat it as the law treats *Fanny Hill*; on the other hand, it might be a rather charming little piece, but that I would never discover if I declined to listen to it. Above all, I was not obliged to choose between the cadenza and the rest of the concerto. It was highly improbable that the cadenza would be a work of such irresistibly seductive bad taste as to put my ear out and ruin my powers of appreciation before the 'pure' and 'proper' music had time to start again.

Yet I strongly suspect that some temperaments do actually fear a corruption of this sort if they let themselves attend to the (tainted word) 'literary' part of an opera—or, indeed, of a painting. A few decades ago it was the fashion to look at a picture such as the Rubens 'Judgment of Paris' and see both a certain composition of diagonals and pyramids and a certain sensuous contrast between the painted textures of naked human flesh, landscape and peacock, and yet deliberately to exclude from one's mind—because, not

being visual, it can't in the literal sense be *seen* — the information
that one of the naked women is Juno and that that is why there is
a peacock in the picture.

To behave like this is certainly artificial: it is to bite back the
first, childish question that comes to mind when you happen on
the picture. If you happened on three naked women and a peacock
in the course of a country walk instead of a visit to the National
Gallery, you would certainly seek an explanation — just as the
purists who make a point of not reading the libretto before sitting
through *Lucia di Lammermoor* would certainly demand what was
going on were they staying in a Scottish country-house-party when
a girl suddenly ran downstairs in a bloodstained nightdress.

Still, to be artificial is not necessarily wrong in artistic matters,
art being by definition artificial. This particular artificiality, however, seems to me mistaken because it is not necessary. It is not a
case of training and concentrating the mind on the work of art by
excluding anything which could distract and interfere. It is,
rather, an inhibition of an irrational kind; the 'literary' element
is dreaded simply through superstition; were it admitted, it would
not interfere and might enhance.

Of course if you had to opt for *either* composition and texture *or*
the 'story' of the picture, you would be bound to take the former,
because those are exclusive to Rubens and constitute what is
masterly in the masterpiece, whereas the subject of the Judgment
of Paris is shared by several quite indifferent painters. But there is
no need to choose — any more than there is to choose between
words and music in opera. The mind is quite sophisticated enough
to take in that one and the same area of paint is *both* a splendid
rendering of peacock-texture *and* the emblem of a goddess, or that
one and the same sound of a certain frequency is *both* top C *and*
the heroine's shriek of distress. With all respect to the debate
between the composer and the poet in *Capriccio*, there really is no
dispute; if it's a question of which is first in importance, the music
wins hands down; and it is of course one's musical ear one takes
to the opera house: but if the experience should offer also to
delight one's literary ear (as happened lately at Sadler's Wells
with the revelation of Congreve's words in *Semele*), it would be the

most wantonly puritanical defiance of the Life Force to slip in an ear-plug. Literary pleasure is not anti-musical but a happy bonus — as though a person one was in love with anyway turned out also to have won £5,000 on a Premium Bond.

As a matter of fact there are resemblances between the sensitivity of the musical and of the literary ear which are still insufficiently explored. Most of the recent approaches have come from the musical side, made by composers seeking a song-speech idiom. But some musical poet might be able to illuminate the strange fact that vowels have inherent (though not constant) pitch. Presumably in a line of verse the succession of vowel-sounds is related to the melody in music; and I have noticed that when someone who (as I do myself) lacks the talent for reading poetry aloud tries to clinch, say, a final rhyming couplet and fails, the displeasingness of the failure is remarkably like that of trying to clinch, but just missing, the final note of a tune. I suspect, in fact, that poetry-reading can be quite literally off key.

On a more fundamental level, my own deepest conviction is that form is one and indivisible, and constant for all the arts. (The most copybook example I know of 'sonata form' is Andrew Marvell's poem 'To His Coy Mistress'.) For what it's worth, I strongly suspect but could not begin to dream of attempting to prove that our appreciation of form is originally kinetic — that, at the bottom of all the layers into which our sensitivity has been educated and transposed by experience, we mentally *travel* the shape of a work of art, in a way we probably learned from being carried round in the womb, before we had any acquaintance with the sensations of touch, sight or hearing. If that is correct, it would make sense to say (as one might in any case on other grounds) that the sensuous content in every art is a metaphor (though never *only* a metaphor) for the underlying form; and in that case it would not be surprising if the metaphors were rather fluid and interchangeable, so that one art could slip into — and quickly out again from — the rôle of deputising, illuminatingly, for another.

In opera, I believe, the business of the literary element is to provide sometimes a metaphor and sometimes a perspective for

the music. Its obvious rôle as a metaphor is to lend specificness to
music's notoriously ambiguous descriptive powers. Almost the
only thing music can represent unambiguously is the cuckoo—
and that it can't differentiate from a cuckoo-clock. Handel's music
to 'As when the dove' is to my ear a very precise account of the
cooing and even the curious little jerks of the head made by doves
in love: but music is *par excellence* like the stain on the wallpaper
which might be a Red Indian or might be a chestnut tree, and if a
musicologist informed me that *Acis and Galatea* was originally composed as a chinoiserie oratorio I should no doubt hear those little
jerks as a perfect description of eating with chopsticks.

The descriptive metaphor a libretto provides is always conditional; it fixes, as it were, one possible aspect of shot silk; and
as if to indicate its conditional nature it is often a metaphor (or a
simile) in the literary sense, a metaphor within the libretto itself.
Acis and Galatea is not *about* doves; it's a case of '*as when* the dove'—
the libretto itself is playing with, trying out, the possible images.
This happens most brilliantly in the work of that grossly under-
rated librettist Metastasio, whose 'comparison arias' are, in the
positively grammatical sense, extended metaphors—which give his
composer the opportunity for a musical metaphor without breaking the unities of the drama. The scene may be a prison; 'when a
shepherd … ', begins Metastasio; and at once a pastoral image
lightens the prison without destroying the audience's prison-
illusion, and a pastoral aria has the opportunity to flower where
the plot gives no excuse for it.

The perspective which literature can lend to opera is a matter
of the characters (and the plot and actions which flow from them).
Music has an enviable immediacy of *mood* — enviable, I mean, to
writers (except, perhaps, to the most lyrical of lyric poets; it is
significant that the word 'lyrical' itself refers to a musical instrument). As a novelist I can much more easily express every nuance
of a character's misgivings, because misgivings at least have an
intellectual content, even if the intellectual content is a rationalisa-
tion by the character, than I can convey the simple fact that the
character is sad or happy. Had I been a nineteenth-century
novelist, I would blatantly have shifted this part of my job to my

reader: 'the reader will more readily imagine than my pen can describe with what happiness Emily ... ', etc. But the composer, should he have the gift of song, has only to put into Emily's mouth a few bars of ravishing melody, to which the librettist need supply no intellectual content — 'I am happy' will do very well, or even just 'Ho ho ho' — and he has made the audience not merely understand but share Emily's happiness.

Moreover, his moods, unlike his descriptions, are quite unambiguous. You could read a third of the way through *Anna Karenina* before you were quite sure the mood of the book is tragic. A hero of Handel's has only to utter three notes in a major key and receive one toot in corroboration from the trumpet, and you know he's in a mood of bravura triumph.

That, however, is all you know about him. Well, no; you know whether he's a tenor or a baritone (or, given that he's in Handel, an alto): but whether cunning, simple-minded, boastful, brave, witty, kind to children or beastly, the music can't in itself convey. He is incomparably, overwhelmingly *present*; but his past isn't implied in his present. It is the continuing individuality of a person which the story contributes. Music is supreme at the moods, the emotions, which only human persons can feel; but it has small means of conveying the individual personality who feels them.

This limitation it shares with painting. (*All* portraits, by the way, are 'enigmatic'.) It is significant that history painting throughout most of its career and opera at its start, before it evolved a narrative technique, both relied largely on mythology or historical fact for their subjects. An eighteenth-century history painting shews personages who often much resemble those of eighteenth-century opera and are placed in similar theatrically architectural settings; their bravura or elegiac mood is made almost as unambiguously plain as in opera; but for the personage's personality and past history the spectator in both cases was expected to apply to the common, educated people's stock of knowledge of the Bible or the classics. Perhaps it was when that stock could no longer be relied on to *be* common knowledge that history painting began to degenerate and opera had to develop a narrative technique out of the simple Handelian succession of arias which is often no more (from the literary point of view) than a succession of moods.

I am aware how dangerous it is to make any claim for even a subordinate importance of plot and character when, for example, Verdi was able to take the musical stuff he had already made up into *Stiffelio* and re-cut and re-sew it into *Aroldo*. Or again, how can one say that 'Dove sono' is a perfect expression of one individual personality, the Countess (Rosina) Almaviva, when virtually the same tune turns up in the Coronation Mass expressing a purely religious mood and attached to no personality? But really the danger is no greater than when one identifies a descriptive passage with the waters of the Rhine. No one is denying that out of context the waters of the Rhine could very well pass for a night on a bare mountain or Don Quixote charging a windmill. Since the music can stand alone, the libretto can be dispensed with if you don't like it; so there is no good reason to refuse to try it and see if you do. The Countess's personality and past history (which is what she is singing about) are a perspective, a funnel, down which one can gaze at that ravishing musical object, 'Dove sono'. The literature in opera is like a well-contrived exhibition or landscape gardening or architectural town-planning: it *arranges* the vistas down which we glimpse the objects. To my mind, the funnel of time and personality down which one contemplates the Countess's aria concentrates one's gaze on the musical essence. But anyone who finds the funnel obscuring it can simply remove the funnel: 'Dove sono' will still be there, quite unharmed, afterwards.

Sentimentality and Louisa M. Alcott

Sunday Times Magazine, December 1964;
New York Times Book Review

Who's afraid of Louisa M. Alcott? Well, Louisa M. Alcott, for one; and, for another, me.

I'm afraid of her in a quite straightforward way — because she makes me cry. Being myself an almost wholly unsentimental writer, I'm not a bit afraid of her example, which doesn't tempt me. It's not as a writer but as a reader that I fear her.

Her own fear of herself was, however, more ambiguous. She is, I suppose, of all writers the one whose name *means* sentimentality: and yet sentimentality is what she and her characters most dread. Indeed, the very reason why Josephine March preferred to be known as Jo (and I would guess the nickname was the final simple stroke which turned her into one of the classic characters of popular-cum-nursery culture, up there with Sherlock Holmes and Little Miss Muffet) is that she found the name Josephine 'so sentimental'.

I was driven back to Louisa M. Alcott, whom I hadn't read since I was fourteen, by the recent revival on television of the old film of *Little Women*. By the old film I mean the one with the young Katharine Hepburn — and there I instantly caution myself not to render unto Alcott credit which belongs to Hepburn. The cinematic personality of Katharine Hepburn (for which I imagine the credit belongs to the real-life personality of Katharine Hepburn) is one of those purely poetic literary inventions like Rosalind or the very idea of a seraph. Tears shed over Hepburn are diamonds, cutting clean and deep lacerations into the cheeks they course down. They have no connexion at all with the synthetically pearled snail-track left by the tears of sentimentality. It was just Louisa M. Alcott's good posthumous luck that Hepburn played Jo and that the high ruffled necks of 'period' clothes (to use the word in its purely evocative or estate agent's sense) set off to perfection the essentially tragic sinewiness of the Hepburn throat.

And yet: one can't say Alcott did *nothing* to deserve her luck. Hepburn was never so ideally cast again. It's already something that Alcott created the character which most perfectly became her. And then — the clinching point — the film provoked tears even when Hepburn was not on the screen.

It also brought back enough memory of the text for me to think that it was sticking fairly reverently to Alcott situations and dialogue — which I soon afterwards confirmed by getting hold of the book or, rather, books; the film is in fact taken from both *Little Women* and *Good Wives*. Buying them turned out to be an exercise in itself in nostalgia for a pre-war childhood. They are pretty well the last genuine *books*, with binding and dust wrapper, to be had for a paperback price. Presumably, therefore, they still sell in commercially worthwhile quantities (though as they are out of copyright there is no author's royalty to add its mite to the selling price). Indeed, perhaps they still sell as a going contemporary concern: for though the publishers admit, by the clothes on the pictorial wrappers, that the stories themselves are 'period', there is nothing to make it unequivocally clear that they weren't written yesterday. You have to consult a reference book to discover that *Little Women* was first published in 1868. The blurb of one edition still speaks of 'Miss Alcott' — which seems to surrender the advantages of suggesting she's immortal in favour of those of suggesting she's still alive.

Having re-read them, dried my eyes and blown my nose (it is itself a sentimentality that this less dignified aspect of weeping is so seldom mentioned: one day I shall go through the fiction in the public library and to every 'His eyes filled' add 'so did his nose'), I resolved that the only honourable course was to come out into the open and admit that the dreadful books are masterpieces. I do it, however, with some bad temper and hundreds of reservations.

For of course to admit sentimentality at all is to play with fire. Sentimentality is always doing something of which art can stand only very small and controlled amounts — bursting out of the conventions of art and making a direct appeal (all art makes an oblique one) to real life. Sentimentality is always playing on your experience of real drowned kittens and real lost mothers—or, worse still, playing on your real dread of losing kittens or mothers. The weepiest of trashy movies is the one which throws in a moment or two of genuine newsreel. And then, having invoked the reality of the real world, sentimentality does the one thing neither morality nor art can stand for—it is hypocritical.

The true artistic impulse is, largely, cruel—or at least relentless. To bring a novel, for instance, to a climax, the artist must drive the situation, and probably the characters, to extremes. He harries his *donnée* until it falls apart and its logical structure is pitilessly exposed. The sentimentalist, on the other hand, is a non-artist who won't take the responsibility of being ruthless. He won't drive his situations to the point of artistic inevitability. Instead, he appears to hold his hand in compunction. He resigns himself—much too soon—to the will of God; but covertly he is manipulating the will of God to suit what he is too hypocritical to admit is really his own taste.

Hundreds of fictional infants were so to speak raped on their deathbeds by Victorian anecdotalists—both novelists and painters —in order to procure for author and audience the pleasure of destroying an innocence but in such a way that the pleasure could pass for the quite innocent, the even creditable, enjoyment of feeling a spasm across the eyelids. Even now one cannot stand quite indifferent beside those deathbeds. I think Oscar Wilde said that no man of feeling could read the death of Little Nell without laughing. But the unwitty and much more terrible truth is that no one can read it without crying. Dickens has made the illegitimate appeal to real life and, no matter what ludicrous nonsense he makes of the death of Little Nell, the death of children *is* sad.

The sentimentalist always breaks the rules of art and frequently those of morality. The most unforgivable of all the occasions when sentimentality has burst through the artistic conventions is the one when Peter Pan bursts through the proscenium and invites the audience to keep Tinker Bell alive by affirming that they believe in fairies. That the audience consists of children is the ultimate sentimental immorality. Christendom's inveterate habit of telling

its children fairy tales and then breaking the convention by
assuring them that the tale is true and they must feel obliged to its
hero, who died for *them*, is, if not justified, mitigated by the fact
that most of the adults concerned really believed the story themselves and certainly believed it would do the children good to
believe it. But I will not accept for a moment that J. M. Barrie
had any more belief in fairies than — well, than the children in his
audiences had.

When Theseus calls the lovers' account of what took place in
that wood near Athens 'antique fables' and 'fairy toys', Hippolyta
objects that their story 'More witnesseth than fancy's images, And
grows to something of great constancy'. So it does: to a fairy tale
genuinely imagined (and therefore genuinely and poetically
moving), which is to be believed utterly — but strictly in the realm
of the imagination. But Peter Pan's telling the audience that
Tinker Bell 'thinks she could get well again if the children believed
in fairies ... If you believe, clap your hands!' is moral torture
inflicted by a wanton — but highly skilled — sentimentalist. Ours is
a paradoxical society which dreads that one of its children might
come on that charming, sentimentality-free little tale *Fanny Hill*
and yet for decades put on *Peter Pan* at the very times of day and
year when it was most likely to be seen by children. (Unless our
winter holiday is in fact built round not the 25th December but
the 28th — which commemorates the Slaughter of the Innocents?)

Not that I am supporting censorship, even for *Peter Pan*, though
if I could see any sense in censorship at all *Peter Pan* would be my
first and probably only candidate. I just think we ought to treat
Peter Pan as a play for adults, as we already sensibly do its runners-
up as sentimental masterpieces for the theatre, *Private Lives* and
Who's Afraid Of Virginia Woolf?

It would certainly be unkind to deprive adults of *Peter Pan*,
because as a piece of craftsmanship it is perhaps the most highly
skilled job in the repertory, and is therefore capable of giving
pleasure to two groups which more usually fail to agree on anything. For, incongruously enough, it is on works of literary craftsmanship that highbrow and lowbrow can often meet. Really, of
course, they are at cross purposes. The lowbrow cares nothing for

technique as technique, and probably doesn't even notice it as such. All he wants is a good read at or a good cry over a good story; and he wants to have that without subjecting himself to the subversive effect—whether of society or of individual emotions—which is inherent in all good works of art. The highbrow, on the other hand, studies technique in order to pick up tips, which he intends to put to use in better appreciating or even better practising the subversiveness of art. But though they are at cross purposes and the lowbrow wouldn't approve of the highbrow's purpose if he knew of it, both highbrow and lowbrow (the two cultures which we really are divided into) are glad, through simple good will, of any meeting place. They could go further and find worse rendezvous than Louisa M. Alcott.

You can measure Alcott's technical skill by asking any professional novelist how he would care to have to differentiate the characters of four adolescent girls—particularly if he were confined to a domestic setting, more-or-less naturalism and the things which were mentionable when Alcott wrote. Greater scope in at least the first and last of those departments has not prevented more than one recent novel from making a hash of almost the identical technical problem. Alcott, of course, triumphed at it (that is why we have heard of her), incidentally turning out for one of her four, Meg, a brilliant portrait of the sort of girl whose character consists of having no character. Girls of this sort are the commonest to meet in life and the rarest in literature, because they are so hard to depict (the problem is a variant of the old one about depicting a bore without being boring): usually it takes the genius of a Tolstoy (who specialised in them) to bring them off.

Whereas Meg was a commonplace of Alcott's own—or any—time, in Amy Alcott actually shewed sociological prescience. Or, rather, I think, it shewed despite her. Try as she will to prettify and moralise, she cannot help making Amy the prototype of a model which did not become numerous in the United States until the twentieth century—the peroxided, girl-doll gold-digger. *Of course* it's Amy who gets Laurie in the end (he's rich, isn't he?): she's had 'Good pull-in for Laurie' emblazoned on her chest from the moment her chest began to bud.

With Beth, I admit, Alcott went altogether too far. Beth's patience, humility and gentle sunniness are a quite monstrous imposition on the rest of the family—especially when you consider at what close, even cramped, quarters they live (two bedrooms to four girls): no one in the household could escape the blight of feeling unworthy which was imposed by Beth. I concur in the judgment of the person with whom I watched the film (and who wept even more than I did) in naming her the Black Beth. (I also concur in his naming Marmee Smarmee.) I think Louisa Alcott may herself have had an inkling that in designing a fate for Beth she was inspired by revenge. She seems, perhaps through suspicion of her own motives, to have faltered, with the result that she committed the sort of blunder only a very naïve technician would fall into and only a very self-assured one could, as she does, step out of in her stride. She brings Beth to the point of dying in *Little Women*, and then lets her recover; whereupon, instead of washing her hands—as not ruthless enough to do it—of the whole enterprise, she whips the situation up again in *Good Wives* and this time does ('As Beth had hoped, "the tide went out easily" ') kill her off.

As for Laurie: well, of course, Laurie is awful, tossing those awful curls (though in *Good Wives* he has them cropped and is told off for it): yet though I will go to my death (may the tide go out easily) denying that Laurie has a millionth part of the attractions he thinks he has and the girls think he has, I cannot deny that he is lifelike. If you want to see the romanticised implausibility which even an intelligent woman of the world (and great novelist into the bargain) could make of a curly-haired young man, look at George Eliot's Will Ladislaw. Laurie by contrast is—if awfully—probable.

In the most important event affecting Laurie, the fact that Jo refuses him, Alcott goes beyond verisimilitude and almost into artistic honesty. No doubt she found the courage for this, which meant cutting across the cliché-lines of the popular novel and defying her readers' matchmaking hopes, in the personality of Jo. Jo is one of the most blatantly autobiographical yet most fairly treated heroines in print. All that stands between her and Emma

Woodhouse is her creator's lack of intellect. Alcott is not up to devising situations which analyse and develop, as distinct from merely illustrating, her characters.

And in fact absence of intellectual content is the mark of the sentimental genre; conversely it is because of her intellect that Jane Austen is never sentimental. I think, incidentally, that the word 'sentimental' may have been in bad repute with Louisa Alcott because in 1868 it still wore eighteenth-century dress. And the reason, of course, why the eighteenth-century sentimental mode, unlike the nineteenth-century one, no longer works on us (the death of Virginie in *Paul et Virginie* really can't be read without laughing) is that the eighteenth century was so double-dyed intellectual that it *couldn't* put aside intellect when it took out its handkerchief: its many attempts to be affectingly simple were made self-conscious and absurd by its (perfectly correct) suspicion that it was being a simpleton.

As sentimentalists go, Louisa M. Alcott is of the gentler and less immoral sort. Beth's is the only really lushed-over death (the canary who dies in Chapter Eleven of *Little Women* is virtually a throw-away): on the whole, Alcott prefers to wreak her revenges on her characters by making them unhappy in their moments of happiness. (They make it easy for her to do so, through their own proneness to sentimentality.) Even here, one can morally if not aesthetically justify her. It's all, so to speak, between consenting adolescents. All four girls are quite masochists enough to enjoy what she does to them.

I rest on Louisa M. Alcott my plea—hedged about with provisos, reduced, indeed, to a mere strangled sob—that we should recognise that, though sentimentality mars art, craftsmanship in sentimentality is to be as legitimately enjoyed as in any of those genres (thrillers, pornography, ghost stories, yarns, science fiction—whichever way your taste lies) which, because they suppress some relevant strand in artistic logic, are a little less than literature. The spasm across the eyelids is not inherently more despicable than the frisson of the supernatural or the muted erotic thrill imparted by a brilliant sado-erotic literary craftsman like Raymond Chandler. It is, however, more dangerous. One should take to heart this stray little fable by Kierkegaard (whose personality is, indeed, to be taken to heart in all contexts): 'In itself, salmon is a great delicacy; but too much of it is harmful, since it taxes the digestion. At one time when a very large catch of salmon had been brought to Hamburg, the police ordered that a householder should give his servants only one meal a week of salmon. One could wish for a similar police order against sentimentality.'

Detective Fiction:
A Modern Myth of Violence?

Hudson Review, Spring 1965

I

The question mark is casting doubt on the violence, not the modernity or the myth — both of which are, indeed, exactly to the point.

Admittedly it is only in a longish historical view that one can call something modern which is a hundred and twenty-two years old. But in that longish view, a hundred and twenty-two is just about the age of modernity itself — of our present, industrialised phase of civilisation. From what went before we are cut off socially by the industrial and intellectually by the French Revolution. People before that demarcation are unaccountable creatures in fancy dress; after it, they are ourselves, modern man, in — if they are men in the sexual sense as well — trousers. There are sound reasons why detective fiction and modernity are roughly coeval. Of its nature, the detective story could not have been invented in the (to us) age of fancy dress. The detective quintessentially wears trousers.

In a longer view still, the contrast with 'modern' is 'ancient' — A.D. is opposed to B.C.; and in this view the detective story has a fairly precise claim to be one of the few equivalents the modern world can put forward to the myths of the ancient. We incline to toss off the word 'myth' inexactly: we call Marilyn Monroe a myth (when we really mean a goddess — a myth being, by etymology, a story and not simply a personality, however touching); novels should be myths, according to some of their theorists (who seem to mean, if anything, that novels should make manifest material from the unconscious). The detective story itself is not a myth in the very strictest sense of an anonymous, undated fiction passing itself off as truth. But it does share one characteristic of myths: it runs to type. In the ancient world, which set so much less store than we do by novelty and originality, many poems or plays, by several authors, might repeat the story of a single myth; and, quite over and above that, the single mythical story itself was often a good deal less singular than it seemed. Very many—perhaps most—of the Greek myths can be divided into groups, the myths in each group being in fact variations on a single skeleton narrative. The countless stories we generically call 'the detective story' resemble a group of myths, inasmuch as there is really only one skeleton detective story, on which detective writers invent variations consciously (which probably separates them from the anonymous and no doubt multiple authors of myths) and more or less ingeniously.

2

In the ancient world itself, Ovid pointed out by implication that myths tend to run to type when he compiled his *Metamorphoses*. The entire collection has a single underlying story: some*one* is transformed into some*thing*. Within this, there are sub-groups, according to why the transformation takes place—as a reward, to save a virgin from a fate worse than metamorphosis, and so forth; and every now and then one of the myths makes a conspicuous, though wholly superficial, bid for independence by tying itself to, and claiming to account for, the genesis of a particular species of bush or the invention of a particular musical instrument. In the same way, a single skeleton lies inside several of the stories of the Greek heroes. A hero was often tied very conspicuously to local patriotism, being claimed for the royal dynasty or as the founding-father of one of those Greek city-states which were so notoriously unwilling to surrender their sovereign independence.

The granular individualism of Greek politics is reflected in the unwillingness of Greek mythology to amalgamate its heroes into a single national hero. Had mythology cared to do it, the job would not have been hard, because the heroes, for all their seeming individualism, are remarkably unoriginal. Quantities of them conform to a type of *the* hero. He is usually of royal or divine parentage, and at his birth someone prophesies for him a future so

disturbing to his father or, which may be the same thing, the ruler
that it is decided to kill him in infancy. But by one mechanism or
another he escapes death—and also the city of his birth. He is
brought up by strangers in a foreign land. Sometimes his foster-
parents disclose his true identity to him when he comes of age (or
when they are about to die); sometimes he has to wait until he is
identified by someone in his native city when he returns there.
Return there, whether by chance or in order to claim his inheritance, he always does; and he always finds the city in urgent
need of a hero. Some innocent party, perhaps the king's daughter,
perhaps the whole population, is under threat from some monstrous tyranny. The hero arrives just in time to destroy the dragon
—or whatever form the monster takes—by a display of heroic
courage or magic or both. He may perform other, incidental
wonders and shew forth the signs of his true identity; he is
acclaimed as a saviour; if he is the king's son he is publicly
acknowledged, and if he is not he usually becomes the king's
son-in-law. Eventually, whether by inheritance, marriage or being
co-opted by the grateful population, he becomes king.

    This story was capable not only of local variation but of cross-
ing a major frontier and adapting itself to the mœurs of a different
civilisation. The Greek custom of exposing unwanted children,
which gave the baby hero in Greek versions of the myth so many
opportunities to be saved by a tender-hearted nurse or fortuitously
found by a humane shepherd, was not practised in Palestine,
where (although the shepherds remain, rather gratuitously, in the
story) King Herod has to resort to the wholesale slaughter of the
innocents. That, it may be, is a rather clumsy and extravagant
variation, but in other items of the myth transplantation brings a
gain in gravity and in the rarity of the hero's standing. In Greek
mythology, with its multiplicity of lecherous gods, the hero who is
the son of a god and a mortal woman was bound to be rather
common. Shifted into the sphere of influence of the jealously
monotheistic and on other occasions sexless Jewish god, the hero's
claim became much more impressive—so much so, indeed, that it
was blasphemous; and that enabled it to fit neatly in, from the
point of view of the mechanics of the plot, with the important and

emotionally very significant change the Christian myth makes in
the ending of the story.

For a modern audience, the Greek hero is in danger of losing
our sympathy. In the contest between the hero (or his Christian
successor, St George) and the dragon, we are apt to take sides with
the dragon. The danger became plain indeed when an ancient,
though not Greek, hero was music-dramatised by Wagner.
Siegfried (one of the heroes, incidentally, who is always seeking the
truth about his parentage) behaves like the nastiest sort of boy
bully when he wantonly wakens, provokes and kills Fafner.
Wagner does, just, make us swallow the situation — he seduces us
by the beauty of the horn calls with which Siegfried summons the
sleeping dragon; but Wagner the impresario was evidently not
quite confident that Wagner the artist had succeeded, since he took
monstrously extravagant — and therefore inartistic — pains to build
up the poor dragon by stage-carpentry into something that should
pass for an opponent of Siegfried's own calibre.

From the danger of creating a sadistic hero the Christian myth
escaped by the nearest masochistic emergency exit. The new
version of the myth was calculated to appeal to a modern
audience and in fact, in making its tremendously wide appeal, it
transformed the ancient world into the modern. In the Christian
version, the population does not recognise the distinguishing
marks which identify the hero as the royally and divinely des-
cended person of whom so much has been prophesied; instead, it
denies him and makes his claim to be his father's son the occasion
for accusing him of blasphemy. He is executed and triumphs only
after death, when he enters into his inheritance of a kingdom that
is not of this world. In this world his part is that of innocent
victim, offering himself in place of the people — who in this version
are not innocent but guilty of sins which culminate in their denial
of the hero.

This convenient exit proved in the end ill advised. It had the
effect of amalgamating the hero's father with the tyrant who
threatens the people, creating a monster-god capable of accepting
his son's self-sacrifice in lieu of the sinful population, at the same
time as requiring the population to do endless penance for their

sins or else forgo the benefits the son has bought for them. The masochistic trap-door had led to a god whose sadistic tyranny was redoubled because it was also sanctimonious. This issue was not, however, foreseen when the new version of the myth appeared. It quickly made enough emotional headway in the Greco-Roman world for its adherents to acquire some political power; and since of all the sects in that world (with the exception of the Jews, who did not, however, proselytise), the Christian was the only one to be absolutely non-tolerating of all the others, the Christians quickly used their political power to shut down the whole of pagan mythology by force of law.

The monster god who then clamped his tyranny over Christendom naturally monopolised Christendom's faculty for inventing and launching myths. That faculty was constrained to flow almost exclusively into the lives of the saints (which often followed a minor heroic pattern) and into the acts of magic performed by their relics, acts which shewed an even greater tendency than the feats of the heroes to reduplicate a type. The myth-making capacity revived a little before it was overtaken and virtually extinguished by a written culture, but many of Christendom's myths are Christian-tinted. The tint is not always so blatant as it is in witchcraft, whose mythology is simply the Christian one written, bravely but un-imaginatively, back to front, but it is usually perceptible. A light and charming Christian varnish washes the whole concept of chivalry, whose ladies do not escape a certain conflation with the madonna and whose knights and troubadours are not wholly distinct from crusaders, while King Arthur suffers the quests of his knights errant to be merged with a quest for the Holy Grail. Perhaps the first figure to revive anything of the heroic pattern in a wholly secular tone is Robin Hood, who seldom enters a church except to rescue the sweetheart of one of his merry men when she is being sacrificed as an innocent victim to a monstrous man she does not love.

3

Compared with the Greek or even the medieval world, ours is short of myths. That does not, of course, mean that our imaginative life has been impoverished. On the contrary. But it is now carried on chiefly through stories which bear a date, an authorship and the open announcement that they are fictions. Great changes have taken place in our attitude to both authorship and fiction—ultimately as the result, no doubt, of the change from an oral to a written culture. Long after Greek culture became literate it remained predominantly, in the very nature of its traditions and conventions, oral—indeed, it remained specifically rhetorical. It did so, probably, because it could. The city-state had a small enough population for the whole electorate to be addressed by an orator, and the Greek world had a small enough geography for a rider or even a hiker to get from one sovereign city to another in a day. Nothing made change pressing; whereas in modern Europe, with its bigger territories and populations, the printing press, which is what eventually enabled culture to entrust itself almost wholly to written media, was one of the few inventions which really have been mothered by urgent necessity. The necessity had already existed, but no one had come forward with an answer to it, in the Roman Empire, whose great areas and population were too unwieldy to be steered with any precision by the rhetorical conventions of Roman law courts and which quickly dropped even the pretence of being governed by the rhetorical conventions of the Roman Senate.

So long as culture remains genuinely oral, it is inevitable that poems and stories will be altered as they are passed on. To that extent, a work of literature in an oral culture really does have no —that is, no single—author; and where the conventions of oral culture persist, they will go on behaving as though there were no authors even when books are in fact circulating with the authors' names on them. Because the stories that are anonymously handed down by an oral tradition count traditionally as history, which provokes pride in the whole community instead of in a single author, fiction was slow to acquire an intellectual standing in the ancient world. History books were in fact written by named historians and fictions by named authors of fiction, and yet neither classical language makes provision in its vocabulary for succinctly drawing the distinction between fiction and non-fiction. The Latin from which we derive 'fiction' also, and significantly, gives us 'feign'. Inventing an original story was not properly distinguished from inventing falsehoods, a circumstance in which authors of fiction might well be less anxious than they are today to own to their work. Rather than see his fiction confused with a falsehood, an author might be glad, even though this involved the loss of his own name from public view, to see his work pass under the anonymous authority of history or the hallowed, semi-mythical and thus almost anonymous authorship of Homer.

In modern Europe, printing led first to licences to print and from there to (under English law, early in the eighteenth century) the first stages of establishing copyright. An author was enabled first to fix his text and thus make sure he *was* the sole author of it, and presently to draw from it not only any kudos but also any royalties it might earn, though it was and remains rare for either to amount to very much. The old prestige of history lingered so forcefully that authors of fiction were for a long time (and in some quarters are still) less esteemed than redactors of facts. Prose fictions, which never acquired a distinctive descriptive name in the ancient world, had to wait a long time before acquiring one in the modern. Fictions long and short had been written and recognised for many years before the ambiguous name 'history' and the morally ambiguous name 'romance' ('romancing' is scarcely better than 'feigning') were driven out, in some languages at least, by 'novel' and 'novella'—words which positively announce that the story is, precisely, new: that is, original to its author.

This claim to originality is not only a boast: it is an obligation. The novelist nowadays is obliged to warrant his publisher by contract that the work *is* his own. This does not mean he must be artistically original: artistic originality is acknowledged to be a virtue, but examples of it are seldom praised or even recognized until some time after they appear. It is only in a letter-of-the-law sense that a novel must be novel. Yet there are departments of fiction in which even this rule is, in a special way, tacitly abrogated. This is not a question of a literary form, which prescribes, exactly, form and not content: no one will accuse me of plagiarism if I publish a series of poems of fourteen lines each, but neither does the sonnet sequence lay down what the poems be about. Again, a literary genre does not say so much what the subject should be as what the treatment should not: not too searching, if it's light comedy; not too subtle, if it's farce. Even the pulp-reading which is often said to be turned out to a formula relies less on a positive than on a negative formula—a set of boundaries which the author cannot cross without losing some of his market. There is a kind of fiction distinct, though at the edges only vaguely, from all of these. It is popular in that it makes small intellectual or imaginative demands on its readers, though its readers in some cases are, unlike pulp-readers, capable of responding to such demands when they are made by a different sort of book; but it is not necessarily popular in the sense of having large sales. Or, rather, it is rare for any one novel in the category to have a very big sale, but the category as a whole may sell enormously, relying not so much on numerous as on deeply addicted readers, who seem to need to consume one novel a week in their chosen category, much as (the comparison is not idle) Christians need to consume one communion wafer a week in their chosen denomination.

It is these fictions which are our latterday myths. Although they carry an author's name (or, very often, pseudonym), they shew the mythological tendency to repeat a standard pattern with variations conspicuous but superficial, and their heroes come close to the mythological type of *the* hero. For the equivalent to one metamorphosed Greek, Narcissus, we have to look to the theatre (and the theatre as depicted by the cinema), where a *vedette*, wearing spangled tights and singing either 'On with the Motley' or 'There's no business like show business', personifies show business holding up a mirror to show business. The vedette has a female version, but apart from her we have few heroines. We have no counterpart to the maiden saved from rape; we can represent her only by her opposite, the tart with the heart of gold, who is closely

related to the female vedette and probably goes back mytho-
logically to St Mary Magdalene—who herself may well be, like
another passage from the New Testament, a plagiarism from the
Greek theatre of Menander. Heroes, however, we have profusely:
the spy (Ulysses?); the mad scientist (Prometheus, undoubtedly
—via Mary Shelley's 'modern Prometheus'); the gangster—who
shades into the outlaw (Robin Hood, Dick Turpin, Ned Kelly);
and, above all, the heroes of two vast and very distinct groups, the
western and the detective story.

The hero of the western borrows from the outlaw tradition and
at the same time exemplifies a modern tradition of chivalry. Like
both Dick Turpin and the knight errant, he is so far inseparable
from his horse that it is tempting to trace him to an ultimate
mythological prototype in the centaur. It is the hero of the
detective story who sticks most closely to the centre of the track
beaten by the Greek hero, though he has abbreviated it at both
ends. The detective story does not finish with the detective becoming king—though he *is* acclaimed by a grateful population. He is a
democratic hero, a superman perhaps, but not by divine right,
and his apotheosis consists of his becoming famous. (Like all
democratic heroes, he has bashfully to deprecate his fame.) At the
beginning of the story, the circumstances of the hero's birth are
omitted; but echoes of the prophecy about the hero may remain
inasmuch as the detective is forerun by his celebrity, and the conspiracy against him, which in the Greek myth happens in the hero's
babyhood, may be displaced to later in the story when the criminal
may feel himself threatened (as the ruler was by the hero's
birth) and make an unsuccessful attempt on the detective's life.
In essence the detective story opens about a third of the way
through the heroic story, at the point where the hero comes back
to the city. For the detective it is not a matter of coming *back*
(though it may be of coming *again*—to another case in his career).
The detective comes by chance or because he has been 'called in'
—he borrows his professional status chiefly from the consultant
ranks of the medical profession. He is accompanied, like the Greek
hero in the Greek theatre (or in the theatre of Racine), by a
confidant (who borrows a touch also from the chivalrous tradition

—he is the detective's squire, his Sancho Panza). In the theatre, the confidant's job is to elicit from the hero in conversation what is going on in the hero's mind and so make the heroic thoughts accessible to the audience. In the detective story he does the same job more selectively: he must elicit some of the detective's thoughts, but not those whose premature revelation to the reader would cut the story too short. The confidant is a device whereby the narrative can keep close to the detective without wholly entering his consciousness. The confidant is also there, of course, as a foil: where the confidant warns that a certain action is dangerous, the detective fearlessly insists on doing it; where the confidant is baffled, the detective astutely sees the sense of the clue. Unlike the Greek hero, the detective cannot shew forth signs which identify him as the long-lost royal son or the prophesied messiah, but he invariably shews forth distinguishing marks—idiosyncrasies of speech, dress and habits which raise him to a heroic level above the other characters in the book. Then, like the Greek hero, he proceeds to perform miracles.

In the detective's case, the miracles are very pointedly not done by magic. They rely on nothing but common sense, which, however, the detective uses to an uncommon, heroic degree. The cause in which he uses it remains the same as that in which the Greek hero uses his magic powers and talismans—the deliverance of the population from a threat. The Greek hero comes to the city and finds the whole people grieving under menace from a monster: the detective comes to a closed community (a family, a house party, a country inn cut off by snow, a school, a campus) where a murder has been committed and the whole surviving community is under suspicion. The writer deliberately makes use of the closed community in order to limit the number of suspects and thereby increase the pressure of suspicion bearing down on each. It may even be that the police are already investigating the crime and about to accuse an innocent person—perhaps even the pretty girl in the story, who plays the same rôle as the King's daughter who is about to be sacrificed to the monster. In this stricken community the detective appears as the saviour. He does not go so far as the Christian hero who takes the guilt on himself. More rationally, he

uses rational methods to discover the real murderer—often
arranging in the penultimate scene a reconstruction of the crime
which brings the murderer's guilt home in the sight of all:
and thus he takes the only exhaustively convincing way available of lifting the suspicion of guilt from the community as a
whole.

Like the heroic myth, this pattern is—and must be—varied. It
can even establish an equivalent to local patriotism: brand loyalty.
Sometimes the publisher tries to set this up for his series of books
by various hands, but it is more successful, and more mythological
in spirit, when it is done by the author, who makes his detective the
centre of a cycle—the case of the this, the case of the that—much
as King Arthur and Robin Hood are the centres of their cycles.
One of the variable factors, the eccentricities and idiosyncrasies
of the detective, may therefore be repeated from novel to novel; the
other, the details and method of the crime, must be fresh for each
novel or short story. Provided I can think up fresh variations at
these two points (or have already invented a detective of my own
in an earlier novel), I may offer my publisher tomorrow a novel
written precisely to the outline sketched above; so far has that
outline become public—anonymous—property that I can in good
conscience warrant him, and he will unblinkingly accept, that it is
all my own work. Yet it is in fact the plot of thousands of detective
novels. Indeed, with one modification (the elaborateness of the
scene where the crime is reconstructed—a scene the detective
tradition has, as a matter of fact, borrowed from *Hamlet*), it is
exactly the plot of the first detective story ever written.

4

That was published in 1841, written by an American and set in
France. Edgar Allan Poe's decision to set *The Murders in the Rue
Morgue*, as well as his two later detective stories, in France is
usually explained by Poe's great interest in and knowledge of
French culture. Strictly speaking, however, those only *enabled* him
to set his fictions there; they do not in themselves provide a positive
impulsion, for which I think we ought to look in a combination of

history and psychology. Briefly, I think that Poe set his detective stories in France because the French Revolution had been set in France.

Moreover, I think it was the French Revolution which was the positive impulsion towards the particular invention of the detective story by Poe and its general adoption as a myth pattern. Here again, there is a distinction between what positively impelled and what merely enabled detective fiction to come into being. Obviously, just as novelists could not set their stories in the neighbourhood of fictitious gasometers until real gasometers had been invented, fictitious detectives had to wait until real detectives and detection had been invented -- which happened in England and in France (where the organisation of an effective police force was a direct result of the Revolution) about 1800. But we are entitled to seek also a positive factor which turned the real-life invention into a much repeated fictitious myth. No such factor seems to exist in gasometers. Evidently the detective, as fictionalised by Poe at that particular moment in history, contained a peculiar myth-creating potential.

Sherlock Holmes, who is still probably the most famous detective hero and the one who commands the greatest brand loyalty, speaks on one occasion of 'my scientific methods'; and they are indeed scientific, but in a restricted sense. They hardly touch on experimental science. Indeed, it was probably in order to borrow some of the kudos of experimental science, which did not rightfully belong to it, that detective fiction evolved its elaborate reconstruction scene, which is at once an experiment in the technique of the murder and, like the play scene in *Hamlet*, an experiment on the criminal's guilty psychology. Again, Sherlock Holmes's methods touch, but only lightly, on technology. His amateur laboratory is sketched in very cursorily indeed: 'the scientific charts upon the wall, the acid-charred bench of chemicals' are enough — the enumeration of his tools goes straight on to 'the violin-case leaning in the corner' (which, in the philistine world Holmes inhabits, counts as one of his eccentricities). Only once in the twelve stories in his *Case-book* do we actually come upon Holmes 'bending for a long time over a low-power microscope'. In fact Holmes himself gives a narrower and more accurate description of his method when he calls it 'my familiar method of logical analysis'. And 'analysis' is the word Poe chooses to epitomise the method of the prototypical detective Dupin in the prototypical case in the Rue Morgue.

In other words, although the detective may call in 'laboratory aids', they are as a rule amateur ones of the sort you might have found in the home of a dilettante, philosopher or man of letters in the eighteenth century—Goethe, say, or Voltaire himself, who expressed his ideal as *'passer d'une expérience de physique à un opéra ou à une comédie'*. Nineteenth-century figure though he is, the detective preserves the fashion of the eighteenth-century Enlightenment in carrying elegantly a veneer at least of both arts and sciences. Dupin is something of a classical scholar; Holmes has his violin as well as his microscope. As for the methods which the detective's scientific smattering helps out, they are less those of science at large than of scientific scholarship, the methods of the historian, the art historian, the textual critic. They consist of pure deductive logic. They are remarkable and specialised only in the rigour and thoroughness of the mind which applies them, a mind which considers no detail beneath and no reputation above scrutiny, and which refuses to accept preconceptions and conventions about what a thing *must* be but insists on enquiring for itself what it *is*.

Here, too, the detective preserves the eighteenth-century spirit. His habit of looking at content instead of nimbus is the essence of Candide's near-naïf vision. Candide is still surprised enough by everything to take nothing for granted. On the battlefield where others have been trained to see honour and glory, Candide sees the actual content of the ground—*'des cervelles ... répandues sur la terre à côté de bras et de jambes coupés'*. It is by a narrowing of Candide's vision to a particular problem that, in the too-familiar-to-be-remarked-by-anyone-else figure of the postman, the detective sees the one person who could have entered and left the scene virtually invisibly. And in fact Voltaire himself did, in another of his *naïf* heroes, Zadig, anticipate the detective's methods—an instance mentioned in histories of detective fiction but, quite rightly, disallowed because Zadig's deductions do not help solve a crime. (In fact they get him unjustly accused of one.) The crime had, so to speak, not yet been committed.

In the widest and most social sense Voltaire might have maintained that his own deductive acumen *was* deployed towards exposing a crime, since it was used to the end he expressed as '*écrasons l'infâme*'. His was only the nimblest hammer in the labour of demolition carried out by the eighteenth-century Enlightenment as a whole. The weapons of *naïf* vision, ridicule, irony, scholarship, textual criticism and logic were used to bring down the whole numinous superstructure, social and theological, of Christendom. Deep buried under the rubble was the guilt European man had consciously entertained ever since he accepted exclusively the Christian hero who died for him. Having refuted the supernatural, the Enlightenment pinned its curiosity and hopes to the natural, by which, since its concept of Nature was barely biological and not at all psychological, it meant chiefly the material—hence all those dilettante hours at the amateur laboratory bench. However, natural philosophy was not yet wholly separated from philosophy, and the philosophers were able to slip between the physicist and his lens the notion that the Nature under inspection must be not merely natural but naturally benevolent. Man having shed his supernatural soul (together with the myth of his Fall), the benevolence of Nature logically extended to human nature, too. The tyranny of Christian superstition exploded, man was pronounced not guilty of original sin and found to be inherently good—though in practice corrupted by unnatural tyrannies. Unfortunately, at the end of the century which had pulled off this enormous intellectual feat, its findings were tested in an experiment. The monarchy which had tyrannised France by virtue of feudal numinous awe was removed, and French citizens were set free to—as Pope had urged at the beginning of the century—'follow Nature': whereupon they proclaimed the noblest slogan ever coined by a body politic and, setting up the guillotine, began severing one another's heads from their bodies in a way that would have horrified the ex-tyrant had they not earlier done the same to him. And, having leapt out of the frying-pan into the fire, they proved unable to call up any fire engine except Napoleon, in whose wars cannon- and musket-fire eventually killed far greater quantities of them than tyrant and Terror combined.

It is impossible to exaggerate the scar left in our cultural consciousness to this day by the French Revolution. The generation immediately after it became all but emotionally and intellectually prostrate in its efforts to sew together the lips of the trauma. The real-life heroes of this period are the first of the anti-heroes, tormented and *maudit*; they are exemplified in Kierkegaard, Newman, Poe himself and Poe's disciple Baudelaire. Reason, it seemed, had led to man's proving himself not benevolent but monstrous by nature. And yet reason had not been wrong: it was impossible to go back with genuine belief to the numinous world: or, supposing one could force oneself to do so, that, as Kierkegaard experienced, was merely to succumb on irrational instead of rational grounds to the conviction of man's guilt. Half of Poe's violently dichotomised imagination was given to creating nightmares in which doom descends in punishment of a guilt whose source is not understood; and the other half was given to constructing stories — those about Dupin's detection, and also Poe's cryptogram and puzzle stories — in which a mystery proves understandable and soluble in strictly rational terms. And in the detective stories, the only ones which laid down the pattern of a myth, it is guilt which is rationally understood and traced to its source.

Having created his detective-hero-deliverer, Poe even tried to make him deliver Poe and solve the mystery of Poe's own dichotomy between imagination and reason. The narrative of *The Murders in the Rue Morgue* is preceded by a discourse on the analytical faculty, in the course of which Poe elaborates Coleridge's antithesis between fancy and imagination in such a way (a way that might have had the approval of Coleridge himself, another of the tormented romantic-rationalists of the period) as to bring imagination and rationality into analogy and almost identification with one another: 'It will be found, in fact, that the ingenious are always fanciful, and the *truly* imaginative never otherwise than analytic.'

Reason, when liberated in the French Revolution, seemed to have laid human nature under the imputation of blood guilt. What Poe invented in the first detective story was a hero who delivers the community — the inhabitants of the 'quartier St Roch' — from just that imputation, and does it not by supernatural means, which would involve a reaction to the *ancien régime* no longer possible, but by a *better* application of reason. One of the strictest rules of the detective-story convention is that the supernatural may be (in the words of Dorothy Sayers, quoted by Howard Haycraft in his history of the detective story) 'evoked only to be dispelled'. The rule was obeyed by Sherlock Holmes ('This Agency stands flatfooted upon the ground ... No ghosts need apply' — this despite his creator's belief in spiritualism) and had been laid down by Dupin in the prototype: 'It is not too much to say that neither of us believe in praeternatural events. Madame and Mademoiselle L'Espanaye were not destroyed by spirits.'

Disdaining the supernatural, the detective disdains also any last attenuated rag of feudal superstition: the last wisp of the heroic tradition whereby the triumphant hero becomes a king or even a god was disdainfully shrugged away when Holmes refused a knighthood. Nevertheless, the detective *is* (witness his disdain) an aristocrat — but a natural one, just as he is merely rational but more incisively so than common people. On a small scale he represents the fantasy which, of all fantasies, post-Revolutionary society wished *could* be true: he offers a way of returning to the aristocratic principle without violating reason. His superiority does not rest on breeding, which is wholly irrational, or on talent, which people may disagree about and which cannot be rationally proved, but on a process of reasoning which, when he explains it, can be followed and concurred in by everyone — including, by implication, a jury, that microcosm of a democratic society. The detective's superiority cannot be rationally refuted, and therefore he is justified, as the aristocrat by blood was not, in exhibiting his eccentricities and his essentially aristocratic disregard of the bourgeois reaction to them. In two cardinal instances, Holmes and Dupin, one of the main eccentricities is keeping irregular hours — the aristocratic mark of the man who does not have to go out to work next morning. Ordinary, blunt-witted rationality—indeed, flat-footed rationality—is represented in the detective myth by the men who do have to go out to work, who investigate the crime by routine methods as part of the routine of their job and not because the problem (or an old friend or a pretty woman) has appealed to them: the flat-foots, the police.

In life, the police came first and were aped by the private detective: but it is significant that in fiction the detective was a private eye from the start. Later detective fictions may deviate from this pattern in fact but not in spirit. The fictitious detective is sometimes a policeman, but he is almost invariably an unorthodox one, whose methods disturb his orthodox colleagues or superiors (this happens to the young Maigret) or bring him into rivalry with another department—which the French judicial system in particular makes plausible. Even English detective writers can postulate a rivalry between Scotland Yard and the local force; Simenon positively pits the Police Judiciare against the Palais de Justice. The middle-aged Maigret has a permanent rival in the judge Coméliau, who '*s'était toujours méfié du commissaire et de ses méthodes*'. The rational-democratic essence of the detective hero is brought out in the fact that between Maigret and Coméliau there is a social contrast: Maigret is plebeian born, but an aristocrat of reason; Coméliau is by breeding an aristocrat but limited to '*le point de vue de son milieu*'. By going beyond police routine and evolving his own unorthodox methods, Maigret becomes, as it were, a private detective who, needing to earn a living, happens to be employed by the police. He sticks to the myth pattern in which both the aboriginal Dupin and the central Holmes are private detectives (Holmes already using the word 'Agency' for his partnership with his slow-witted confidant). Holmes is the aristocratic consultant who receives fees, the police the routine artisans who are paid wages. Dupin actually mentions the famous real-life French policeman Vidocq—as 'a good guesser, and a persevering man', who, being 'without educated thought … erred continually'.

In fact, the competition between the detective hero and the police is indispensable to the myth, because it is the police, with their propensity to err continually, who are the threat to the population of the story. The pattern is already firm set in *The Murders in the Rue Morgue*, where the police arrest an innocent man. The lax reasoning of the police in detective fiction is the inheritor of the lax reasoning whereby the Revolutionary juries condemned innocent men; the detective is the hero who rescues the innocent — not, like the aristocratic Scarlet Pimpernel or Napoleon himself, who founded a new aristocracy as well as a new tyranny, by a plunge into reaction and irrationality, but by superior rationality.

To recognise the detective as primarily a deliverer is in itself to refute — or at least greatly shift the emphases of — the theory most usually advanced as a psychological account of the detective story's popularity. There is, of course, another but this time quite superficial theory, namely that it is popular simply as a puzzle: but that is easily disposed of, since it does not explain why the puzzle grew into a literary myth. Poe's purely puzzle stories laid down no myth pattern and have few imitators. It seems that the actual content of the detective puzzle, unlike, say, the significance of the words which answer the clues in a crossword puzzle, is a material and indispensable element. This is in fact assumed by the usual psychological theory — which also assumes, however, that the important part of the content is violent death: the death of the victim and then the death of the murderer in expiation. According to this theory, the detective story is an opportunity for reader and writer to commit at least one murder in their imaginations; the writer is said to have a *nostalgie de la boue*, and both reader and writer are said to have a 'blood-lust' which can be 'sublimated by reading and writing fiction murders'. The words are those of 'Nicholas Blake', a detective-story writer who contributed an introduction to the Howard Haycraft book (*Murder for Pleasure*) I have already cited. The book was published in 1942, and the introduction by 'Nicholas Blake' goes on to suggest that, had the Germans sublimated their blood-lust through detective fiction they 'would certainly have less zest for murdering real Poles'. This 'certainty' is supported by two arguments: that the Nazis banned imported detective fiction; and that in any case detective stories were not popular in Germany. These facts (if the second *is* a fact — after all it was in the German language that *Emil and the Detectives* had carried the detective myth to the very nursery) cannot have been very telling even at the time. (The Nazis banned a good range of cultural imports, not all of which offer an opportunity for sublimating murder.) Now that we have seen some of the post-1942 behaviour of the countries, America, England and France, where the detective story undoubtedly is popular, they do not seem a very solid support for so large a hypothesis.

The view that the reader commits murder in his imagination is not always stated explicitly, yet it seems to be implied by a very commonly drawn contrast. 'Nicholas Blake' himself, in the same introduction, draws it when he asks 'From what dark incentive, by what devious and secret psychological passages have detection writers—timid and law-abiding persons for the most part, who faint at the sight of blood and tremble when the eye of a policeman is turned upon them—first set out upon the sinister paths of crime fiction?' A hundred other cliché-writers have said the same thing in not very different words. It all goes back, I rather think, to some journalistic commonplace of the 'thirties, which still turns up in the English press on Sundays, to the effect that detective stories are the favourite reading of bishops. What with these (presumably) Anglican bishops, the fictitious detective Father Brown and the detective-fiction writer Father Ronald Knox, it must have seemed in England in the first three decades of this century that detective aptitude was conferred by the laying on of hands.

As a matter of fact, to see so prompt a contrast between murder and the priesthood is an example of our un-Candide-like vision, our habit of heeding people's professions about their professions rather than the content of their professions. Were we to see the priest as a man whose daily routine is to feed first himself and then others with the body and blood of a person who was tortured to death, we might think it less surprising if the priest's imagination *were* blood-boltered. Yet if the detective myth really is analogous to the heroic one, then in fact the priests must be acquitted of blood-thirst at least in their spare-time reading. The detective myth appertains to a different priestly function.

The place of the detective story in our society does distantly

imply a general confession of blood guilt — but of guilt which is
there before, and quite independently of, the story. Reading the
story does not bring the guilt into existence: rather, it is the
existence of the guilt which impels the repeated writing and
reading of the story in its many variations. The detective myth,
which did not exist before it, is a repeated admission that the
French Revolution took place. It admits a wish to kill as inherent
in human nature, inasmuch as it repeatedly builds a fictitious
situation in which all the human beings involved need to be
cleared of the suspicion of guilt: we might all be murderers.
(Before the French Revolution it was possible to disbelieve that
proposition.) But the detective story does not pile yet more guilt
onto its readers by seducing them into imaginatively participating
and concurring in a murder. On the contrary: its form is carefully
calculated to make participation impossible. By the very terms
of the puzzle, the reader cannot follow the act of murder through
the consciousness of the murderer.

Some recent detective stories do slip in a passage seen through
the eyes of the murderer, but he has to remain anonymous to
the reader — a device which in itself tends to set him beyond the
reader's power to identify himself with the characters; and
the device is usually employed to arouse fear in the reader of
the person who is least identifiable with oneself, the stranger, the
prowler who may jump out at you; indeed, if anything, the device
identifies the reader with a potential victim rather than the
murderer. The reader cannot be in a position wholly to identify
himself with the murderer in a detective story until the story is
over. Only when the puzzle is solved does the reader come into
possession of the facts — the murderer's name and the technique
of the crime — which enable him to put himself in the position of
the criminal during the act; and by then the act is finished and
done with. If the reader can follow the murderer's consciousness at
the time, then the story is by definition not a detective story but a
thriller or psychological thriller like *Crime and Punishment.*

In the detective story proper, murder is less an act than stage
machinery. It sets the scene and starts the story moving. (Further
murders may re-set the scene and give the story a fresh impetus.)

More often than not the murder happens off-stage, frequently before the story opens. Neither the act of murder nor the hunting down of the murderer (which in societies which still practise capital punishment may imply a further murder, committed in vengeance for the original one) occupies the centre of the narrative stage, because it is not on those that the suspense in the story rests. The suspense is generated by the race between the detective's powers and the doom of unjust suspicion which is descending on the population. Blood there has, admittedly, to be; admittedly, without the pre-existing blood guilt there would have been no story; and usually a murderer has to be indicted because that is the only way to provide the rest of the cast with an acquittal wholly satisfying to reason. But the psychological purpose of the story is summed up in that acquittal. The detective myth exists not to provoke or endorse guilt but to dissipate it. The solution pronounces the general absolution.

Usually that can be done only at the cost of excepting one person and accusing him of murder, but it would be wrong to think the myth exacts his blood and makes the reader an imaginative participator in the act of vengeance. The murderer is required as a piece of machinery without which the solution would not be plausible. The narrative is often a touch shame-faced about its need to employ him — more shame-faced, in fact, than it is about requiring a victim to be murdered to start the story off in the first place. If that often happens off-stage at or before the start, the murderer, once detected, is positively rushed off-stage at the end. His death on the scaffold, so far from being gloried in, is scarcely hinted at. In this the author may be following the sound commercial practice of not offending the susceptibilities of any class of readers, even if it is probably a minority, when there is no need to; and commercial practice certainly makes it clear that the pattern of the story does *not* need an emphatic and blood-thirsty revenge against the murderer. Or the writer may be acting on his own convictions, many detective writers being no more in favour of capital punishment than of murder. (And in one notable instance at least, when a detective writer conspicuously played the detective in real life, it was with the same essential purpose as the fictitious detective, namely to establish innocence. Conan Doyle worked strenuously to clear the wrongly convicted Oscar Slater—just as Voltaire earlier gave his deductive and literary brilliance to clearing Callas and Sirven.) With no matter what motive, the detective writer regularly makes not the most but the least of the criminal's punishment. If he plausibly can, he often takes the comparatively humane way out by suggesting that the murderer will be found insane or by allowing him to commit suicide.

Even the rule that someone must be guilty is not absolutely essential to the myth pattern. All that really matters to it is innocence. This is clear from the first detective story, which laid the pattern down. It is highly significant that, in that story, there are murders but (although Poe may have intended an allegory about the bestial aspect of human nature and certainly perpetrated a slander against orang-outang nature) what the solution shews is that there is no murderer.

Some Writers
and Books

Crime   Simenon

The Train

Translated by Robert Baldick
[Hamish Hamilton, 1964]

Maigret's Special Murder

Translated by Jean Stewart
[Hamish Hamilton, 1964]

New Statesman, April 1964

The Train is probably the book everyone has been expecting from Simenon. (The French public had to wait only till 1961.) If we aren't satisfied now, we are ingrates.

It has been a problem of, precisely, satisfaction. Despite the fame and the high-class praise, Simenon's reputation has never been quite established *enough*, and I think it's because, up till now, no one book has ever clicked quite satisfactorily home. He has been a master—an acknowledged master—without a masterpiece. Virtuoso technician, he was eluded by some tiny technical knack. Novel after novel was without fault; something much less important, some mere and hardly more than mechanical flaw, disrupted their proportions. This is nothing, of course, to do with the absolute size. *The Train* has the usual Simenon brevity: he simply gives more condensed value than the standard package.

In the puzzle or suspense novels, the disproportion is inherent in the genre. Anticlimax is inevitable when the resolution of a book includes the solution of a mystery or the sudden dispersal of terror. Stories in this form are always a little less than legitimate —they really do deceive. When you sit down with them, they present magnificent, athletic torsos: only when it's time to rise do

145

you discover that their legs are withered away. With Simenon the maiming is all the more conspicuous because the torso is *so* fine. The dénouement shews him up as the victim of his own genius for building suspense to Colossus size. But even in his most 'straight' novels there is, if less noticeably, a top-heaviness. Probably it comes from the resolute defeatism, the low relief, of his vision. Since this is implicit in the very manner of his writing from the start, it makes for an overloading of the first third of the book: a little too much of the conclusion is already stated in the major premise. The conclusion therefore doesn't carry quite the right weight, doesn't make quite the decisive home-coming click of surprise plus inevitability. To work, as Simenon determinedly does, with a muted — a rainy — palette invites the same difficulties about the moment of home-coming as singing in a minor key. Simenon is too versed a craftsman to go sour on the key note, but one senses his having to feel round for it; he comes to it, finally, with not quite enough breath.

In *The Train* he achieves perfect breath control. So far as I can scrutinise it, the miracle (artistically it's nothing else) is worked by almost literally invoking heaven. Simenon always composes on two planes (perhaps the ultimate disproportion in the other novels is a flawed gear-change between them): he incarnates the universal in the particular. Like Chardin, he creates an artistic archaeology — people are implied by their possessions and their utensils; and his method, like Chardin's, is to *super*-saturate these objects in their own essence, so that something spills over into universality. And when you come to his people — come on them, as it were, *in* their things — they in their turn are *so* particularised, just as his settings are *so* localised, as to become general. I think the psychology of it must be that he makes the habits and idio-syncrasies of his characters so known to the reader that each and every reader emotionally equates the character with the person of his most intimate acquaintance, himself. Similarly, localities realised in such exact and penetrating detail can be treated by the reader's emotions only as the one locality we have all apprehended in truly vivid detail, the setting of our childhood.

The Train is built up by this method: but also, in counterpoint, by its opposite. Simenon's favourite theme, a personal moral failure, is set against a whole nation's failure of morale. The time is the early summer of 1940—as he establishes by a single observation of period clothes, of the kind that the Nevers episode of *Hiroshima mon Amour* took a whole sequence to convey: a woman on the train is 'wearing a blue serge skirt, which was too tight and riding up her hips, and a white blouse marked with rings of sweat, through which you could see her brassière.' You always could see the brassière through 1940 blouses. The train itself is taking refugees from near the Belgian border deeper into France, but it hardly outstrips the German armies. Marcel, the first-person narrator, decides to abandon his radio repair shop and his hens (all over Europe, wartime must be evoked by the importance taken on by hens) and, with his wife and small daughter, join the train. On it, his family rate better accommodation than he does; he is separated from them, and presently their carriage is shunted off. Marcel goes on, in the overcrowded cattle-truck, to—it turns out—La Rochelle. In transit and at the reception centre at La Rochelle he has, with a fellow-refugee, one of the most poignant love affairs in twentieth-century literature.

As always in Simenon, the love is foredoomed. Myopic, ex-tubercular, Marcel has never expected to achieve a 'normal' life—a metaphor, in terms of the external, real political world, for the sense we all have of inward handicap: no sensitive person has ever expected to achieve a normal life. Marcel cannot rise to the occasion of his love affair and transcend his marriage—because the marriage itself seems higher than he could have aspired. It is implied all through that he conscientiously will pursue his enquiries through the disorganised channels of bureaucracy, discover where his wife has been taken and return to normality, which he knows will mean abandoning, and half knows will eventually mean betraying, his mistress. But Simenon has for once opened this closed world, this inevitably open-and-shut case, to the sky. Not only does the puddle reflect the heavens; the heavens are invoked to reflect the puddle. Simenon has done nothing so pretentious as write an allegory of the fall of France. He has used that as, in the jeweller's sense, a setting: he sets the feeling of

wartime extraordinariness against the extraordinariness, the sense
of a détour taken out of normal time, of a love affair. The much-
played-on irony that France fell in a brilliant summer is in
Simenon's hands doubled back on itself. The blue sky of national
disaster is the blue sky of happiness, of childhood recovered, for
his hero. Simenon, who has evoked so many moods by means of
weather, now employs the pathetic fallacy at its most biting. The
perfect sky which rains machine-gun bullets is also the sky of a
pastoral idyll.

Simultaneously translated with *The Train* is an exceptionally
good Maigret, *Maigret et son Mort*. I have long held that the
Maigret books let us into Simenon's workshop, Maigret himself
being essentially a novelist. Eternally dispossessed, eternally a
Belgian in Paris, the novelist sits on the Métro wondering about
the man opposite: what does such a man carry in his pockets,
what sort of room does he go home to at nights? If Maigret is a
detective, it's because only the detective — once the victim has been
opportunely knifed — has the chance to search the room and
itemise the contents of the pockets. Maigret's relationships are
almost always more with the victims than with the assassins. He
doesn't really want to know whodunit — only what it was like to be
the victim before it was done. Other detectives demonstrate the
triumph of ratiocinative, Maigret of imaginative reconstruction.
They sit and think; he sits and imagines. He has a novelist's
passivity. (One of the few blunders in the workmanlike transposition of Maigret to television was that in one episode Maigret
drove a car. The real Maigret can't drive. He is, to his marrow, a
passenger.) *Maigret's Special Murder* is a refined example of the
novelist-detective method. Maigret is tantalised by having spoken
to the victim on the phone, by having *almost* caught sight of him
from that window on the Quai des Orfèvres, before he becomes a corpse reconstructable from its effects. When he does,
the corpse becomes Maigret's property: 'Alors, Maigret, et "votre
mort"?'

The book also adds to our knowledge of Maigret's ineradicable
lower-middle-classness. Here, as in so many of his cases, Maigret
is contrasted with the well-born and *au fait* judge Coméliau, who

is in charge of the *instruction*. Maigret's social standing probably represents Simenon's own Belgianness, a motif Simenon cannot leave alone even in French settings: this time, the former proprietor of a Parisian *brasserie* ('of the sort Maigret liked, not yet modernised') announces himself as a Belgian and adds 'I'm not ashamed of it, you know!' It is in this book that we learn that Maigret addresses his wife, on the phone, as 'madame Maigret'. The translation can't give the full incongruity, since he combines the formality with tutoyer-ing her: 'C'est toi, madame Maigret?' She addresses him as 'Maigret'.* Not until (in *Maigret chez le Coroner*) he goes to the United States do people ask Maigret point-blank what his first name is. Then (since '*il ne pouvait pourtant pas leur dire qu'il n'en avait pas*') he admits to Jules.

Not until *Les Mémoires de Maigret* did he recount the conspiracy against him when he was a young, *pudique* and easily-blushing inspector of the Police des Mœurs: his colleagues at the Quai des Orfèvres did not know his first name but the prostitutes of Paris contrived to find out; as he patrolled his (and their) beat, one after another would murmur from doorways as he passed 'Bonsoir, Jules!'

Highsmith

New Statesman, November 1965

Literary pages which, unlike the *New Statesman*'s, still segregate the crooked from the straight, usually review Patricia Highsmith under 'Crime'.

The classification is unjust but correct. Miss Highsmith writes not simply fiction about crime but, in the technical sense, crime fiction, instantly recognizable as such by addicts of the genre, which is by now thoroughly established as a distinct sub-compartment

* But in a story (included in the volume *Maigret et l'Inspecteur Malgracieux*) written eight years later Simenon added an apparently post-dated explanation of the habit: 'Depuis toujours, peut-être parce qu'une fois ils l'avaient fait en riant, ils s'appelaient Maigret et Mme Maigret.'

within the line of descent from Poe's invention, the detective story. Neither could an addict be disappointed in Miss Highsmith, who is a very good crime novelist. But there's the injustice. For as a novelist *tout court* she's excellent.

Although crime has long been on its way up in the literary world, the genre is still considered as something a little lower than literature—and not, in general, through mere snobbery. In my judgment and experience (that of an addict under control), Miss Highsmith and Simenon are alone in writing books which transcend the limits of the genre while staying strictly inside its rules: they alone have taken the crucial step from playing games to creating art.

Although Poe was a literary person, his prototypical detective story was a sub- or at least a para-literary form. Like his cryptogram stories, it was a puzzle—one of those bits of hard work we undergo to refresh ourselves and not, as we undergo life and art, as its own justification. Yet the actual content of Poe's story, as well as its formal propensity for puzzling us, is already essential to the effect. And the actual content already includes violent death. From the start the genre reflected, though it did not place its chief emphasis on, the violent fantasies of the unconscious. Indeed, I believe that (as I've argued in my article on detective fiction) Poe invented it in reaction to the irrational violence manifested at the French Revolution and in token of that (as well as to correct the methods of Vidocq on his home territory) set the first detective story in France.

Still, the detective story acknowledges the fantasies only as a ritual or a neurotic symptom does—by exerting itself to master them. The detective makes sense of inexplicable and threatening events and in doing so relieves all but one of the *dramatis personae* from suspicion. Suspense in the detective story proper consists in the fear that the wrong person will be punished for the crime before the detective can discover the truth. The detective does the Ego's work: making sense of the irrational and acquitting us of blood-guilt. (For those murders in the Rue Morgue the whole human species was acquitted of guilt.) And meanwhile the story itself, in its conundrum aspect, is directly providing the reader's

Ego with therapy—on the magical principle of all games, 'if you can master the puzzle, you can master experience.'

When the private detective developed into the much tougher private eye, the form loosened. No longer much of a conundrum, it was less of a grind for the intellect (no more having to follow those plans shewing the library in relation to the butler's pantry), and perhaps less therapy; but it made up for that by ceasing to rub the intellect up the wrong way. A literate Ego could now get its therapy without offence from stilted dialogue contrived solely to plant clues fairly but not too squarely or from detectives characterised and humorised only by an idiom (homage to Poe) literally translated from supposed French. Indeed, safely beneath the notice of intellectual pretentiousness, the crime genre evolved immense technical flexibility. I suspect more fertile experiment has been made in B-feature writing than in all the avant garde schools. The narrative strategy of Dashiell Hammett, the witty narrative tactics of Chandler, and now the quite brilliant narrative surface of Mr Ross Macdonald,* their successor and, perhaps, culmination, constitute a superb repertory of technical expertise applied, like Hitchcock's mastery of cinematic technique, to (a quite precise critical term, which I use in full consciousness of ingratitude for the stunning entertainment I've had) high-class hokum. It's all, on an unbelievably polished plane, so much play-therapy.

When the suspense reaches the point of pain, or when the violent events are admitted in too nasty a verisimilitude (were they in *Psycho*?), it can be shock therapy, but it's therapy none the less, even if the principle is that of banging your head on the wall so that it will be pleasant to stop. Crime is a genre dedicated to reassuring the Ego. However frightening the material that erupts, it erupts round—not in—the hero, who is clever and tough enough to carry the thing through to the resolution, when the irrational events are seen to have been subject all alone to a logical (as distinct from psychological or artistic) pattern. The hero's integrity can survive even a shift of the story's sympathies onto the criminal side. It's a fallacy of ill-read sociologists that the glamorous

* Most recently in *The Far Side of the Dollar* (Collins, 1965).

criminal is new. Even if you discount Robin Hood and Dick Turpin, whose sagas ante-date the crime genre, the hero of that genre turned criminal quite soon after it was established, though he then incurred the penalty that the violence in the story must in the end turn against him. As early as 1899, E. W. Hornung took his brother-in-law's detective pair, Holmes and Watson, and re-incarnated them on the wrong side of the law as Raffles and Bunny, who pursued the Ego's business of getting a living by the entirely logical method of stealing it—though the price was that, whereas Holmes proved unkillable, Bunny ended the first volume of their career in prison and Raffles ended the second dead.

If Miss Highsmith and Simenon deepen this already flexible therapy-form into art, I think it's done by dissolving the hero's integrity as an Ego. Whichever side of the law he's on, he's no longer undivided against himself. He may or may not be so to the police, but to himself he is a prime suspect. The suspense is no longer whether the violent events will catch up with him; it's whether he will do them. And even if he doesn't do them in fact, he does in fantasy; he's admitted ownership of the violent material in the book. Thus the suspense which is the crime genre's currency is translated into mortal horror, through which the thriller becomes capable of the moral ambiguity of the straight novel.

Both the artists of crime fiction express the hero's unease with himself through a social metaphor. They create characters who do not quite belong to any class, who are (Miss Highsmith is brilliant at this) neither happily nor unhappily married, who are not stupid but are somehow *shifty* in relation to the intellect; and their shiftiness is mirrored, by an extension of the pathetic fallacy, in a physical seediness of settings and atmospheres. And both writers enlarge their genre by a simple, very bold act of psychological naturalism: they admit that their characters have imaginations. I've said before that Maigret is a novelist, reconstructing by his imagination what the criminal is like; and Simenon's pure crime studies present as it were the view through the window, with the frame of Maigret's imagination removed. Miss Highsmith's new novel* makes space for its hero's imagination to the full, logical extent: he is a writer.

In literary status, as in his marriage, his class and his very nationality (he's an American living, though not quite settled, in Suffolk), Sydney Bartleby is ambiguous. His books have neither succeeded nor failed; he is on the edge of success as the ideas man of a free-lance two-man TV-script-writing team, the scripts being, of course, in the crime genre. An ideas man Sydney is *par excellence*. His mind runs on the idea of violence and teems with fantasies of murder. He can scarcely see a living body without fantasising how he'd dispose of it were it dead. He can't rid himself of an old carpet without surreptitiously digging it a grave. When his wife ambiguously (holiday or desertion?) goes off, his very jokes with friends elaborate a fantasy that he's killed her. He is a man whose stream of consciousness resembles the unconscious in Freud's characterisation of it: 'our own temptation to kill others is stronger and more frequent than we had suspected.' And the frequency and fertility of Sydney's violent fantasies give Miss Highsmith an entirely plausible opening for an astounding metaphor whereby she brings Sydney's temptations home to us.

I have in mind Freud's observation that, because the *Oedipus Rex* is a tragedy of fate, many authors have tried laying a doom on their heroes but, since they failed to hit, as Sophocles and the myth did, on a doom which is in fact a temptation unconsciously present in everyone, they failed to move the audience's emotions and produced mere nonsense. What Sophocles did for the tragedy of fate Miss Highsmith does for the melodrama of coincidence, whose long arm, when wielded arbitrarily and unpsychologically, has produced so much entertaining but mere hokum. In both this novel and *The Cry of the Owl*, of 1962, someone disappears and is thought, incorrectly, to have been murdered; and the hero has in fact wished to commit the murder.

The device is a perfect dramatisation of two Freudian remarks: that, for the unconscious and children, 'being dead means ... much the same as "being gone" and ceasing to annoy the survivors'; and that 'in the unconscious mode of thinking even a

* *A Suspension of Mercy* (Heinemann, 1965).

natural death is perceived as murder.' Even, one might add, a death that hasn't happened. In both these novels of Miss High-smith's (they are pendants), the 'survivor' is the hero, innocent of the deed but guilty of wishing it. His spoken and acted-out fantasies weave a net which, by a development of the suspense in the classic detective story, threatens to trap him from two direc-tions. He is in danger of being wrongly held guilty by the law; but all his actions and evasions are directed by his unconscious wishes towards bringing about the death which has not yet taken place.

As Sophocles hit on the incest, so Miss Highsmith hits on the murder which is in the unconscious and will out. *The Cry of the Owl* builds up Websterian tragedy. In *A Suspension of Mercy*, also, the doom is too precisely determined to be dodged, but the story reaches it by the comedic methods of ingenious plot-making and social observation. (As some of the Italian dialogue in *The Two Faces of January* shewed, Miss Highsmith's ear is a touch faulty for foreign languages, and here her English-born characters some-times speak American, but there is no mote in her eye for an elderly, middle-class English lady with a novel by Pamela Hansford Johnson beside her bed.) In the characters who volun-tarily disappear and thereby assume the condition of having been murdered, and again in the suicidal Jenny in *The Cry of the Owl*, Miss Highsmith even tackles what Dickens more than once approached but veered away from, the psychology of the self-elected victim.

When we can spare long grave consideration for trilogies of re-arranged, de-intellectualised Proust and for scatty light novels with a trimming of Catholicism, it is absurd that the Websterian intensity and the Sophoclean constructions which issue from Miss Highsmith's imagination should be docketed in ten lines—a mere report, for addicts, on the alcoholic strength—under the heading 'Crime'. Simply to take Miss Highsmith straight would do justice to her and the public but injustice to her chosen, and wisely chosen, genre. It says something for *it* that it can be transmuted into art. I think Dickens was on the point of transmuting it as it then stood established by Wilkie Collins; but it's as if, flinching

from his own moral horror and turning on himself the violence
Hornung turned on his criminal hero, Dickens died rather than
finish *The Mystery of Edwin Drood*. Miss Highsmith has superbly
carried out Dickens's task of making the crime story literature.

Scoop and *A Handful of Dust*

by Evelyn Waugh
[Chapman & Hall, 1964]

New Statesman, September 1964

In literary calendars 1945 is marked as the year Waugh ended. It was the year of *Brideshead Revisited*. To be precise, Waugh made one further appearance — in 1948, with *The Loved One*. After that it was clear he had been conclusively eaten by his successor, Mr Evelyn Waugh, English novelist, officer (ret.) and gentleman. Mr Waugh writes a prose as fluent, lovely and lacking in intellectual content as a weeping willow: Waugh had written — and, almost as much as written, *omitted* — in fragments and ellipses, like a fiercer Firbank. Mr Waugh has still only to give what *Brideshead* calls 'a twitch upon the thread', and he twitches tears into your eyes — but they are the weeping-willow tears of a sentimental sensibility: Waugh could appal your imagination. Mr Waugh, after stating that *Brideshead*, in contrast to the first novel by Waugh, was '*not* meant to be funny', declared its 'general theme' to be 'romantic and eschatological': the really extraordinary thing is that precisely the same is true of the general theme of Waugh's novels.

Two of those, dating respectively from 1938 and 1934, have now been republished in hard covers. *Scoop* has always struck me as a mere, though entertaining, after-flutter of the fine imaginative flight which had produced *Black Mischief*; it is a *Black Mischief*

without the great Seal set on it, and starting from a springboard
of mistaken identity which is not quite bouncy enough to get the
invention into the air. But *A Handful of Dust* is a major work in the
canon. It is the most open of Waugh's books about having a tragic
intention (even though it is *The Loved One* which is subtitled a
tragedy), and this makes it Waugh's equivalent to *The Flower
Beneath the Foot* (*Vile Bodies* being his *Pirelli*). The characters break
the classical rules for tragedy by being in themselves shallow and
vulgar-minded. But the essential advantage of the fragmentary
method is to put perspectives round the characters beyond their,
or conceivably the author's, vision. The irony and poetry echo in,
so to speak, the interstices of the narrative. For all the vulgarity of
its characters' values, the book is not a vulgar tragedy. The
adultery of Lady Brenda Last and her parasite John Beaver
catches a particular cold lust in action—in the very action of cold-
sweating; theirs is a sado-masochistic relation which is expressed
and enjoyed in social terms, in the actual mental vocabulary of
snobbism. At the moment (one of the miracles of English fiction)
where Brenda is told that John has been killed and takes the John
concerned to be her lover instead of her small son, the plot-making
has plunged into contrivance: yet it is the poetic contrivance of a
baroque conceit, and the plunge is not into sentimentality but into
the moving and nauseating depths of authentic bad taste.

The holes in Waugh's narrative, unlike those of Firbank, who
often drops stitches through sheer giggling inattention, compose
into a deliberate vista pointing in a single relentless direction. Like
the thoughts of his Father Rothschild during the Channel cross-
ing, Waugh's imagination works towards the Four Last Things.
This the preface to the new edition emphasises by recording that
the ultimate doom of Tony Last, the horrific perpetual motion in
which he rereads Dickens aloud to Mr Todd in the jungle to all
eternities, was the first part of the book to be conceived. It was
published on its own as a short story, so when the whole book was
serialised an alternative ending had to be written. It is printed
now 'as a curiosity'; it is deft but falls flat, because it falls short of
the Last Day.

As a matter of fact, the eschatology of Waugh's imagination, like that of Catholic doctrine, distinguishes between a Particular and a General Last Judgment—which gives Waugh's characteristic form a climax and then a coda. In *A Handful of Dust*, Tony's particular doom is followed by the general devastation of his beloved, neo-feudal domain by middle-class heirs—a bourgeois sack of a fake-Gothic Rome. In *Vile Bodies*, Agatha Runcible is immolated in *her* perpetual motion, as she continues in hallucination round and round the motor-racing track; and then comes general destruction on 'the biggest battlefield in the history of the world'—an end-of-the-world landscape imagined by a *funny* Signorelli. There are three, perhaps four, novelists now practising who write like angels. Only Waugh could write like a baroque cherub—a baroque cherub on a funerary monument, forever ushering in the *Dies Irae*.

Hortense Calisher

Extreme Magic
by Hortense Calisher
[Secker & Warburg, 1964]

New Statesman, September 1964

Hortense Calisher is certainly one of the writers I had in mind among the rare angels. Her latest volume, consisting of eight magazine stories plus a longer novella which lends its title to the collection, displays a new flexibility in her imposing, idiosyncratic talent. Some of the stories are loosely, anecdotally spun—though always into firm shapes. One story adds farce to Miss Calisher's accomplishments; it is a sort of surrealist embroidery on the bosom of the surrealist corset advertisement about dreaming one has stopped the traffic. In a Nabokov-like setting of Europeans on the campus, and again in contrasting French phonetics with French of Paris, Miss Calisher uses her intense sensitivity to words as a probe into comparative linguistics. A monologue addressed, in Florence, by an older to a younger American woman writer opens a dazzling Jamesian corridor of mirrors in which literary mind reflects back literary mind. The longest is the finest story, a marvel of condensed realisation. A small cast of eccentrics, including a girl of sixteen and a half in whom Miss Calisher captures not youth but youth's appearance to middle age ('the flesh at that age was aureoled in its own fuzz'), is set down and reshuffled on the under-populated shoreline of the Hudson River; Miss Calisher's talent is such that she moves you by the eccentricity even of the landscape.

Tale for the Mirror
by Hortense Calisher
[Secker & Warburg, 1963]

New Statesman, June 1963

Hortense Calisher is an American of European sympathies, taut artistry and stupendous talent. European culture in the very act of being déraciné—and letting out a mandrake shriek—is the motif Miss Calisher builds into a grand fugue in *False Entry*, published here last year, a huge novel you can nibble round for twenty or thirty pages before you are suddenly in, hurtling through its exciting plot, dazzled by its delicacy and stunned by its sheer Dickensian creativeness. Her effects are necessarily smaller but at their best just as cogent in *Tale for the Mirror*, which consists of thirteen stories, all bearing the marks of having had to earn their living. Literally, they are magazine stories: it is sad that the only one which could be called so derogatorily is the one from the *New Yorker*. The atmospheres range from suburban to Southern to Yiddish; there is even a superb period piece set at a 1918 victory parade, as condensed in its evocations as a bit of dusty bunting. The themes are mostly metaphors of loneliness. In the title story —the longest—the hero is led, through a Jamesian series of social scenes, to recognise that he himself is no less isolated in American

society than his Indian and possibly charlatan neighbour. Loneliness is tied into a neat, rather Dorothy Parker parcel in a
story about two solitary American women in Rome, and carried
to a chill intensity in 'The Scream on 57th Street', a story about
— or, I rather think, a story which achieves the classic expression
of — widowhood.

Occasionally Miss Calisher's intricate prose flattens into
doodling, her narrative swoops towards sentimentality or melodrama and she herself seems engulfed in a second's loneliness,
where she cannot believe her own imagination. But she is only
plummeting in an air pocket. One even comes to accept her
scoopings, like those of a supreme soprano. Most of the time her
decorative manner is as firm and economic as rococo wrought
iron. Her talent is a naturally brilliant exotic, cutting a figure of
stylish idiosyncrasy. Muscular and slender, it picks its fastidious
way over the mudflats, leaving a print beautiful, elaborate and rare.

Textures of Life
by Hortense Calisher
[Secker & Warburg, 1963]

New Statesman, September 1963

Hortense Calisher's second novel attempts, and pretty well pulls
off, something of a *Golden Bowl*. This one could not be symbolised
by the extravagant *objet d'art*, with its bizarre flaw, conceived by
James. Miss Calisher's material is the American bourgeoisie at
home, and the textures of the lives she interweaves are homely.
Hers is a Golden Bowl in, so to speak, basketwork. But the work
is Jamesian indeed in firmness of structure and subtlety of superstructure. Sometimes she uses the master's very idiom — not in
pastiche but as legitimately and creatively as Tiepolo used
Veronese's.

The story starts at the wedding of Elizabeth and David, a social
event which thrusts together the bride's mother and the bride-
groom's father. Not long after their children have done so, these

two marry. This second pairing implies none of the moral ambiguity of Adam Verver's marriage to his son-in-law's mistress. But the unspoken Oedipus motif is just as strong, and so is the shock to the first couple. The novel consists of the effects of each marriage on the other; the implications each holds for the sympathetic relation between David and his father, and for the impatient, dissatisfied relation of Elizabeth and her mother; and the response of the characters, severally, in pairs, as parents or grandparents, to the younger couple's baby daughter, who sustains the Principino's rôle at the heart of the knot. James aerated the closeness of his four principals by allowing them a third couple as chorus or confidants; but, although Miss Calisher's people sometimes have to confide in acquaintances, their situation acknowledges that in modern urban society marriage is the only voluntary relationship that will bear weight, and the parent-child relationship the only involuntary one that cannot be dodged. Nothing remits the intensity with which each of these four needles, threaded with its own colour and ply, is compelled to stitch in and out of the others' stitching.

In such a quadrille, the performers need not, perhaps cannot, be equals, but they demand equal treatment from their author. In James's nexus the Prince is admittedly not up to the other three. Yet it is not simply as a weak character that he lets the dance down. Weak characters can be boldly portrayed; but James is too relenting towards the Prince to make him a Vronsky or a George Osborne; the weakness lies not only in the Prince but in James — where it is perhaps a weakness for Italian young men, or just for princes. Miss Calisher's construction has a comparable flaw, and again in the younger generation. *Jeune premier* parts are always the hardest to do. Her David may not properly exist — there is little to him but a trick of letting his glasses slide down his nose — but he is waved into being by adroit sleight of hand. It is Elizabeth, reacting against her mother's 'taste', bohemianly disregarding material objects except such as she herself, as a sculptor, makes, in whom one suspects a lightweightness of character and a college-girl pretentiousness of intellect — which the author seems not to realise. With the older couple Miss Calisher can do nothing wrong. The vivid, invalid's life of David's father, the vaguer but penetrating vision of Elizabeth's mother—she splendidly creates both and superbly counterpoises them. Miss Calisher is not only that rarity, a talented novelist, but that double-blossomed rarity, a talented novelist who is serious about art.

Elizabeth Taylor

A Dedicated Man

by Elizabeth Taylor
[Chatto & Windus, 1965]

New Statesman, July 1965

Mrs Taylor is the poet of the Thames Valley, geraniums (a post-man in a Thames-Valley heatwave complains that their bright red hurts his eyes; an Oxford couple arrive at a Moroccan hotel and are offended that it is so Europeanised as to have a drive bordered with 'scarlet Thames-Valley geraniums'), the brink of social disaster, and people's relations with their moral image of themselves. This last, which is also the theme of her most recent novel, occurs *passim* in her new volume of stories, of which there are twelve, all previously published in the *New Yorker*, and every one a stunner.

Mrs Taylor is not after the farcical contrast between the banal flesh and the fantasy self who gallops nobly about on a white steed. Her much more exacting and intellectual concern is to explore the gap between the Ego and the Ego-ideal. A mother shops and house-cleans, and seems to hear a voice comment, 'Hilda's managing well.' The benefactress, in a story of that name, believes she bustles 'about the countryside doing good. "No one knows what people in this village owe her." The words were clear, though the person who said them was only dimly imagined.' The poetry of Mrs Taylor's work lies in the passionate exactitude with which she pins down the self's need to invent a self *moralisé*; what makes it also authentic high tragi-comedy of manners is her tacit acknowledgment that without the disembodied agencies of approval people probably could not behave morally at all.

Neither are Mrs Taylor's social discomfitures precipitated by anything so crass as class. The people who fail to mesh at her dreadful social occasions belong to the same stratum (which may be high or low) but simply don't get on. Even when a rich schoolgirl takes a poor one home for the holidays, they come from the same school and *ipso facto* (it's in England) the same stratum. What Mrs Taylor is really contrasting, through the girls, is their mothers: the puritan, who wins the unseen agencies' approval by martyring herself (her poverty serves rather than causes her martyrdom), and the expansive one, who does it through generosity—and not only her own: when the poor girl puts on a shabby dress, her rich friend does likewise, and the rich mother, seeing them come down to dinner looking 'unbelievably dowdy', has to turn away for a moment (a moment Mrs Taylor makes like the moment of biting into a lemon) 'because her eyes had suddenly pricked with tears at the sight of her kind daughter'.

These two mothers Mrs Taylor keeps physically apart until she can manœuvre them into a miraculously dank tea-party. Other ill-met characters skirt disaster at luncheon: Mrs Taylor's mastery is such that she can express her characters' feelings about one another through their exasperation with one another's children and chows. In a story which attains the almost irascible nervousness of Katherine Mansfield, the sheer youth, sexual attractiveness and narcissism of an uninvited guest disrupt a dinner-party like a too heavy pollen in the air giving everyone hay fever.

Mrs Taylor has always been an excellently unpretentious writer: if she had a fault it used to be that she was (artistically) under-ambitious. These stories seem to me to rise wholly to her talent. The title story is a classic—in the simple sense that, now she has revealed its shape, it is perfectly obvious (and unforgettable): it is what all our imaginations ought to have discovered while dwelling on (as they surely all have done) the graven presence of a waiter in a staid hotel. I can only express my gratitude for *A Dedicated Man* and declare myself Mrs Taylor's dedicated fan.

Kathrin Perutz*

A House on the Sound
by Kathrin Perutz
[Heinemann, 1964]

New Statesman, July 1964

If a reviewer had the self-control not to read the author's first name or the information on the jacket, I doubt if he would guess that *A House on the Sound* is by a woman, and I am sure he would not guess that she is only twenty-five. Both these observations are compliments to the author, and no dispraise to reviewers. If Miss Perutz's youth doesn't shew, it is because she is in full command of the technical resources of fiction. If her sex doesn't, it is simply because she is an imaginative writer.

There is still some superstition reducing visibility round this subject, so let me insist that in writing, as indeed in handwriting, there is (spontaneously, at least) no such thing as 'a feminine hand'. Critics sometimes imply the existence of a genre, the feminine novel. Two of the characteristics ascribed to it, sensibility and concern with emotions, are simply common to all good novels. Two others, miniaturism and intuition, are unwarranted insults. The miniaturist insult derives, I suppose, from that over-modest reference to 'a little bit (two inches wide) of ivory' which is the only remark of Jane Austen's I would wish unwritten: it has given too many people a pretext for not noticing that Jane Austen's

* Alluding to the content of this review, the Literary Editor of the *New Statesman*, Mr Karl Miller, gave it the title 'K. Perutz'. When I saw this in proof, I insisted that the review be signed not, as usual, with my full name but 'B. BROPHY'. I was delighted to see the publishers of the book under review quoting my favourable opinion as by 'B. Brophy'.

ivory is in fact a tusk, with which she gores deep into the essence of everything. 'Intuitive' just means in practice 'of second-rate imagination and no intellect'.

This may operate as a spurious gallantry. Atrocious writing by women gets off more lightly than it should on the theory that, though it is to all appearances tripe, it must be tripe marinaded in some specifically feminine but otherwise unspecifiable virtue. But while bad women writers are allowed—or, rather, allotted—the unfair advantage of playing over a lower net than men, those who are honourable and capable enough to play over the standard net sometimes incur an unfair obloquy for doing so. All exercises of imagination and intellect are inherently subversive, and therefore provoke animosity. If it is known that the imagination and intellect are being exercised by a woman, the animosity may be doubled. That an original thought, irrespective of its content, should be clearly and concisely uttered by a woman is automatically subversive in itself.

I stress *if* it is known—because, above a certain level of literacy and imaginative intensity, a novelist's sex is discernible only in the light of extraneous information. Most women novelists could, by publishing under a male pseudonym, deceive reviewers and readers as easily as George Eliot did; and if all novelists of whatever sex published under surname and initials only, a 'feminine hand' would no more declare itself than it does in that frequent social dilemma when you receive a letter from an unknown person who signs only initials and surname. Of course, the correspondent may use mauve scented paper, and a novelist may stamp his sex all over his prose—which, however, thereupon becomes a pose, a restraint on the imagination's power. (The miracle of imagination is not that the novelist can enter a personality of the other sex but that he can enter another personality.) The most one can securely tell about an affectation is that it *is* an affectation. The letter on scented paper comes either from a man posing as a woman or from a woman posing as a woman. Had Hemingway shunned publicity and published as E. Hemingway, it would have been a toss-up whether the poseur behind the manly prose was a man or a butch lesbian or—which at the depths of Hemingway would have looked the likeliest—a very feminine but very unimaginative woman trying not very hard to work out what it must be like to be a man.

It will be an instance of postjudice (prejudice through hindsight) if Miss Perutz's second novel gets labelled 'feminine' or 'catty' (I see her first was called 'kittenish') or, through her youth, 'promising'. Far from promising, it fulfils. An account of a dinner (and bathing) party on Long Island Sound, it slices into American society sharply but compassionately: down to the coloured servant, and out to the European immigrants and the visiting English. Host and hostess are a middle-aged publisher and his just-grown-up daughter. (Miss Perutz's virtuosity is such that she implies the mother *in absentia*.) Perfectly orchestrated, the narrative moves with ease from one consciousness to another, while the evening descends from mood to mood and the themes—half-relationships —emerge: jealousy, a love too old to be revived, a sado-erotic ambiguity between two young men, an incestuous ambiguity between father and daughter, a sexual act *gratuit*. The *tour de force* is an ageing Russian woman who actually bears out the intelligence and the baroque poetic quality ascribed to her, a character it must have been as hard to fit into the novel without stunting either her or the others as it would be to fit her into a dinner party. Miss Perutz's one fault—and it is less fault than psychological curio—is to keep misquoting Marvell's 'To His Coy Mistress' although (or because?) she obviously adores it. Ostensibly about the hopelessness of the liberal rich, the desperation of social drinking and the vicissitudes of party conversation, Miss Perutz's accomplished, witty and moving novel is really—and without the least strain or faking—about the depressions and silences of society itself: a statement about—but since it is an excellent work of art, not of—despair.

I. Compton-Burnett

A God and his Gifts

by I. Compton-Burnett
[Gollancz, 1963]

New Statesman, December 1963

Novels by Miss Compton-Burnett can no more be read for their
narrative impetus or their development of character than those
problems in which Harry is taller than Dick, who is shorter than
Bill. Miss Compton-Burnett gives her characters more distinguished names but scarcely more distinguishing marks. You
are not invited into their consciousness: you are set the problem of
working out their relationships—including, as a rule, their blood
relationships.

The dialogue—that is, virtually, the whole novel—is full of
lesser conundrums of its own. It's not always easy to identify the
speaker: Miss Compton-Burnett plays fair but close to the chest;
she will give you the information only if it's absolutely impossible
to deduce it from other sources. Whatever the clues you employ,
they won't be individual tones of voice. Everyone in her novels
speaks in the same idiom, and the idiom itself is instinct with
conundrums. Miss Compton-Burnett's speakers seem to be applying a course of remedial exercises to the relaxed muscles of
English syntax. They invent, as it were, private equivalents to a
preceding direct object and test the reader's alertness to the agreement of the adjective. 'I shall not see the life as ordinary,' says the
hero of her new novel. 'None is so to me.' 'How do you see your
own life?' asks his interlocutrix. 'It is even less so to you?' Give a
full account, one seems to be being bidden between the lines, of the
significance of the second 'so'.

To my senses, Miss Compton-Burnett is not exactly an artist.
She is something less valuable but rarer—the inventor of a wholly
original species of puzzle. It is probably the first invention of the
kind since the crossword, which it far outdoes in imaginative

depth. Indeed, it is only a touch less profoundly suggestive than chess or formal logic. An extra attraction is that, though her novels are not themselves works of art, the rules of the puzzle are allusions to literary forms and conventions. Reading them is like playing some Monopoly for Intellectuals, in which you can buy, as well as houses and hotels, plaques to set up on them recording that a great writer once lived there.

The social nexus in which Miss Compton-Burnett assembles her speakers is such a memorial—to Jane Austen. The centre, the permanent set, in the new novel is a baronet's home in the country; the milieu consists of those grouped round the magic 'Sir'. At the start, the baronet's son Hereward is refused by a tenant, marries instead the daughter of the neighbouring house and brings her to live in the baronet's. Hereward is a popular novelist, which occasions a discussion in which the baronet and his butler gently disparage novels—a tacit allusion to the novels passage in *Northanger Abbey*. But the resemblance to Jane Austen is never more than allusion-deep. The composure of Jane Austen's prose is adaptable to expressing every nuance of social and individual idiom, whereas the sedateness of Miss Compton-Burnett's is wooden-featured. Where Jane Austen is concerned above all with her heroines' consciousness, Miss Compton-Burnett shuns—indeed positively and in panic flees from—the idea of entering anyone's consciousness. Only one paragraph in *A God and his Gifts* makes any attempt (and it is a sketchy one) to give the reader direct access to what someone feels.

In flight from the novelist's freedom to wander into minds, Miss Compton-Burnett is logically driven to embrace the restrictions of a dramatist. Her allusion now is to classical drama, whose conventions she abides by to the extent of having major events happen off-stage—though in her new book some curiously intimate ones, including a proposal, happen in public. Her text is as bare as Racine's of furniture or handkerchiefs, and you might say her speakers resemble his in all speaking alike; the trouble is that hers don't speak poetry. Their language is in fact a let-down. They exchange big, imprecise banalities, seeing paths plain before them, keeping a light touch, letting things loom large.

Still, they toss these clumsinesses about with some grace, achieving the form if not the content of wit. It's like reading a Wilde comedy in algebra, the aphorisms reduced to 'All a's are really b's. Only y's ever think them z's.' Occasionally a speaker strikes off at least a common-sense-ism. When the baronet dies, his widow is offered the consolation of yet another banality. 'You will live in the past. That will always be your own': and she has the wits, if not quite wit, to reply 'I have lived in it. But then it was the present. And that was much better.'

The setting is not so much subject to the conventions as plain conventional—'book-lined'. Period is not indicated—you can't make much of the absence of cars and telephones when so few material objects are present anyway; the butler, however, has a presence which seems unmistakeably Edwardian. (He is named, by the wittiest stroke in the book, Galleon.) The devices of the plot-making seem borrowed from the Edwardian theatre. Where except in a mustachio'd melodrama would a man betray, as Hereward does, that he is the real as well as the adoptive father of a child by letting himself be overheard exclaiming above the child's head 'blood of my blood, and so deeply derived from me'?

Indeed, Miss Compton-Burnett creates a positively farcical pile-up of skeletons tumbling from the Edwardian cupboard. Piecemeal it is disclosed to his family (an allusion to the strip-technique of the *Oedipus Rex*) that Hereward is a man of unconfinable sexual appetite and charms. He, not the baronet (who is financially dependent on his son's royalties), is the head of the family, the boss stag in the herd who takes all the females as his right. This, since the herd is rather restricted and close-knit to begin with, involves him in the near-incest of taking his wife's sister and his sons' wives; when these have children by him, apparent cousins are really half-siblings (liable, of course, in the restricted milieu, to fall in love with one another) and the close-knit family has become inextricably inter-ravelled.

As a matter of fact, Hereward's unions always *are* fertile. I take it Miss Compton-Burnett is tacitly referring to the doctrine of pagan theology that gods never mate fruitlessly; for by the end Hereward's family have explicitly recognised him as the god of the title, identifying the paradox of their continuing respect for him with the paradox of the Greeks' basing their own restrictive sexual morality on a lecherous and incestuous pantheon. Presumably the particular god concerned is Zeus: the incest in Zeus's own ancestry is represented by the fact that Hereward's parents are distant cousins; Hereward is a Zeus with no need to usurp his father, having reduced him to financial impotence, but when, on the baronet's death, the butler greets the son as 'Sir Hereward' we understand that Zeus has come into his inheritance.

Inside this classical box, Miss Compton-Burnett's Chinese puzzle implicitly places another. The situation is an outline of Freud's theory of the primal horde. Indeed, I suspect Hereward's name of being compounded of 'herd' and 'horde'. The situation is, however, pointedly worked *out*, and not worked, in psycho-analytical jargon, *through*: and that the reader is not called on to involve his emotions is, I suppose, why the book remains an admirable and diverting puzzle rather than a work of art.

Miss Compton-Burnett's technique is all directed to avoiding the need for technique, just as her dialogue is to avoiding the need for a consciousness. It is, in fact, the technique of a *faux naïf* painter—one who, unable to render either adults or children, depicts both as charmingly wooden dolls. Miss Compton-Burnett's children and servants charm and astonish the reader by speaking as gravely and syntactically as her educated adults: the real sleight of hand is that her educated adults are not flesh and blood, either. Time Miss Compton-Burnett treats exactly as the neo-primitive painter treats perspective. Not only does she make no indications of period to start with: generations elapse at the turning of a page, and still Miss Compton-Burnett gives not the least sign or sense of change either in period or in personalities. Her eighteen novels make a pretty, quirky terrace inhabited by grave dolls, each villa an ingenious little puzzle box, depicted, without perspective and with a most meticulous absence of technique, by the cunningly *naïf* hand of a Grandma—no, Moses has the wrong connotations: Grandma Oedipus.

Janice Elliott

The Somnambulists

by Janice Elliott
[Secker & Warburg, 1964]

Sunday Times, April 1964

Janice Elliott's new novel is beautifully strange. When the red-headed Purdy children are orphaned, Jessie, the eldest, is already forceful enough to hold at a distance the adults whose 'moon faces' loom above, offering succour. She accepts a minimum of material care for herself and Andy, her fat brother: but emotionally she creates round the two of them a world the adults cannot enter. When she and Andy become adults themselves, it proves a world they cannot get out of.

Even their brother, the youngest Purdy, does not impinge on his siblings. He lives in his own fastness: by one of the strokes of bizarre poetry with which Miss Elliott's book effloresces, he is a deaf baby. He wins the notice of Jessie and Andy only once in childhood, when he is likely to die, and once in adulthood, when he does. The child Andy, put in charge of his deaf brother and finding him a burden to amuse, conducts him into the local Catholic church and, without rancour, leaves him on 'one broad, blue-painted thigh' of a plaster Virgin.

Jessie and Andy begin to arrange their childish impressions according to the logic of the real world. At twelve, Andy wonders if orphanhood is, 'against all his inclinations, his speciality'. He explores Jessie's as well as his own character through their separate relationships with the violet-scented 'Mummy Schultz' —who is in fact not a mummy and to whom the orphans are therefore emotional prey. But the brother and sister, though they learn to make sense of, never make contact with, reality. Jessie grows up to join the British Union of Fascists; she is an oddity among (brilliantly sketched) oddities. In the war, the younger brother, cured of deafness, goes into the R.A.F., Andy, who has

171

incurable flat feet, to Oxford. Andy and Jessie have a love affair apiece. But those are their utmost 'attempts to live in the world of people and events'. During the Victory celebrations, they return to each other.

The book is marvellously wrapped in the somnambulistic sensation of the title. In their submerged world, Jessie and Andy move 'like dancers beneath the sea' — but a tropical sea, in which everything is visible with sharpest clarity. Miss Elliott's fabric is sprigged with knots of condensed observation (the river at night *smells* cold) and shimmers with lyrical metaphors: girls lying in the sunny park are so impressionistically equated with flowers that a tulip can button her cardigan. Miss Elliott remarks that 'in a sense, nothing happened' to her hero and heroine. Yet the narrative is deeply exciting — through the sheer, unforced *bizarrerie* of her vision, which has the utter, almost alarming truthfulness only pure imagination can achieve.

Gillian Freeman

London Magazine, May 1963

Among the novelists who have made their name in the last ten years, Gillian Freeman is one of the most purely *novelist*. The back flaps of her books will tell you that she took a degree in philosophy. Nothing inside the books would even hint it. I mean this, of course, as praise. Indeed, I mean it to mean that Gillian Freeman is a wholly unpretentious writer. There is absolutely no claim one can advance for her except her talent.

A novelist who possesses talent has always been a rarity, but nowadays a novelist who trusts it is rarer still. Too often the post-war novelist spreads his risk. Just in case his novel should turn out no good as a novel, he puts forward an extraneous claim as well — that his novel either documents or, by its very existence, exemplifies some social trend we can't afford to miss, the Lolita Thing or the Teenage Syndrome (to neither of which does *Lolita* itself, to its credit, make the smallest contribution) or the situation of women since sexual emancipation. Too often the post-war reviewer lets himself be bought off by these irrelevancies with relief. They spare him the pain—it *is* pain—of making an artistic judgment. He is perfectly justified, and at much less expense of spirit, if he commends the book as an interesting phenomenon or an interesting, quasi-Kinsey report, without broaching it as a novel at all.

It is possible that some of the praise reviewers accorded Gillian Freeman's first novel in 1955 was, though utterly deserved as praise, the result of a mistake. *The Liberty Man* recounts the love story of a sailor and a middle-class schoolmistress. Small wonder if reviewers took it for a contribution to the sociology of the class problem and picked it out in the way that old-fashioned critics of painting (with the same propensity to seize on any problem rather than the artistic one) used to pick out the 'problem picture' in an exhibition.

In reality, *The Liberty Man* is simply (not 'only') a novel— whose subject matter is class. If the reviewers misunderstood it, perhaps the rather middling notices they gave its successor *Fall of Innocence*, shewed their disappointment that that did not mention class at all. Or perhaps they were only treating *Fall of Innocence* as the usual case of 'second novel hurdle'—an expression reviewers love to toss off as though it were a technical term, without realising that the hurdle is created wholly by themselves and consists of their biting back the generosity which a kindly tradition has obliged them to expend on the first novel. Either way the reviewers were wrong about *Fall of Innocence*, which is much surer in technique than *The Liberty Man* (where the scenery sometimes wobbles) and which, considered as a novel (though not considered as reportage), has exactly the same theme. In *Fall of Innocence* it is not classes but generations which meet in a love affair: the contrast is between generation-mannerisms and generation-assumptions, instead of class ones. A middle-aged widower goes to bed with one of his daughter's schoolgirl friends. As in *The Liberty Man* (whose title has two meanings), there is a liberation for both sides in the affair—though for the schoolgirl it is hardly more than the relief of concupiscence; in his realization that she is in fact not innocent, it is the man who falls from innocence; yet his loss of innocence is at the same time his release from puritanism. Apparently deadpan, the novel is so accurately aimed that it can be left to make its own ripples, which expand with an implicit yet perfectly palpable ambiguity.

Three of Gillian Freeman's five novels are concerned—if not positively preoccupied—with class. (The count comes to five, by the way, through the inclusion of *The Leather Boys* by 'Eliot George'. That this must be included is clear in any case on the internal evidence; and a blatant hint is given by the film—due this autumn—which has a 'script by Gillian Freeman, based on the novel by Eliot George'.) In *The Liberty Man* and again in *Jack Would Be A Gentleman* (her third novel, now in Penguin), Gillian Freeman explores class by positing a class-contrast within the story—not for any extraneous but for the artistic purpose of revealing the working-class characters and their lack of perspectives on themselves through the larger consciousness possessed by a middle-class character or assumed by a middle-class narration.

The method inflicts on the schoolmistress in *The Liberty Man* an accidental touch of priggishness. Even in *Jack Would Be A Gentleman* there is, about the working-class family bumped up by winning a football pool, a suspicion not of displeasing but of rather Lowry-like quaintness. It is *The Leather Boys* which is the most complete success among the class novels, and it secures the effects of a class-contrast while suppressing the contrast itself. Indeed, it suppresses the middle class, which, unless you count the court of law at the end, is not represented. The whole novel, which straightforwardly describes a love affair between two proletarian youths, is confined to the working class but not submerged in it. Events, rather than anyone's consciousness, are used to reveal what the characters do not know about themselves. The boys fall in love without knowing what homosexuality is, and become caught up in violent events with no more understanding of their implications than the functions of the court which eventually pronounces on them. The novel is not about the *problems* of class, homosexuality or violence: those are forces which impel the characters without being perceptible to them, though they are made perceptible to the reader. It is almost like a baroque painting where the mortal characters are without knowing it brushed by angels inhabiting a realm above: except that Gillian Freeman's imagination is not at all mythological — is, in fact, rather close to the ground — so that instead of putting in the angels she leaves a space. It is by an intimation of their own lack of intimations that her characters are brushed, and it is by leaving an emptiness round them that she creates an upper dimension where they are more moving than they know.

The near-obsession these novels shew with the trappings of working-class life is not intellectual but sensuous. Accuracy for its own sake fixes on detail for its. Gillian Freeman's eye knows what ornaments *would* be on the mantelshelf, just as her sense of touch knows the discomfort of washing and sleeping in a working-class home. Her proletarian dialogue displays almost a linguist's gift: she delights in getting it not merely right but idiomatic. If she is not posing us a social problem, still less is she giving us social information. Her whole method as a writer — not only as a writer about the working class — depends on our possessing the information already. The response it provokes is recognition. Like wit, her talent consists in getting there a second before we do or being an inch more ruthlessly precise. When the hero of *Fall of Innocence* stays overnight in an hotel, 'The tooth glass, as he discovered when he lifted it from the metal hoop, contained a white sediment from the last occupant's liver salts.' Lagging an instant behind, we can only comment we might have known it would. As with the detail, so with the major motifs. We almost know them already. Gillian Freeman spins an exciting narrative out of events that are all but obvious, and by means of it she grapples our interest to almost extraordinarily ordinary characters. It is done by sharpening the focus just beyond ordinary vision.

Her new novel* marks the opening out of the method implicit in the others. It is entirely confident: it entirely justifies its confidence. It puts its trust in the novel as an act of imagination: it succeeds in its bid to take over the reader's consciousness and leave it enlarged

* *The Campaign.* Longmans, 1963.

after immersion in the cosmos a good novel creates. The campaign of the title is a fund-raising campaign in a Church of England parish. The hero, himself an atheist (not an agnostic as the blurb timidly makes him), is newly trained by the organization. The seaside parish he is sent to is his first assignment. This is the nucleus which the novel expands and exploits—almost explosively in the force of its narrative tension, yet with control. For all the urgency with which one devours the concise, firmly shaped story, the book makes an impression of having plenty of room. Without the least forcing, it can encompass sheer brilliant horror in an abortion scene and a scene of sheer inspired farce about a contraceptive syringe. Rather than point a single contrast between classes or generations, *The Campaign* takes—but economically—time to slice obliquely into a whole community, in such a way that each of its cross-sections illuminates the others. The old-fashioned and the 'with it', the innocent and the weathered, the provincial and the faintly shifty urban are not only contrasted but seen through one another's minds; they even aspire or are forced to aspire to see how they themselves must appear in one another's minds. An ambiguity both moral and psychological no longer hovers above the characters but is progressively driven by events down into their—especially into the *moyen sensuel* hero's—awareness. The detailed vividness ('a Cornish pasty like a dinosaur with a ridged spine') of the author's vision, appropriately like the just extra vividness of seaside light, fixes the rather Greene-like seediness of the out-of-season resort. Gillian Freeman is an author who knows exactly what rubbish has been thrown under the seat in the shelter on the promenade. And as a matter of fact in choosing her seaside setting she has consummately chosen a metaphor of the whole. There is a sense of seaside detritus being blown through the entire book: you feel it grittily shift under your feet while you read: by the time you finish you have recognized it as the actual sensation of ambiguity.

Shaw

Platform and Pulpit

by Bernard Shaw
Hitherto uncollected material edited by
Dan H. Laurence
[Hart-Davis, 1962]

London Magazine, March 1962

Unfortunately, not a word of this book (and the first one was spoken in 1885) is out of date.

Mr Dan H. Laurence has gathered the contemporary reports of thirty-seven (that is, about two per cent) of the occasions when Shaw used the platform as a pulpit and the pulpit (of the City Temple) as a platform. Mr Laurence has annotated the local allusions, reduced the text to coherence where the reporter had broken down, and translated them into Shavian spelling; and the publisher has put the whole into a type-face, binding and format so delicately in the mood of the Shaw Standard Edition as to count as architectural reconstruction.

The result is indeed a monument: to Shaw's resolve to make himself a master speaker; and to his audiences' complete inability to master what he was speaking about. Hence the tragic topicality of speeches half a century old. Shaw on vaccination during small-pox epidemics; Shaw (irrefutably) against vivisection; Shaw for smoke abatement: we still haven't taken the point. 'I have said enough' (so he winds up one speech) 'to make myself thoroughly misunderstood.'

In fact, it wasn't Shaw who was misunderstood, but his subjects. Audiences knew well enough what Shaw was. The reports record

their acquiescent laughter whenever Shaw, borrowing the effron-
tery of Oscar Wilde, informed them he was a man of genius. Of
course, people did shew the resentment they always will of anything which is new to them and original to the person who tells it
them. But this resentment passes with the newness. By the time
Shaw was fifty and the author of several excellent plays and one
masterpiece, the world no longer held it against him that he was a
genius and an originator. What we have still not forgiven him is
that he reasoned.

If you are the sort of genius who presents a vision so alarmingly
personal that only you *could* have had it, and providing you have
the stamina to keep yourself before the public and the fortitude to
withstand abuse, you need only hang on and you will be praised
in the end. Keats would have had to live to only half the age Shaw
reached and address only half as many public meetings, to be
made Poet Laureate. Shaw's trouble was that he presented a
vision *everyone* could have had. It was part of the eighteenth-
century quality he often remarked in himself. Thus Shaw, in one
of these speeches, on the soldier: 'a cheap article who has but to
obey orders, charge with the bayonet at men with whom he has no
quarrel, shoot and be shot at, and give three cheers when titled
persons inspect his buttons.' The purity of vision might be Candide's. (Ten years later it *was* Candida's.)

If everyone had seen as lucidly as this in 1885, we should have
had no more armies and no more wars. That is why there was
really no alternative left to us except to misunderstand.

Likewise, if everyone had seen the force of Shaw's socialist
vision, we should have had no more class war. Picking up Samuel
Butler's point that illness is an eyesore and an offence, and applying it where it fits much better, namely to poverty, Shaw announced
that the poor were 'useless, dangerous, and ought to be abolished'.
If he had been prepared to announce that blessed were the poor
and that anyone who would not embrace their poverty ought to be
abolished, he might have led a political party (tributes to his
oratory make him seem twice the spellbinder Lloyd George was)
and eventually played Lenin to a communist Great Britain. But
he persisted in reasoning. The result was that he had to work

through the Fabian Society, which he describes here as 'in many ways a feeble and ridiculous society'. He spoke as a celebrated author and declined to speak as one having authority.

Shaw chose to go on speaking as well as writing not merely because it gave him an opportunity to use his preliminary sketches (a chunk of the Preface to *Back to Methuselah* was delivered, rough-hewn, to the Hampstead Ethical Institute two years beforehand) but because it perfected his expertise in his natural medium, spoken words. 'Platform' is only another name for 'stage'.

In the report (drafted by himself) of a paper he read to the Church and Stage Guild, Shaw describes his early novels as 'bad sermons'. They are bad precisely because novels have to be read instead of heard. All that is wrong with them is that they are not plays. Such narrative as *The Irrational Knot* possesses is pastiche Jane Austen of the stiffest kind. The dialogue, however, is already brilliant; and so is the opening chapter, because Shaw is, without knowing it, employing the idiom of stage directions and scene-setting. We are shewn a room, with a closed door leading to the adjoining room. A noise is said to be audible behind the closed door. It ceases; and a young woman enters. Shaw already has no use for the novelist's privilege of penetrating closed doors.

When he did take to dramatic art, Shaw made his major *dramatis personae* just what he had already made himself in real life: captivatingly articulate public speakers, with a fluent turn for repartee. Adherents of naturalism will always object to this type of drama on the grounds that in real life people do not speak like this but in grunts. (Grunts are at present occupying our theatres, but the only new thing about them is that they are often working-class grunts. The middle-class grunt was popularized decades ago by Noël Coward.) The best answer is not to enter into the artistic ethics of naturalism, a very soggy problem, but to make yourself a masterly speaker, thereby proving that people *can* speak like that in real life. That was what Shaw did. That, he would have explained, is how evolution works.

It worked, however, to the perfecting of Shaw, not of the rest of us. Shaw knew this, but evidently he could not abandon hope. Hope, combined with his tremendous generosity, accounts for one

of the few illusions he entertained. He over-estimated his contemporaries. He must have found it unbearable to admit that even
the best brains evolution had produced in his own time were
feeble. Only that can have persuaded him that Dean Inge had
'a splendid mind' and that Gilbert Murray 'reincarnated Euripides'.

On the subject of himself, whom he if anything under-estimated
and who really did bear some likeness to Euripides, Shaw had two
further illusions and gave them currency in his speeches. He
thought he was a puritan, and he thought he was visually sensitive.
That Shaw, like most of his compatriots, had no visual sensibility
whatever is demonstrated to the eyes of anyone who has seen from
photographs the way he furnished his house and the still more unfeeling way he furnished his body — with tweed apparently woven
from the clippings of his beard. I possess a postcard on which
Shaw told an editor who had inquired about Shaw's education
that he was educated in the National Gallery of Dublin, at musical
rehearsals and by books. As a matter of fact the National Gallery
of Dublin is not a collection capable of giving anyone a compre-
hensive visual education; and it shews the conventionality (that is
the blindness) of Shaw's response to visible beauty that he bothers
to mention the Gallery but not that he was brought up in the most
architecturally beautiful city in Europe. Even the fact that Dublin's is eighteenth-century architecture could not make him *see* it.

Most Irishmen think they are puritans, and most are. But not
Shaw (unless visual deficiency is puritanical): not the man who
described intellect as a passion, diagnosed philistinism as a species
of puritanism and never shaped a sentence without making it
sensuously attractive. Even about sex directly, he was much less of
a puritan than he made out — which he did in order to point up the
pruriency of the proper. In his open letter to Frank Harris
(*Sixteen Self Sketches*) he wrote: 'You were amazed and incredulous
when I told you that … I lived, a continent virgin, … until I was
twenty-nine.' Any Irish puritan worth his salt would comment
'Only till then?'

This same open letter contains a clue which so far as I know
Shavian biographers have not yet picked up, and which suggests

Shaw must have begotten a child — though that is not to say it was born. Writing of his sexual experiences as a young man, Shaw asserts: 'I was not impotent; I was not sterile; I was not homosexual.' Unless this is the sole moment in history when Shaw used a word imprecisely, there seems only one way he could have known he was not sterile.

So far from being a puritan, Shaw in these speeches is still in a position to shame *our* puritanism. In 1928 he was warning a conference of Chief Constables of the dangers of making rules about obscenity. He himself had taken a 'sun cure' in Italy, and the illustrated papers had been full of 'pictures of me with nothing whatever on except a bathing slip. I can remember the time when that would have been considered shocking indecent exposure'. This sort of thing is obviously out of date, the very language drooping: 'sun cure', 'bathing slip' (what was it, and how much did it expose?). Yet consider the case of the young man who pleaded guilty to using insulting behaviour after going for a run in Shoreditch wearing only 'a singlet, a brief pair of briefs and a peaked cap.' A police inspector told the court how 'anxious mothers tried to shield their children's eyes'. This took place on (I have been quoting the *Guardian* of the day after) January 30th, 1962.

I wish Shaw was still alive and that it was he who had gone for a run in his bathing slip. At least the mothers would have told their children to be certain to look. But I suppose it is foolish to hope they would have told them to go home and find out what he had to say.

Virginia Woolf

Virginia Woolf
by Dorothy Brewster
[Allen & Unwin, 1963]

Orlando and *A Room of One's Own*
by Virginia Woolf
[Penguin, 1942, 1945]

New Statesman, March 1963

'Fond as she is of her subject,' says the blurb, 'Dr Brewster can criticise unfavourably when necessary.' What sort of literary criticism or even fondness would it be which—'when necessary'—couldn't? However, Dr Brewster is hardly writing criticism, for or against. Her unfavourable remarks turn out to be the faintest of disapproving murmurs to the effect that Virginia Woolf shared the period weakness for 'the Russian soul'. Everywhere else, Dr Brewster's part is to keep up an approving murmur, and occasionally genuflect, when the procession goes by. Much of her book is a précis of Virginia Woolf's books. An opening chapter gives a résumé of Virginia Woolf's life. A brief final section, though called 'Toward a Conclusion', heads nowhere much. Yet *the* conclusion is foregone: Virginia Woolf is on Parnassus. To be literal, she is on the syllabus. Dr Brewster's book (which is written and spelt in American) seems cut out for examinees: a handy prayer-wheel which should save them—in all reverence, of course—the bother of reading Virginia Woolf.

Like many works of piety, this one makes allowances for the simple. As though assuring her readers 'No one *need* be afraid of Virginia Woolf', Dr Brewster has been through her text with the sandwich flags. The *Daily Worker* becomes 'the Communist *Daily*

182

Worker'. Restoration drama gets for tag a potted Margaret
Lockwood film of the 'forties—'Restoration drama, with its
witty, corrupt, intriguing and double-dealing fops and ladies of
fashion.' To her first mention of *The Times Literary Supplement*
Dr Brewster adds 'hereafter referred to as TLS'. *And how* she
thereafter refers to it. By the time you reach 'Toward a Conclusion' you gather that it is by the corporate, anonymous and
infallible act of TLS reviewers that the canonisation has been
performed.

Dr Brewster's book rests its existence on an absurd over-estimate
(two, if you count that of the TLS). Great novels are devastatingly
particular. Virginia Woolf's novels are too devastatingly vague. I
lost patience when I discovered (from the luncheon in *Between The
Acts*, a scene Dr Brewster does not mention) that she thought you
need a corkscrew to open a bottle of champagne. For evocation,
subtlety of mood, atmosphere—all the qualities the Lupians praise
—the sensitive Mrs Woolf can be shamed by an old toughy like
Simenon, who has the literary good sense to approach the intangible through the concrete. Dr Brewster quotes the passage in the
Diary where Virginia Woolf listed the portraits and memories she
was intending to incorporate in *To The Lighthouse*; the last item is:
'and all the usual things I try to put in—life, death, etc.' In practice, the meshes of her attention, set wide in order to catch life,
death etc., often catch surprisingly little, life, death, etc. having
slipped through under their incarnation in the particulars she is
too vague to focus on. Perhaps only Aeschylus and Shelley have
made great literature out of pure generalities. Both poets had
the gift of an angelic ear. Virginia Woolf brought to English
prose an ear quite outstandingly defective, with the result
that onomatopoeia cannot make good the imprecision of her
images.

Dr Brewster is convinced it was the search for an expressive
form which 'pushed' Virginia Woolf to experiment. Sceptics may
think it just as likely that the whole experimental fabric was spun
to conceal a hole—the absence of characters and incidents, those
sheer gifts which are as indispensable to true novelists as tunes to
true composers and which can only come, not be summoned. It is

hard to believe the famous 'stream of consciousness' method (such a wispy, chiffon-scarf stream) was mothered by artistic necessity — certainly not the necessity to give expression to characters, since in the result it is so poor at realising or even differentiating them. To my eye the device reads like the reverie of a clever, thoughtful literary person determined to fabricate from *somewhere*, since the Muses just would not descend bearing it, material that should make her 'a creative writer'.

An instance of a novel more factitious than fictitious is *Orlando*, one of two new Woolf Penguins — the other is the feminist essay *A Room of One's Own*, issued, as though to ratify the canonisation Dr Brewster is promoting, as a 'Modern Classic'. The astonishing thing is that novel and essay are virtually the same book. It is a non-fiction — indeed, a sterile — book: a whimsical, frequently facetious panoramic stroll through English history and literature. (Virginia Woolf was to do it yet again in the pageant in *Between the Acts*.) Orlando him/herself is a thread sewing together a *son et lumière* commentary (at Knole?). His distinction is to be equally unconvincing as a man and as a woman. I confess I prefer the marmalade cat — he makes so much less the impression of being neutered.

Virginia Woolf *was* a clever and thoughtful literary person. Her sense of humour was genuine, though self-conscious: too much pondered, it comes out ponderous. Even through Dr Brewster's condensations one can see that the literary person was a deeply literate and often interesting commentator on other writers. The contrast is plain, if piety would only read it, when Dr Brewster moves to the novels. Dab-hand though she is at a précis, she can make nothing of the plots, nothing dramatic of the incidents and nothing that is not commonplace of the characters ('Maggie, a sensible likeable girl'). Her account is thick with enormous but undefined lumps of ectoplasm like 'the Self' and 'the External'. She describes but says it is preferable not to analyse Virginia Woolf's wave symbolism. In the end, Dr Brewster can get the symbol off her hands only with the remark of an exasperated high-class florist: 'If you prefer roses to waves, here too the harvest is rich.' No, Virginia Woolf may not deserve the compliment which the existence of Dr Brewster's book implies, but neither does she deserve the insult of its execution.

The only charming part of Dr Brewster's book is on the jacket — the photograph by Man Ray which, touched with surrealist insight, makes Virginia Woolf resemble a large, lost dragonfly.

A. L. Rowse's Shakespeare

William Shakespeare

by A. L. Rowse
[Macmillan, 1963]

Queen, October 1963

People who have thought Shakespeare a good writer all along will probably not be holding any special celebration for the Quater-centenary — on whose 'eve', say the publishers, stretching the vigil a bit, there appears this new, long biography which famous men have described as a 'wonderful work' and a 'great book'.

The jacket, admittedly, seems too droopy to be celebrating anything. In a pattern of Tudor ironwork (rusty presumably, since the colour is of aniseed balls), a spy-hole has been made, through which peep the Bard and his quill pen; the lettering, picked out with fake Italic flourishes, indulges in a not very vivid fantasy of having been *done* with the quill pen; the whole might have issued from Bouverie Street *circa* 1919 in a series of Great Lives For Girls And Boys.

However, our tourist publicity often does have an old-fashioned look: it is a deliberate part of promoting Quaint Britain. Such publicity is not, of course, intended for foreigners, who, should they take it literally enough actually to come here, quickly discover that we have made no provision for them. The Quaint Britain image is meant for home — indeed, positively for Home Counties — consumption. Dr Rowse's volume is a ponderous contribution to the campaign. Most of the preface is given up to personal boasting.

By adopting an historian's approach to his subject, Dr Rowse says, he has 'produced discoveries that have astonished me, shed light upon problems hitherto intractable, produced results which might seem incredible'. Even so, the preface finds room to presage the national boasting which is the key in which the book as a whole is composed; there is a pronounced foreboding when it speaks of English people as 'English folk'. And with Chapter One Dr Rowse plunges breast-high into his far from alien corn. 'Warwickshire', he begins, 'is the heart of England.' (Six pages later he acknowledges the metaphor to Michael Drayton.) Right at the start you recognise the noble—the in fact slightly martyred—tones of the travelogue commentator, and realise you have only to wait for that long-drawn library shot in which the corn is positively rippled in the spectator's face. You can also predict that, halfway through, the commentary will take a more virile, even a martial, turn. Dr Rowse reaches this point with a chapter he ringingly entitles 'London: The Armada Years', in the course of which he quotes some of Shakespeare's military-patriotic prose and comments, in his own, 'There is the very voice of England.'

Not that we're allowed to reach London (or anywhere) quickly. First, we must map that heart—and we are, as a matter of fact, in the literary equivalent to the department where they sell expensive prints of olde worlde countie mappes. The first thirteen of Dr Rowse's large pages are spent in a slow tour of Tudor Warwickshire and its classier monuments—Dr Rowse has a penchant for the Elizabethan nobility equal to Shakespeare's own but less prettily expressed. The next fifteen pages elapse in a slow stroll round Tudor Stratford. 'Let us', says Dr Rowse, 'perambulate.' (I swear he actually says it—on page 14. It is given a paragraph to itself.)

Dr Rowse conducts the trip in a prose half-timbered when it is not half-baked, thatched with disintegrating archaisms and inspired by the principal belief of the men who write the travel posters, namely, that to string three epithets together without an 'and' between them will make anything on earth evocative, poetical, dignified. Unfortunately, Dr Rowse is often undignified through verbal ineptitude, which shews worst when he tries to be with-it. There is almost an implication that Shakespeare actually and physically wrote with his ear (and not, after all, that quill pen) when Dr Rowse remarks, apropos of Shakespeare's schooling, that a phrase in Ovid 'fastened on his ear to pop out again at different times in his writing'. Still, the ineptitude of the manner is nothing to the jejune bathos of the thought. Dr Rowse comes near to rivalling the lady who said 'How unlike the home life of our own dear Queen' when he gives us, as *his* comment on (or, as he would say, upon) *Antony and Cleopatra*, 'There was little information about Egypt to go upon.'

To his own clumsiness Dr Rowse adds that of a Victorian guide-book, writing 'Back down Henley Street now to the High Street' and 'Or from Henley Street we could follow the stream into Rother Street.' Reaching on our right the Birthplace, we find that in literary terms we have drifted out of the olde mappe department and into reproduction antique furniture or at least reproduction antique accessories. Dr Rowse's style begins to give off copper and pewter gleams as, warming-panning to his task, he points out that 'At the back is the kitchen with wide open hearth for all the cooking-pots.' Before delivering his comment ('It is touching to stand there looking at the scene, simple and intimate'), Dr Rowse also draws our attention to 'upstairs the big family bedroom dominating the house, the place of birth and death'.

The same sort of meditation visits him on the way to Stratford church, where 'We follow the road down which they were carried at the beginning of their lives to christening in the church and at their end for burial in the church or churchyard.' (I have not, in quoting, made it clear who 'they' are—and in fact Dr Rowse doesn't: I think he means Shakespeare's fellow-citizens.) Not the least of the bathetic disappointments to which Dr Rowse subjects his readers is that, after all the preface's boasts about the historian's method, the best discovery the historian can come up with in the first section of the book is that Elizabethans were born and died.

This disappointment is, however, bettered when Dr Rowse reaches the Sonnets. Blurb and preface agree that this is where he has made his chief contribution to scholarship. He tells us his method 'has enabled me to solve for the first time, and definitively, the problem of the Sonnets, which has teased many generations'.

Many people will feel that Dr Rowse himself is a bit of a tease when they come, after reading about a third of his thick book, to his revelation that the Sonnets are addressed to (as many people have thought for many years) Southampton.

The historical method does not exactly *prove* this: it merely assumes it, from the start and throughout a long discussion, towards the end of which Dr Rowse slips in an admission that the point he claims to be clinching had occurred to one or two people before — 'we know now, as it was fairly clear all along, that it was Southampton.' In Dr Rowse's reconstruction, the 'rival poet' is Marlowe (Shakespeare's statement that his rival wrote compliments to the young man is fitted in by asserting that Marlowe's Leander is a portrait of Southampton); the identity of Shakespeare's mistress 'we are never likely to know'.

Dr Rowse makes no mention of Oscar Wilde's theory that the 'master-mistress of my passion' to whom the Sonnets are addressed was a boy actor for whom Shakespeare had written the parts of all those girls who dress up as boys — 'Thou art all my art, and dost advance / As high as learning my rude ignorance.' Dr Rowse was under no obligation to mention this, since Wilde put it forward not in a scholarly paper but in a work of fiction, as the theory of a fictitious character: yet it has the merits of social and psychological plausibility, argues more closely from the text of the Sonnets than Dr Rowse does and incidentally points out an item which goes a good way towards refuting Dr Rowse — that Sonnet 25 makes it plain that, whoever the person addressed might be, he was *not* a lord.

As for the theories that Shakespeare wasn't Shakespeare, the historical method has a quick way with those. Taking, I presume, though he doesn't say so, a swipe at the theorists who favour the Earl of Oxford, Dr Rowse affirms 'We can be quite sure that it was no aristocrat who wrote the Sonnets: there is no aristocratic reserve.' Evidently, to the historical method, 'aristocratic reserve' is a tangible, discernible *thing*, and as reliable as the evidence of a document. (I am not, by the way, defending the Oxfordians or Baconians. I have never been able to lend a moment's belief to the notion that the author of the Works was anyone except the petty bourgeois from Stratford—but Dr Rowse's conducted tour of Stratford makes me wish to heaven I could.)

Identifying the *dramatis personae* of the Sonnets is really the smallest of the problems Dr Rowse has to clear up. There is also the question of the relationship between the two main characters. This is dealt with by simple assertion: 'There is not the slightest trace of homosexuality in Shakespeare.' I suppose Dr Rowse has actually *read* the Sonnets whose puzzle he claims to have 'solved'? Of course, Dr Rowse concedes, Shakespeare (and, on his reckoning, Marlowe too) fell in love with Southampton's *beauty*, but this is apparently quite different from falling in love with *Southampton*; and in any case, 'These were men of the Renaissance, and they were infinitely more sensitive to physical beauty', etc. etc.—I forbear to quote more, all the argument and most of the phrases having appeared in a hundred books before.

Dr Rowse's appreciation of the poetry of the Sonnets does not go beyond clichés. Of one of them he says 'There is heartache in every line.' But the personality of Southampton, which he is so certain is material to the case, prompts him at least to switch to a new cliché-station. He reports in his usual bluff English persona that Southampton 'became, in the end, a politician and—God save the mark!—something of a Puritan'; but then it is in an unaccustomed, almost Hemingway persona that he comments (with what meaning I can't, however, guess) 'This is what life does with people.'

With the homosexual question tidied away, Dr Rowse needs only one more touch to make his Shakespeare acceptable and even eligible ('Shakespeare's attitude towards women was perfectly normal', he assures us) in the Home Counties: 'He loved horses.' This is expanded into the statement that Shakespeare writes of horses 'with either fellow-feeling or sympathy'. Why Dr Rowse makes this pointed dichotomy between these two near-synonyms I no more understand than why, having called the Sonnets 'unprecedented', he thinks it adds something worth saying to go on to call them also 'unlike anything else'.

There, then, is Shakespeare, peeping through the ironwork, his floppy white collar laundered, his face cleaned up by Dr Rowse

just in time for his Quatercentenary : a decent, patriotic, country-
loving, horse-loving, lord-loving (but in the nicest way) Englishman, perfectly—'perfectly normally'—fit to be held up to our
admiration on those dignified British travel posters : the man, in
fact, in the Anne Hathaway shirt.

John Horne Burns

Sunday Times Magazine, October 1964

I would guess that only a few of those old enough to remember will in fact remember the literary splash that went up in 1947 (in the United States) and 1948 (here) about a book of fictional or fictionalised sketches called *The Gallery*. The author whom it made briefly famous, John Horne Burns, was an American in his early thirties and newly out of the army. The subsequent career of his reputation illustrates not so much the viciousness as the whirligig irresponsibility of literary circles.

Horne Burns's next publication (in 1949) was a longish novel, *Lucifer With A Book*, set in an American private school — a sort of American Gordonstoun, which Horne Burns satirises in broad, lethal swathes and with hideous hilariousness. I've heard it suggested that this exposure of an American institution from the inside (Horne Burns himself had done some teaching both before and after the war) was more than the American critics could forgive. However, most of the English critics, who presumably were less tender on that point, seem to have shared the American response to the book: a response of furious attack or even more furious silence. The next novel, *A Cry Of Children*, appeared in 1952; it was again set in the United States but written in Italy, where Horne Burns had gone to live. About this one, his English publisher, David Farrer (of Secker & Warburg), presently commented to Horne Burns by post that it 'must hold the record for being the most savagely and *unfairly* criticized novel of the century'.

In 1953 Horne Burns, still in his thirties, died at Florence. His name, already out of fashion, began dropping out of remembrance. His books trickled out of print. This October, however, two of them (*The Gallery* and *A Cry Of Children*) are to become Panther paperbacks — an act of justice not only to Horne Burns but to the public: in my very serious opinion, John Horne Burns was by far the most talented, and the most *attractively* talented, American novelist to emerge since the war.

Probably it was the war which occasioned the misunderstanding
in the first place between Horne Burns's talent and his critics.
Literary criticism had spent the war years asking (unanswered)
'Where are the war poets, the Rupert Brookes of this generation?'
When the war was over, it made decent allowance for the fact that
most novels take longer to write than most poems and then started
asking 'Where are the war novelists?'

The Gallery must have looked a plausible answer. Its title is a
pun: the book is both a gallery of portraits and a series of medita-
tions on the Galleria Umberto Primo which was the Piccadilly
Circus of American soldiers in Naples. However, Naples is only a
thematic centre. The sketches cover North Africa as well as Italy—
they follow, indeed, the route taken by the American army and
Horne Burns with it.

This obvious factualness made it easy to misread *The Gallery* as
a book about war reported in tranquillity. Moreover, Horne Burns
carried many of the marks to be expected in the much expected
soldier-prose-writer. He obviously felt he would burst if he could
not explain what the war had really been like, as opposed to what
films and magazines had made it look like. He was bitter with
awareness of the irreconcilability of army-reality with civilian-
reality. He even loosed at the civilians a few of the blows
they half wanted in order to cancel their sense of being in
debt.

The very form of *The Gallery*, a discontinuous narrative with
different characters for each section, helped it to pass for naturalistic reportage: a soldier's experience of war *is* episodic. At the same
time, this broken surface concealed that in conception the book
was unified; thematically considered, it was a novel; and the
conception was a large one. Horne Burns was working on a wide
social front: he was concerned not with American-Italian encounters but with the inter-penetration of two civilisations. More importantly, he was working in depth as well. His psychological
theme was the agony of a personality obliged to choose between
two systems of reality. That these came out, in his first book, as the
irreconcilable realities of the army and of civilian life was an
historical accident—an accident which made it possible for the

critics to appreciate his brilliance but appreciate it superficially. Almost inevitably they overlooked that what they had, to the credit of their discernment, got hold of was not a war writer but a writer. What distinguishes *The Gallery* is not its 'brilliant observation' (though that *is* brilliant) but its imagination.

This is not to deny that Horne Burns was one of the writers who use (but imaginatively and psychologically use) their own experience. His fiction after *The Gallery* continues to invoke the war as a climactic experience, a fence which now lies behind his characters but which they can never forget having surmounted. The hero in each of his novels is a 'veteran', that word which the American language, with perhaps a stab of unconscious cruelty, pins on young men returned from wars as though to label them as prematurely superannuated — 'pins on' much as if the general, in affixing the medal, were to stab the pin into the soldier's chest. To David, the hero in *A Cry Of Children*, the parish priest remarks 'Permit me to tell you, my son, that the Navy has changed you. You used to be such a spiritual little fellow.' Guy, who in *Lucifer With A Book* has come from the army to teaching and finds himself out of patience with the school's hypocrisies and, presently, its reviving militarism, carries from the war a scarred face — not, I think, a corny symbol of a scarred soul but something more subtle and also more psychological, the equivalent, in fact, of an hysterical symptom: the scar is an engrained wince.

On the naturalistic level, this use of the war and the figure of the veteran is simply novelist's justifiable opportunism: it made for socio-historical plausibility. More and more, however, it becomes clear that it was by socio-historical accident that the war coincided with the climactic experience in Horne Burns's and his heroes' past. More and more he used his veteran-figure to express not just the serviceman's resentment of the civilian but a passionate and poetic individual's indignation against society. No doubt the moment when this development became conspicuous was the moment when the critics parted from him. The motif had, however, already been enunciated in *The Gallery*, where a second lieutenant of the engineers foretells a society where 'The queer, the beautiful, the gentle and the wondering will all go down before a

race of healthy baboons with football letters on their sweaters.'
('Queer', incidentally, is to be taken in both senses.)

The second lieutenant who says this has been accosted in a bar
in Algiers by a corporal. (It is possible that both figures represent
Horne Burns, who entered the army as a private and became an
intelligence officer.) The lieutenant turns on the corporal in a way
that brilliantly sums up what must, I think, have been Horne
Burns's own state of mind during his army service. 'How', the
lieutenant asks without preliminaries, 'do *you* know you're in
Algiers? Or for that matter what proof can you give me that you're
alive?'

The same state is described in one of the meditative 'promen-
ades' which interleave the 'portraits'. The 'I' of these is not necessarily, and sometimes obviously isn't, Horne Burns's literal self,
but I am sure it is Horne Burns's autobiography the 'I' is writing
when he says: 'I got lost in the war in Naples in August, 1944.
Often from what I saw I lost the power of speech. It seemed to me
that everything happening there could be happening to me. A kind
of madness, I suppose. But in the twenty-eighth year of my life I
learned that I too must die.'

He was right in supposing it a kind of madness. (More than one
sketch in *The Gallery* touches on madness.) It was, I surmise, an
extreme neurotic prostration precipitated by traveller's trauma —
which is no doubt more acute in armies but may overtake even
tourists; indeed, it is too little appreciated how many people are
slightly mad while they are abroad. Horne Burns is describing the
moment when the alienness of a foreign country becomes depressing, and the knowledge that 'I too must die' verges on the suicidal
determination that I *will* die. 'I got lost' — or I lost my 'I': the self
suffers the loss of the very cell walls which keep it distinct from the
outside world; everything which happens out there 'could', as he
says, 'be happening to me'. It is the sensation of unreality which
comes from being unable to choose between two realities.

The realities are irreconcilable because they are shocked by
each other. Horne Burns was shocked by Italy (as he would eventually have been in any case, by the sensual life *somewhere*): but his
imagination made him, by sympathetic adoption, an Italian, and

he was then shocked by America. The American habit of 'Having Sex', says the 'I' of *The Gallery*, 'began to strike us in Naples as being so cold-blooded ... we came to look upon this ... ejaculation without tenderness as the orgasm of a frigidaire'. The wince scarred into the veteran Guy's face is the wince of a puritan — but a Janus-puritan, shocked both ways.

Horne Burns's dustjackets were reticent about his history ('born in 1916 in the State of Massachusetts') and his friends not much better informed. I can't even guess (I never met him) whether his native puritanism was Catholic or Protestant. (I *feel*, but without evidence, that it was Irish.) One of the 'I's in *The Gallery* remembers back to a childhood which includes the First Baptist Church : yet in *A Cry Of Children*, where all the main characters are Catholic or lapsed, Horne Burns not only saturates his characters' behaviour and thoughts with a sly Catholicism ('Dear Father Rushton had a way with serviette and teacup ; he balanced them on his knee with a grace that only schismatic Anglican clergymen are said to have') but strings the images of his own writing like the beads of a rosary — 'The trees on Brimmer Street looked like arthritic nuns, too numb with orisons to get off their knees, with a veil of sleet and ice weighing down their old heads.' Perhaps Horne Burns was (an Irish fatality) the child of a mixed marriage : the most rollicking section of *The Gallery* concerns the friendship of a Catholic and a Baptist army chaplain, who pussyfoot round each other in their dog collars and combat boots as they try both to score off and to be tolerant of each other, and who end in comradely disaster in Naples over drink and a prostitute.

With most other writers, one *could* guess. Non-Catholic writers seldom *dare* to conceive Catholic-reared characters from the inside. But the distinguishing mark of Horne Burns is the boldness of his imagination. It is comparatively easy to have the courage of one's convictions, to *think* nothing human alien from oneself. It takes artistic genius to have the courage of one's imagination.

Horne Burns can plunge not just into female minds but into a female institution, the staff common room of the girls' school which is twinned with the boys' school in *Lucifer* — and he brings it off with tremendous funniness but also tremendous finesse. A homosexual himself (a friend described him to me as 'the most *committed* homosexual I have ever met'), he is quite honest about the homosexual themes in his books and yet does not hesitate to create heterosexual love. No more does he hesitate to create Italian minds. As a theme, Italy figures to him much as it did to the early E. M. Forster, as the instinctual life in opposition to nordic puritanism: yet compared to Horne Burns's, Forster's Italians have the pretty impossibility of shop-window dummies, small men's size. Horne Burns's imaginative daring shews even in his naturalistic observation. Even an overhear depends on the auditor's *daring* to catch the words: just as one often finds after saying 'I beg your pardon?' that one has in fact heard after all. Horne Burns dared catch the whispers of the unideal in the nation he had made his ideal. He captures for instance—and for ever—the leaden over-elaboration, the fatigued classicism, the nineteenth-century comic-paper quality of Italian jokes, when he records a snatch between two prisoners of war cleaning the latrines in an American army VD clinic: 'Sa che cos'è la sifilide? Un'ora con Venere e dopo sei mesi con Mercurio.'

From passively suffering, as a neurotic affliction, that dreadful feeling that what happens to others might be happening to oneself, Horne Burns developed a positive—an artistic—comeback on life, plunging his imagination into *being* his characters. He draws in bold strokes, sometimes caricaturing, sometimes creating a sort of farce of indignation. He is bold in scale. He is not afraid to bid to be universal; and he can justify his bid because the depth of his penetration into alien minds lets him use colossal perspectives. Perhaps the finest of all the sketches in *The Gallery* is the one about a queer bar in Naples, a meeting place for the homosexual soldiers of six nations. Without losing the immediacy of this to him most immediate of subjects, Horne Burns has chosen the one artistically right—and at the same time the boldest—method of 'placing' it in a perspective both ironic and compassionate: he displays it through the eyes of the middle-aged Italian woman who—in demi-innocence—runs the place. Again, in *Lucifer*, where Guy's struggle with the school is so palpably Horne Burns's own struggle with schools and post-war America at large, he builds so steep a perspective (an historical one, this time) that the book as a whole resembles a dizzily high historical monument. It is done by the simple bravery of opening the narrative in the nineteenth century and in the mind of an old, dying, high-born American Protestant spinster—in accordance with whose will the school where Guy eventually comes to teach is founded. Conversely, the final paragraph of *The Gallery* creates a geographical perspective, down which the book recedes from the reader—the reader sails away from the book: 'Outside the Galleria Umberto is the city of Naples. And Naples is on the bay, in the Tyrrhenian Sea, on the Mediterranean ... '

Such perspectives served Horne Burns, who always composed on two planes, as great conduits of poetic illumination down which his two planes comment on and contrast with each other. The positive come-back of the affronted puritan in him was to achieve a compassionate irony about sex; and as a baroque designer he missed no chance to redouble his irony by exploiting the theme of bisexuality. The sergeant in *The Gallery* who has got into the hellish VD camp ('We ain't interested in making these shots painless,' says the GI who gives him his first injection) through a love affair with an Italian girl finds himself solicited by an American sergeant on the staff of the camp.

A similar design is worked out with more elaboration in *A Cry Of Children*, where Horne Burns takes off into so towering a flight of imagination as almost to leave the naturalistic plane out of sight below. The events retain just enough probability to make the characters' sensations of nightmare terrifyingly convincing. The dialogue falls into cadences not quite naturalistic, yet flexible enough to *represent* natural speech—an idiom, a Racinean convention, of Horne Burns's own evolving (though I think it may be developed out of a self-mocking manner of talk current in New York: a not dissimilar idiom is used in a novel which was published here last year, *Textures Of Life*, by that excellent American writer Hortense Calisher).

The centre of *A Cry Of Children* is the love between David, a rich ex-Catholic pianist (there is evidence in all the books of Horne Burns's musicalness), and Isobel, a poor, ex-Catholic slut. This centre is, however, immediately fissioned by the fact that Isobel has a twin, Fred. David is in divided relationship—in relationship not to each of the two, but to the twins. His love for Isobel is shadowed by an unrealised homosexual love for Fred: but that in its turn is shadowed by an erotic cruelty between the two men, which is realised when David deserts Isobel, and Fred, to punish him, straps him to the bed and beats him up.

It is easy to guess that Isobel and Fred were created by Horne Burns's consciously splitting a single original; in the early part of the book Isobel reads like a woman faked-up out of a character originally conceived as a boy. But if Horne Burns has faked it he has done so for no dishonourable reason: indeed, through artistic necessity. Isobel had to be a woman if the design was to be brought to the point of perfection where the east wing could echo, ironise and set off the west wing. And Isobel's agony, by the end, though most particularly female in circumstance, has refined away everything that is not simply and universally human. David has not only deserted her but made her pregnant. The abortionist she goes to is a lesbian Negress (who advises her, as the seducing sergeant in the VD camp advises *his* patient, that the way to keep out of trouble for the future is to stick to homosexuality). Losing her nerve, but too late, Isobel has to be strapped to the operating table, in echo of David's being strapped to the bed. Her child is taken from her almost by an act of rape. The death-dealing operation is equated with the act of love. ('I don't think I care to say goodbye to Madam,' Isobel says when she is well enough to leave. 'She don't care to see you either, honey,' replies the assistant. 'It's like a one-night stand.') The ultimate irony at the end of all the perspectives of Horne Burns's imaginative world is a kind of bisexuality not between homo- and heterosexuality but between sexuality at large and death. The monumental design proves—which may be true of all baroque designs—to be a tombscape. From its superb height one is looking, chilled, into the lesson Horne Burns learned 'in the twenty-eighth year of my life', that 'I too must die'.

If it comes to my mind to see Horne Burns as a designer in marble, it is probably because his was an inherently streaky talent.

No one could deny that he offered tooth-holds to the critics who savaged him. The idiom he evolved for *A Cry Of Children* occasionally melts into an anticipation of Salinger-like babytalk. Towards the end of *Lucifer With A Book* Guy sometimes takes on a goody-goodiness which makes the narrative resemble those last five minutes of flag-stirring patriotism which used to be tacked on to otherwise sophisticated Hollywood films. Indeed, in certain lights the handsome and athletic Guy, like at least one of Scott Fitzgerald's autobiographical heroes, forces home to me that it may be the utmost handicap to a novelist to be good-looking. Like Fitzgerald (there are fleeting similarities to be caught in their artistic personalities, too), Horne Burns was handsome — and, unlike Fitzgerald, large. What must have been even more disconcerting to him is that he looked, in every meaning of the word, normal. To meet, I have been told, he was just 'an American college boy' — perhaps one of the 'healthy baboons with football letters on their sweaters'.

However, although the critics were right, they were also utterly wrong. It would be impossible to have the good in Horne Burns without the thin streak of bad. Both come from the tremendous generosity of his imagination — which was like the sort of mouth called generous: capable of great tenderness but also of slobbering over. He is not one of those simple cases where a classical novelist is waiting to be let out of his own tomb of flesh, one of those cases whose prototype is George Eliot, who could be transformed tomorrow not merely into one of the greatest (which she is already) but one of the most perfect of novelists — by any competent editor with the arrogance to set up his own judgment against hers and strike out all those paragraphs of non-fiction she littered through her novels in the puritanical belief that imagination was not enough. Horne Burns had the courage, and sufficiently overcame his puritanism, to commit himself to his imagination, even where it was artistically unsafe. His prototype (and he is of a stature not to make the comparison belittling to him) is Dickens.

No doubt Horne Burns's streaks grew larger as his achievement grew larger, just as the pattern on a balloon gets larger as you blow the balloon up. I have every reason (that is, both a knowledge of the nature of Horne Burns's talent and a knowledge of the critic's perceptiveness) to accept David Farrer's judgment on Horne Burns's last—and never published—novel, namely that it contained both his best and his worst writing. I have not seen this last novel and indeed do not know if the typescript still exists. I know of it only through David Farrer's courtesy. It was set in Italy and concerned a love affair between an Italian, Mario, and an American, Helen (who in the course of the story visited a fictionalised Bernard Berenson); it was called *The Stranger's Guise*.

Horne Burns's American publisher rejected this novel. Secker & Warburg sent him back the typescript with David Farrer's detailed recommendations for revising it. From Italy Horne Burns replied: 'Perhaps I'm getting older, for I find the report 98% just in its findings ... I know now precisely what must be done ... I cannot afford another scalping this time ... No, your remarks were not harsh. I should prefer to be brought up short by my editors than by the critics and the public.' He said that he hoped to finish the final draft 'within a month'. But within a month he was dead.

From the distance of England his friends could not make out the circumstances of his death. They were certain it was tantamount to suicide, but uncertain whether he literally killed himself or drank himself to death. He had lately had a disastrous love affair with a Florentine boy.

I do not for a moment imply that Horne Burns was killed by a reviewer's paragraph. It seems likely he had suffered a return of the neurosis which had attacked him during his army service in Italy. Since his distress lay precisely in a dissolving of that narcissism which attaches a person's instinctual love to his own ego, and so attaches him to life, it is possible that some public appreciation of his writing (appreciation equals love) could have tided him over. But it could have been only tiding over. That his distress came from his own personality is clear from how much of his love affair with death is pre-implied in his books, even as far back as the first book and even down to details. *The Gallery* already contains the theme of neurotic drinking (the one part of the American myth expatriates seem unable to shake off with the soil of America). The meditative 'I' in *The Gallery* seems, when he writes 'There'll be

Neapolitans alive in 1960. I say, More power to them', not to expect to live to 1960 himself. Even the Florentine boy was fore-ordained. He enters the queer bar in the Galleria in Naples on the last page of the section, in the company of his lover, a Captain Joe. Their entrance sets off a rough-house in which the clientele smash up the bar for ever.

We have, but John Horne Burns hasn't, lived until the 1960s. May he not be one whose name was writ in water.

Henry James

Henry James And His Cult

by Maxwell Geismar
[Chatto & Windus, 1964]

London Magazine, April 1964

On Thursday, January 9th, 1964, an assassination was attempted. A heavy book (444 pages), which had already been published in the United States (to what reception its English edition does not hint), was dropped on the reputation of Henry James.

Mr Geismar's accusations against James are (in summary and tidied up) these. James's fictions arose from his own infantile fantasies, not from knowledge of sociology and economics. He wrote about American financiers and European aristocrats without understanding the workings of either capitalism or feudalism. He was 'non-historical, since his notion of "history" was that of legend, romance and the picturesque'. His picture of Europe as a place of culture and history was an adolescent romantic daydream, his picture of America as a place of no culture and small history an adolescent prejudice. He thought democracy inimical to culture, and often endowed his characters with private incomes because he thought those helpful to culture. He was ignorant of the proletariat. He was ignorant of sex. His view of sex was through the keyhole. Emotionally he remained an infant *voyeur* with oedipal and preoedipal obsessions. He did not know this about himself. He was 'absolutely non-Freudian'. He was not Theodore Dreiser. The characters in *The Golden Bowl* deceive and prey on one another.

Out of his portrait of James as antidemocrat ('He was non-political; that is to say, he was a "royalist" in the politics which he disdained') Mr Geismar spins a secondary attack—against James's admirers, to whom he gives the—in his context—witty name of Jacobites. The James cult, he maintains, developed in the 'forties and 'fifties because James's 'royalism' chimed with conservative feelings in American intellectuals reacting away from the Leftism of the 'thirties. Alternatively, he thinks, the Jacobites may be conspirators of a merely opportunist kind, 'sensing in this new literary trend the fastest, best way to a university chair, a book-reviewing podium ... '

On the Sunday immediately after its publication, Mr Geismar's book was noticed from only one of the big three book-reviewing podia, the *Observer*'s, where Mr Philip Toynbee wrote, 'For years the notion of "exposing" the cult of Henry James has been slug-gishly turning over in my mind; and it is a special satisfaction to me that the task has now been so ably performed by Mr Geismar.'

This left the Jacobites to live through their anxiety till the Friday. Rescue then arrived in force: John Bayley, Tony Tanner and Richard Mayne (in, respectively, the *Guardian*, the *Spectator* and the *New Statesman*) came to the vindication of James. At the second week-end the other two Sundays reviewed the book. In the *Sunday Telegraph* Miss Janet Adam Smith routed the first of Mr Geismar's two theories about the cause of the James cult by shewing that the James revival began before the 'forties, took place in England as well as America and was not 'the peculiar interest of the radical when disillusioned'. In the *Sunday Times* Mr Connolly finished off the rescue with 'Aren't we all *voyeurs*?'

All's, in the immediate sense, well that ends well. Yet on a slower look a more apt title for the little drama would be The Skin of our Teeth. This is not to be ungrateful to the rescuers, who very effectively accomplished the immediate job and manœuvred agilely in the short space and time available to weekly reviewers. But when the skirmish was over I felt (as—in Mr Geismar's sense only—an intense Jacobite) much as I would if a friend had just been let off on a charge of breaking a law I believe ought not to exist. The acquittal was the urgent thing; but now one ought to set about persuading public opinion to reform the law. In criminal cases reformist belief rarely goes beyond the negative assertion that the law should not be there: many liberal people hold, for instance, that homosexual acts should not be crimes; few go so far as to proclaim them positive good deeds. But in the case of Geismar *v.* James, as in that of Meletus *v.* Socrates, the defence can and should go precisely so far — so far as to proclaim that the counts on which James is accused are in fact the very glories for which he should be honoured in the canon of perpetual remembrance.

To establish that, there is no need to make out a new case for James. The only brief needed is Mr Geismar's book, whose two most surprising characteristics are that it is a good book and that it constitutes an excellent critical anatomy of James. Mr Connolly allowed, and, with one exception, the other reviewers more or less agreed, that 'Mr Geismar both writes well and argues well'. The dissenter, Mr Mayne, found that Mr Geismar's prose 'reads like early tape-recorder or vintage Presidential press-conference, complete with hesitations, unfinished sentences', etc. The description is accurate but not, to my taste, against Mr Geismar. His manner *is* a verbatim manner. He writes (a rarity nowadays) rhetoric — not of the formal but of the crackerbarrel kind. He has the folksy eloquence and much of the conviction of a fundamentalist preacher. However, his fluency takes on a tint both ironic and idiosyncratic from the fact that many of his mannerisms — many, even, of those hesitations Mr Mayne remarks — are borrowed from the writer he is attacking. When Mr Geismar asks about James 'How else could he have been, also, so obviously, so patently, sometimes so ludicrously ignorant about his own motivation ... ?', the reader may well ask how Mr Geismar could have been so obviously, so patently, sometimes so ludicrously ignorant about his own mannerisms as not to notice that they are parodying — or paying tribute to? — the master's. His blend of the unblendable — homespun forthrightness and no-nonsenseness plus shavings and slithers of meaning teased off the Jamesian bacon-slicing machine — makes Mr Geismar just what he calls James, 'a phenomenon never before glimpsed on literary land or sea', which Mr Geismar intends as dispraise of James but which I insist on applying as praise of them both.

Time and again the rhetorical jets under which Mr Geismar means to drench if not drown James turn out brilliantly to illuminate him—as when Mr Geismar says 'this rococo artist went so far out of his way to contrive a notable series of "terrible things" which the heart of man, or his mind, had never imagined—and very likely never would again', or when he calls James 'a writer ... utterly consumed in projecting a baroque personality under the universal guise of art'. Mr Connolly's review commented 'After a successful piece of debunking one feels one can never read the author again ... In fact I doubt if I shall ever read Mr Geismar again'; and no doubt most of Mr Geismar's readers would agree that a second total immersion would be supererogatory. Bits of the book, however, might be re-read repeatedly: most of all, the analysis of *The Golden Bowl*, a novel through which Mr Geismar stalks at length and in detail, trying, like a perfervidly puritanical prosecuting counsel, to rabblerouse our disgust by pointing to corrupt goings-on in the corners: 'please note', Mr Geismar writes, 'that this solemn pledge and seal of sexual love is another ironic scene of hypocrisy and duplicity, in which the two "lovers" are trying, probably without success, to dupe each other ... ' What one actually notes is the beauty with which James has designed his imbroglio of hypocrisy and duplicity. Mr Geismar's exposure is in practice an illuminating exposition, a *son et lumière* commentary that at once lays bare the cogency of the ground plan, floodlights the overall shape (the sustained image of the bowl itself, which has only to be inverted to become the most baroque of motifs) and picks out, where the commentator means to shew up dirt in the cornices, details of master-joinery which even Jacobites may not have noticed before. More clearly than ever one recognises *The Golden Bowl*'s similarity in spirit to *Les Liaisons Dangereuses*— though this, too, is no part of Mr Geismar's intention and probably would not count with him (more 'hypocrisy and duplicity', more serpentine Europeanness) as a virtue. Mr Geismar has, as it were, brought us here in order to appeal to our horror of snakes; and we have stayed to admire and delight in the snake's stunning markings.

One can of course go through Mr Geismar's counts against James defensively citing precedents. Shakespeare wrote about Moorish generals and exotic islands without understanding either the immigrant or the emigrant problem. Mr Geismar's remark that James's 'notion of "history" ' was a matter of legend, romance and the picturesque would admirably describe the notion of history entertained by Keats. The *Oedipus Rex*, more than any of James's fictions, betrays the psychology of the infant *voyeur*. Moreover, Sophocles, too, was 'absolutely non-Freudian'. Few people with any 'notion of history' would expect Sophocles to be otherwise, and it is hard to see how Mr Geismar expects James to be better informed: James's *œuvre* had reached its grand culmination by 1904, and the first English edition of Freud's first cardinal work, *The Interpretation of Dreams*, did not appear until 1913.

However, the defensive is not enough. Merely to cite the precedent of Keats's legend- and romaunt-born notion of history is to imply that Keats somehow *got away with it*. What one should be asserting is that it is just *because* of his impressionistic notion of history that Keats is a great poet. It is through the elastic trappings of 'history' that Keats expresses the very exact and very true emotional history of infancy. Just so, James's impressionistic notions gave him freedom to write novels which in their deepest sense are not at all about *déraciné* Americans shut out from classy European *salons* but about the dispossessed and forever excluded infant *voyeur* who is the oldest and deepest-buried self in each of us. To create drama out of one's infantile oedipal fantasies is not an activity in which Sophocles merely *happens* to provide James with a distinguished predecessor (as though one were to justify James's baldness by pointing to the baldness of Aeschylus): it comes close to being *why* Sophocles' drama is a great one, and close to defining what artists *ought* to be up to.

Even in the immediate crisis several of the reviewers did make time to utter a reformist protest against some of the laws Mr Geismar lays down. Most of them remarked that not to be Theodore Dreiser is not a demerit. Only John Bayley, however, offered a defence so sweepingly bold as to amount to counterattack. Mr Bayley summarised Mr Geismar's accusations and then commented 'One is inclined to say "Yes, of course" and "So what?" ' So, one might on consideration complete, James is a great artist—precisely *so*.

For the whole Geismar indictment really boils down to the one charge that James wrote from his imagination. The fault lies in our literary public opinion if that can be accepted as a matter of reproach; and there is an ignorance in public opinion, not in James, if imagination is taken to be antithetical to a sense or a knowledge of 'reality'. Even in the more superficial meaning of the word James was a better realist than his accuser. There *is* a conflict between 'democracy' and culture. Private-income patronage *has* advantages over 'democratic' patronage by the TV-mass or by committee. Many of us share Mr Geismar's passion for social justice without persuading ourselves that the justice of our passion wipes away the problem. In the more penetrating sense of the word, James's novels are, with exactitude, penetrations into reality. He was, Mr Geismar asserts, 'innocent ... as regards the real nature of ... finance capitalism': 'Love', Mr Geismar says, '*meant* money to Henry James; and in accordance with those oral-anal, pre-oedipal and pre-sexual temperamental patterns ... money meant love.' But in what sense 'real nature' of capitalism? Might it not quite probably be that the real nature—the most deeply causal nature—of finance capitalism is that, to capitalists and proletarians alike, money does mean love? Might it not be that James knew nothing whatever about either capitalists or proletarians except—thanks to his oedipal and pre-oedipal imagination—the inmost truth about them?

Vanity Fair

(Expansion of radio talk, B.B.C. World Service, May 1965)

Chapter 39 of *Vanity Fair* is entitled 'A Cynical Chapter'. In a sense—a sense I mean utterly as praise—*Vanity Fair* is a cynical book. Thackeray is a cynic who knows the price of everything—its price in human pain and disillusion—and who leaves the value of nothing unquestioned.

The image of Vanity Fair is a borrowing from *The Pilgrim's Progress*, where the Fair, an allegory of worldliness, is a market— not only for worldly goods but for worldly pleasures and honours. Thackeray's Fair, too, is animated by buying and selling. It is a place of trafficking. Men are for sale in the City or on the fashion or politics market, women for sale on the marriage market: as Thackeray comments,

> a title and a coach and four are toys more precious than happiness in Vanity Fair: and if Harry the Eighth or Bluebeard were alive now, and wanted a tenth wife, do you suppose he could not get the prettiest girl that shall be presented this season.

Becky Sharp, having missed the chance to sell herself in marriage to a baronet (one who would himself like to buy a peerage), marries Rawdon Crawley in the hope that he will inherit his aunt's £70,000—a £70,000 which every member of the Crawley family is hoping to lay hands on by selling the old lady his personal charm or his solicitude for her health. When she does die, old Miss Crawley leaves a small annuity to her companion Miss Briggs, who goes into well-earned retirement—only to be driven quickly out again:

> Briggs tried to live with her relations in the country, but found that attempt was vain after the better society to which she had been accustomed. Briggs's friends, small tradesmen in a country town, quarrelled over Miss Briggs's forty

pounds a year, as eagerly and more openly than Miss Crawley's kinsfolk had for that lady's inheritance.

With that sardonic backhand about Briggs's being accustomed to 'better' society, Thackeray refutes the whole concept of 'good', let alone 'better' society. The little history of Briggs's annuity slices through the social layers and exposes that, in Thackeray's view, big fleas have little fleas all the way down. Likewise, of course, up. When Becky becomes (or as good as becomes) the mistress of the Marquis of Steyne, Steyne believes he has purchased Rawdon Crawley's complaisance as a husband.

> My lord had bought so many men during his life that he was surely to be pardoned for supposing that he had found the price of this one.

As it happens, Steyne is mistaken: Rawdon Crawley is stupider than Steyne thinks. The innocent, in *Vanity Fair*, are innocent only inasmuch as they are stupider or more gullible than the rest. They are the ones who get sold. When Amelia Sedley throws herself away on the lightweight, unloving George Osborne (a portrait of an *homme moyen sensuel* even more telling, and far more economical, than Tolstoy's Vronsky), it is with no passionate affirmation of All for love and the world well lost. Amelia is merely, supinely, duped. She no more embraces her destiny than her merchant father embraces holy poverty when he goes bankrupt and is (that persistent buying and selling motif) 'sold up'.

Whereas Bunyan's pilgrims are only passing through Vanity Fair on the way to the Celestial City, Thackeray's Vanity Fair is not only 'the world' in its allegorical sense but a closed world. His is the tragedy of an ironist; the tragedy which is half an abrupt joke and which can be so much sadder than tragic tragedy. If the values of this world fail, and Thackeray demonstrates they do, the abrupt tragic joke is that there's no other world.

Not a ray of celestial illumination enters Thackeray's book—which is one of the hundred contrasts between Thackeray and Dickens, whose chiaroscuro nightmares gleam with infernal if not celestial light. Thackeray has none of that sense of evil which Dickens expressed graphically, by making his evil characters *look* evil. The worldly Thackeray has a subtler and more sceptical appreciation of people's surfaces; where Dickens (in the photographic sense) blows up the surface, Thackeray penetrates it. Dickens's genius is to draw us down to a child's eye view; reading Dickens is to stand at knee height, looking up at people who have the monstrous big heads of caricatures. Thackeray's genius is to oblige us to see through adult eyes. He won't let us romanticise or prettify. The subject-matter of *Vanity Fair* is comprehensible to a child of fourteen; its tone can be caught only by the disenchanted.

Thackeray's vision is through an immensely penetrating lens but from an immense distance. One of the distancing devices in *Vanity Fair*, one that's often forgotten, is that it is an historical novel. It is a sort of more intellectual *War and Peace*. The story opens at a time when Thackeray himself was a baby; at the Battle of Waterloo, which gives the novel its halfway climax, Thackeray was still a month short of his fifth birthday. *Vanity Fair* was published, in monthly instalments, in 1847–8; spiritually, however, it belongs to the time not of its writing but of its setting. Thackeray, chronicler of the Four Georges, was a man spiritually born into the eighteenth century, which he factually missed by eleven years. A political history of England in the eighteenth century is written in miniature (along with an almost Vicar of Bray story of the sycophancy and place-seeking and place-buying which went on beneath the grand political surface) in the very names in the Crawley family tree, where a Sir Walpole Crawley is succeeded by a Sir Pitt.

Vanity Fair gets its period detail not merely right but lovingly right—even when it is factually wrong: either Thackeray or Becky Sharp has made a slip when Becky, recounting her arrival as governess at Queen's Crawley, writes to Amelia 'Sir Pitt is not what we silly girls, when we used to read *Cecilia* at Chiswick, imagined a baronet must have been. Anything, indeed, less like Lord Orville cannot be imagined.' Lord Orville (who isn't, anyway, a baronet—but Becky at this green stage of her career is sufficiently ignorant of baronets to expect Sir Pitt to wear court dress perpetually) is in *Evelina*, not *Cecilia*. But what is overwhelmingly right is that the schoolgirls should have read *a* novel by Fanny Burney — indeed, they would probably have read them all and, to be fair, would have (who wouldn't?) mixed them up; what is brilliantly right is the Jane Austenish syntax of 'imagined a baronet *must have been*'; what is almost movingly right in its sensuous, linguistic feeling for the period is that Becky ends her next letter by apostrophising Amelia — like Keats to Fanny Brawne — as 'dearest girl'. Thackeray's invention is wonderfully historically-minded. Miss Pinkerton wears a turban (the pretentious old thing would like to be an English Madame de Staël); the very incidental music, as it were, in the book is by Stendhal's idols, Mozart and Rossini; the charades by her participation in which Becky shocks her respectable in-laws might come direct from *Mansfield Park*.

Thackeray's, like the Regency style itself, is built firm on the eighteenth-century Enlightenment. Thackeray has only to toss off a history-in-a-paragraph of the school where Lord Steyne places the younger Rawdon Crawley (presumably Thackeray's own school, Charterhouse — before going on to which Thackeray had been, like Amelia and Becky, at school in Chiswick), and he unconsciously speaks in Gibbon's voice, remarking that Henry VIII hanged and tortured some of the monks of the old foundation 'who could not accommodate themselves to the pace of his reform'. Time and again, Thackeray's artistic taste inclines back to the eighteenth century. In 1847 it was by no means obligatory to characterise as 'beautiful', which Thackeray does, a quotation from *The Rape of the Lock*. In contrast to the architectural taste Dickens reveals in *Our Mutual Friend* (' ... Smith Square, in the centre of which ... is a very hideous church with four towers at the four corners' — that is, Thomas Archer's church there, which was completed in 1728), Thackeray obviously admires 'the great filagree iron gates' and 'the narrow windows of the stately old brick house' in Chiswick Mall from which his story takes its departure; and by 'old' he means, if one may judge from the non-fictitious houses which survive in Chiswick Mall, dating from 1700 or 1730.

And indeed *Vanity Fair* itself is a literary equivalent to those London houses which went on right into the 1840s and '50s being

built in the eighteenth-century manner. Thackeray is the con-
tinuer of Jane Austen. Taking up her moral concerns (Thackeray
is a moralist, concerned with good and bad, whereas Dickens is a
supernaturalist, concerned with good and evil), and also taking
up her nexus of young marriageable people who can be put
through the formal permutations of a mating gavotte, Thackeray
expands the social nexus onto further social levels and extends her
moral pessimism into his own sharp despair. He continues her,
moreover, in a quite literal way: by taking his story beyond the
point, marriage, where she regularly brings hers to a stop.
Thackeray achieves, between the lines of the Victorian literary
conventions, a singular sexual frankness. When Becky and Rawdon elope, he manages to give us the unambiguous information
that their marriage, though already solemnised, is not yet con-
summated. He lets us know unequivocally that George Osborne
finds Amelia dull in bed. Continuing the story beyond marriage,
he has continued it into disillusion. His narrative edifice rests on
two great pillars, Amelia's marriage to George and Becky's to
Rawdon Crawley. Both marriages, unlike Thackeray's structure,
give way.

Moreover, when Amelia, at the very end of the story, marries
again, her feelings of affection and gratitude towards Dobbin are
already known to be much paler than the romantic, duped love
she felt for her first husband: but for Dobbin the marriage is the
attainment of the ideal he has yearned romantically towards
almost since the book began: and he is disappointed. His disappointment is even known, no doubt disappointingly in itself, to
Amelia. In almost the last breath of the narrative Amelia thinks
to herself (and sighs) that Dobbin is fonder of their small daughter
than he is of Amelia. Thackeray does not contradict her thought:
he confirms it with the 'but' by which he introduces the disclosure
that Dobbin, having achieved the marriage which represents his
romantic heart's desire, is in that marriage moved less by passion
than by tenderness and duty—'But he never said a word to Amelia
that was not kind and gentle; or thought of a want of hers that he
did not try to gratify.' It is Dobbin's married plight which directly
provokes the second question in that final groan of commentary

where Thackeray asks 'Which of us has his desire? or, having it, is satisfied?'

The entire book is daringly built on disillusionment suffered and scattered by the twin sources of the action, Amelia and Becky. Thackeray has dispensed, as Jane Austen never quite did, with the heroic ideal. (*She* still creates heroes who are halfway between the unromantic position of entertaining no illusions to be disabused of and the authoritarian position of being able sufficiently to master the young women they marry to prevent them from broadcasting disillusion.) All Europe lost its last and indeed desperate attempt at a hero and master when the glamour of Napoleon went up in cannon-smoke at Waterloo. But Thackeray has never subscribed to Stendhal's romanticism. *Vanity Fair* is, its sub-title states, 'a novel without a hero' (and, one might add, without a heroine either). It forgoes a hero even before it loses George Osborne on the battlefield, and he is already discredited and de-heroised before he is left 'lying on his face dead, with a bullet through his heart'.

Vanity Fair is a sequel to Jane Austen's œuvre by virtue not just of its formal structure but of its *analytical* formal structure. The famous opening, where Amelia and Becky drive away from school into the world (into Vanity Fair) and Becky tosses her leaving-present, a Johnson's Dictionary, out of the carriage (by what I take to be another period accuracy but one whose significance — archaism? genteelism? vulgarism? — I cannot trace, Miss Pinkerton and her sister pronounce dictionary 'dixonary'), must be the most concentratedly pregnant acorn from which a novel has ever grown. The single kernel gives Thackeray at once his plot and his historical, ironical point. He is going to place the two female friends vis-à-vis two young men who were also friends at school (and again he manages to make plain the erotic quality in Dobbin's idealising love for his handsome junior George); from this social nexus he will precipitate Becky, bouncing like a mis-hit ball out of her fiasco with Amelia's brother, into the higher social world of the Crawleys; the bankruptcy of Amelia's family and the near-rupture of her engagement with George having given him his quarter-climax, he will bring his two social worlds together, and assemble most of his main persons, at his halfway climax at Waterloo. Then the groups split up again. Since Amelia and the faltering in her engagement have provided the quarter-climax, it falls to the other pillar, Becky and *her* marriage, to provide the three-quarter one, which Becky does by her intrigue with the Marquis of Steyne and its dramatic detonation (which shatters her marriage to Rawdon).

At that point Johnson's Dictionary comes back into the story: Rawdon uses it to help him spell his challenge to the Marquis. But it comes in as no mere formal echo. It is not even confined, like the intimation of Anna Karenina's death by train which enters the book at the moment of her first meeting with Vronsky, to echoing within the personal psychology of one character. Tolstoy's train motif is pinned down only by Anna and in other aspects flaps loose—aspects in which it is arbitrary, occurring at what is merely the point where Tolstoy chose to begin the relationship. *Vanity Fair* could not have begun otherwise than with Johnson's Dictionary. When Rawdon has recourse to it, he is falling back on the old Johnsonian rules and ideals, the *gravitas* and gentlemanliness of Johnsonian England. It is just these Johnsonian rules and ideals which Becky flings away at the start of her career and of the story; and it is not only George Osborne but Johnsonian England, eighteenth-century England, which was killed at Waterloo.

Vanity Fair has one of the most perfect, least forced skeletons in the whole repertory of the novel. The beauty of its structure is inextricable from the intellectual content of its structure. Whereas Tolstoy in *War and Peace* deploys his narrative strategically, a general responding *ad hoc* to the ground he has to cover, and impresses us by sheer size and sheer naturalism, Thackeray *uses* his lovely symmetrical structure for analytical purposes. Becky, as an adventuress who can swarm up and tumble down in social level, not only serves to stitch together the several milieux of the plot but actually and dramatically demonstrates the social fluidity of commercial England. The generations of Sedleys, Osbornes and Crawleys are spread out not simply to impress and move us, as they do, by the sheer human processes of ageing and breeding, but to allow Thackeray to explore causes. Unremitting analyst, he anticipates psycho-analysis itself, probing whether George Osborne's weakness is caused by his father's *nouveau riche* indulgence and whether Rawdon Crawley Junior will be brutalised by his mother's lack of love. At the same time he frets away at the possibility of an economic causation of personality. The nub of Thackeray's scepticism lies in the moment when Becky says to herself, 'I think I could be a good woman if I had five thousand a year', and in Thackeray's comment, 'And who knows but that Rebecca was right in her speculations.' *Vanity Fair* is the work of a moralist inquiring what kind of goodness it is that can be conditioned by five thousand a year.

Pursuing the metaphor of a sideshow at the Fair, Thackeray speaks of his people as puppets—the 'Becky Puppet' and 'the Amelia Doll'. That is not to imply they lack life of their own. The world has produced few books so utterly *created*, few assemblies of characters so completely self-propelled by great internal springs of the Life Force. The whole beauty of the book lies in the tension of applying the most rigorous conceivable analysis to an unfailing imaginative fertility—and only because the imagination and invention *are* unfailing can Thackeray in artistic terms afford and dare to press on to that ruthless point where nothing is left in the book that is sentimental or wishful. If the people are puppets, it is not Thackeray who is pulling the strings; he has pushed through all illusions to the disturbing and despairing speculation that human beings may be pulled by strings of circumstance, by the chances of upbringing and the mere accident of five thousand a year. And having brought us to this almost intolerable adult, unillusioned vision, this most sardonic of novelists compounds the exquisitely artistic pain he has inflicted on us by addressing us as children, and finishes his book

Ah! *Vanitas Vanitatum!* which of us is happy in this world? Which of us has his desire? or, having it, is satisfied?—Come, children, let us shut up the box and the puppets, for our play is played out.

Lucky Jim

Sunday Times Magazine, January 1964

Many people's response to the reminder that Lucky Jim is coming up to his tenth birthday will be that that's just about how old they thought he was all along. This estimate of Jim's mental age is roughly correct, though there is evidence, which I shall mention presently, that the precise age at which his emotions and intellect are fixated is eleven. His sociological age is another matter. As a phenomenon in English popular fiction, Lucky Jim is a good deal older than he lets on to being.

When Kingsley Amis's first novel appeared in 1954, several critics took it for a new sort of book—which illustrates the difficulty of telling a revolution from a counter-revolution while it is going on. From the distance of a decade later, Jim can be recognised as a literary throwback. Recognition is all the easier because, while many people and most fashions have changed during the last decade, Jim has stayed where he was. He has marked time in the sense that Jim Mark I has been followed by Jim Mark II and so on up to (the present score) Mark V. Among the dozens of imitators of *Lucky Jim* the most assiduous is Mr Amis. At re-writing much the same novel under different titles and with different names for the characters he is beaten only by Miss Compton-Burnett—who, however, invented in the first place a prototype of much greater subtlety and potentiality for development. The only development in Mr Amis's series of novels is that—in the words of one reviewer of the latest—'Kingsley Amis's heroes have got progressively more nasty.'

No one is seriously blaming Mr Amis just because he (like Stendhal, Proust and Dostoievsky) writes about nasty young men. Most people nowadays have discarded the artistically pernicious doctrine which used to be urged by dear old ladies that painters should depict only pretty things and novelists only nice people. What serious critics ask is whether Mr Amis *knows* how nasty his heroes are. Even that may be unfairly put. Mr Amis is not obliged

to think his heroes are nasty at all. Writer and readers need not
share a moral standard: if they had to, no socialist could appreciate Evelyn Waugh, no atheist Graham Greene and no woman
Henry de Montherlant. The pertinent question concerns not Mr
Amis's moral but his artistic standards.

If morals seem to come into the question, it is because Mr Amis
allows his heroes moments of moral debate. There is a moment
when Jim Dixon (Mark I) would like to apologise but dare not,
and a moment when Roger Micheldene (Mark V) is asked by his
mistress: 'Why are you so awful?' and doesn't deny that he is.
In other words, Mr Amis has voluntarily entered the genre of
moral comedy. This is, precisely, a literary genre and not a branch
of ethics. It does not demand any particular moral viewpoint in the
author — or even that he have one. Many of its finest practitioners
have remained morally deadpan or actually morally ambiguous.
What it does demand is that there should be absolutely no artistic
ambiguity. Here Mr Amis fails — through every layer of the
novelist's art, right down to technical rockbottom.

Mr Amis consistently ignores the elementary requirement that
a storyteller should distinguish between straight narrative and
reporting of the characters' consciousness. When he writes, in
Take A Girl Like You, 'Jenny felt she must be blushing down to her
belly-button,' we have no means of knowing whether it is Jenny or
Mr Amis who has chosen the vocabulary of an exceptionally coy
gym-cum-hygiene mistress. And it's no good trying to go by
whether the words would be 'in character' for Jenny, since her
character and idiom are so inconsistent as to be barely recog-
nisable from chapter to chapter. The ambiguity is even more
embarrassing when the style turns whimsical. Patrick Standish,
who eventually rapes Jenny, is a slightly more coherent character
than she is. Yet none of the traits Mr Amis has tried to build up
for him includes the tone of a Lord Leighton heavily at play, so
we are unable to guess whether it is Patrick or Mr Amis himself
who should be held responsible for this thought on the subject of
Jenny: 'he had not been altogether mistaken, he was prepared to
bet, in his earlier assumption that the Great Sculptor and
Colourist, particularly in his latter capacity, had fashioned her

primarily as a bedroom amenity.' Conceivably this is parody: but
of what, and with what relevance to the story or Patrick's character? More probably Mr Amis is just trying to make his readers
blush down to their belly-buttons. He can hardly be surprised if
some of them feel a moral disquiet when his ambiguous form of
narrative moves from whimsicality to passing moral judgments. A
journey Patrick takes by car is described like this: 'Turning off at
the electricity showroom, he was lucky enough to send the greater
part of a puddle over a sod in ragged clothes who was doing his
level best to blow his nose into the gutter.' Is it Patrick who thinks
this lucky or Mr Amis who is saying 'Lucky Patrick' (that is,
Lucky Jim, Mark IV)?

We cannot tell whether Mr Amis shares his heroes' morality:
but his own practice makes it clear that he does share another of
their conspicuous qualities. The Amis heroes are militant phili-
stines. The 'policy' of Mark I is 'to read as little as possible of any
given book'. Mark V, coming on a novel said to be in 'the tradition
set going by Jane Austen and kept going by Henry James',
responds by yawning and feeling 'as always, that what he could
not do with was a good read'. The apex of philistinism comes in
Lucky Jim itself, when Jim hears a tune by the composer whom
either he or Mr Amis (the passage is again in Mr Amis's ambiguous
reported speech) thinks of as 'filthy Mozart'.

This philistinism Mr Amis endorses by writing as though to
contradict the very principles of art. He himself has entered the
genre of moral comedy practised by Jane Austen and Henry James
in order, it seems, to trample it. It is as though the next best thing
to destroying the great novels written in this genre was to contribute to it what are, in a positively destructive sense, anti-novels.
For quick, cheap effects Mr Amis sacrifices the novel's artistically
logical form no less than the psychological consistency of his characters. His heroes' bloodymindedness is not permitted to flower
into the gangrenously poetic beauty of a sick joke: it remains
unimaginative bloodymindedness, easily convertible into the
blubber-lipped sentimentality of the ending of *Lucky Jim*. Satire
is sacrificed to petulance. If Mr Amis does not consistently build
up his heroes, still less does he accurately send up his foes. He

merely splutters like Colonel Blimp—with whom he shares the distinguishing mark of social ignorance. Colonel Blimp believes that the weirdies who want the Bomb banned are the same people as the bureaucrats who create his parking problems, who in turn are the same people as the pop singers who refuse to get a haircut. The great target and rival (defeated in the happy magazine-fiction ending) of Lucky Jim (Mark I) is an equally muddled and socially unlikely amalgam: a pacifist painter (beard and beret) with social-realist subject matter, high Tory opinions and the vocabulary sometimes of a commercial traveller ('One of the best, she is') and at other times of an empire-builder guyed in a 'thirties revue ('Very fine body of men, the gentlemen of the Press').

Mr Amis's own vocabulary is borrowed basically from the banalities of the fiction read—and very likely written—under the hair-drier. His people get badly rattled, throw glances over their shoulders and give looks of pain and incomprehension. On this base he superimposes the fatty facetiousness—the polysyllables and archaisms—of an old-fashioned prep school master. Much of *Lucky Jim* can be readily translated into classroom idiom. 'Dixon had forgotten ... that Welch ... was "out for his blood". How would Welch manifest his pursuit of that entity?' (Translation: 'I am out, as they say, for your blood, Dixon Minor. And how do you suppose I will manifest my pursuit of that entity?') At the thought of subtlety Mr Amis's prose seems to reach for its pea-shooter.

What passed in 1954 for the fresh and original 'comic gusto' of Lucky Jim was in social-historical fact a revival of the facetious style and the farce of situations (finger stuck in the sardine-tin key) of the novels of Jerome K. Jerome. Having set up his farcical situations, Mr Amis went on to labour them even more violently than Jerome had done, as though he could do to death the whole conception of artistic economy and elegance. It was an appeal to the philistinism of a middle class which suffered from cultural claustrophobia, believing itself obliged to be literate not through love of culture but as a badge of class. Naturally the appeal used the idiom of those precariously middle-class schools where master and pupils share a hatred of education combined with a resolve to keep up the accent of the 'educated classes'. Lucky Jim, sometimes confounded by journalists with the proletarian writers and characters who at about the same time were emerging into articulateness in the traditionally bourgeois enclosures of the English novel and theatre, belongs quintessentially to the middle class, and the frightened and reactionary middle class at that. He is hanging on with all his snobbish, opportunist might to the white collar that accompanies his job as university lecturer, minor public school master or publisher, even while he bucks against the yoke of superficial literacy it implies.

Jim's ancestry in the history of fiction begins with Jerome K. Jerome, continues with schoolmastering real or reported, and finishes with Richmal Crompton's William. The immediate precursor of Lucky Jim is Just William (as he was called in the first of the series), the hero of the epic in (so far) thirty-one volumes which, set in a family just but resolutely middle-class (when William wants to have Fisty Green to his party, the answer is 'He's a butcher's boy, William! You *can't* have him!'), began circulating among middle-class children, especially during measles epidemics, just before Mr Amis was born. From William comes Jim's persistence from book to book. (Though Mr Amis changes the names of the major characters, he leaves a token of ancestry in a minor and offstage character called L. S. Caton who continues from one novel to the next.) From William comes Jim's habit of getting into, and with talismanic luck out of, farcical scrapes; his sentimentalised, tousled, would-be endearingness; his superficial truculence and basic truckling to authority; his apparently racy but quite unrealistic idioms of speech; his anti-bookishness plus the facetious dignity of its expression ('William lay on the floor ... engrossed in a book. This was a rare thing with William.' For the sentiment, compare any Amis hero; for the style this, from the latest: 'Then he wanted very much to cry and started to do so. This was unusual for him when sober'); his suspicion of artists (there is a poet in, for instance, *More William*, who is treated as crossly—and inaccurately—as the painter in *Lucky Jim*); his unfeeling aggressiveness ('Looking out of his window he espied the gardener ... The gardener had a perfectly bald head. William had

222 SOME WRITERS AND BOOKS

sometimes idly imagined the impact of a pea … with the gardener's bald head … He took up his pea-shooter') together with his moments of moral remorse ('To William the idea of reform was new and startling and not wholly unattractive'); his sex life (William, like Jim, is usually involved with an unattractive girl who worships him and a pretty one whom he worships but feels to be unattainable); and even his habit of drinking until he feels sick, though in William's case it is eating. Indeed, even Jim Dixon's well known repertory of funny faces is a development of William. William, for example, 'assumed his famous expression of innocence, and felt distinctly cheered' or — a pure Amis sentence — 'William had discovered that his smile annoyed her, and since then had given it little rest'.

William has remained eleven since the early 'twenties. Jim has kept it up so far only for a decade.

Bette Davis

The Lonely Life
by Bette Davis
[Macdonald, 1963]

London Magazine, February 1964

The eyes that pop, the cheeks that pout from the flattened and pursed little face on the jacket might belong to a pekinese. The personality inside the book could belong to a pekinese only if the pekinese had been endowed with telling speech by a super-Saki.

And really a talking animal is only a whit more startling than a talking star — a star, that is to say, talking both *in propria persona* and sense. As all the reviewers have made clear, Bette Davis's autobiography is eminently *not* the gush and ghosting of the standard star memoirs. To be just, there had been exceptions before: the witty Tallulah Bankhead; the intelligent, unintentionally sad Mae West. Miss Davis can be witty — 'I wonder how Michelangelo would have sculptured and painted today? Would all that beauty and nobility be sacrificed to the grafitto [*sic*], John Loves John?' She can also (witness her book's title) be sad. But it isn't unintentional. 'Whatever I did,' she writes, 'I did. I alone am responsible.' That is how far she is removed from the gushing norm. It is all the difference between the gushing and Holy-Ghosting St Thérèse (of the Child Jesus and Lisieux) and St Teresa of Ávila.

As a matter of fact, it is St Teresa's autobiography I would seriously propound as an analogue to Bette Davis's. Not that Miss

Davis has a religious vocation—or even, one gathers, belief. (But then had—in her heart of pierced hearts—St Teresa?) The resemblance lies in another sort of faith, exemplified in the childhood fancy entertained by Miss Davis, who was born during a thunderstorm, that 'the Finger of God was directing the attention of the world to me'.

Miss Davis is essentially a star rather than an actress: or, lest that should be read as disparagement, of which I would not utter a syllable, she is not so much an actress as a great actress. Among the distinguishing marks of greatness, she has (like Edith Evans, Chaplin, Barrault) the power to command you to believe her beautiful. That is much more useful than real beauty, about which half the audience will always say 'Yes, but it leaves me cold': it is more like the open-ended creativeness of the novelist, who can cunningly write 'beautiful' and 'handsome' and leave it to each reader to fill in the description. Miss Davis's star quality is, like all her qualities, conscious and deliberate: 'The purists have much to say about personal magnetism, style and star quality. I will defend all three to my death.' Herself the most disciplined and hard-working of players (eight films during her first year at Warners'; at one period she was making one film in the daytime and another at night), she is against the actor who is 'an emotional slob, spilling his insides', and not much in favour of the technically accomplished chameleon. 'The public makes its stars and loves them. They should recognize them and welcome them ... in straight drama one would have to have repeated plastic surgery to keep from being "the same in every rôle".' And likewise 'There is a part of you that must hold the reins and control the projection ... I was always Bette Davis watching herself become another person.'

In point of fact, Bette Davis herself was in a sense the result of 'becoming another person'. The name did not exist until its bearer was adolescent—old enough to be 'the most dedicated Girl Scout that ever lived'. It was at that period of her life that Miss Davis created Bette Davis—after *La Cousine Bette* ('The fact that M. Balzac's Lisbeth Fischer was a horror didn't come to my attention until I read the book some time later'). When she signed her new name to a letter to her father, he replied that it was just a passing fancy. 'That', Miss Davis writes, 'did it—it always has. Just tell me I'm not going to do something. I do it.' Perhaps the change of name has as much ritualistic significance in the psychology of a star as in that of a dictator—or of a nun taking the veil.

To her assumed self Bette Davis is so remarkably true that her 'sameness in every rôle' extends even to her rôle as autobiographer. There are turns of phrase in her book—particularly inversions, like her 'Off to England were we'—which demand to be read not as a text but as a musical score. They do not come to sense unless the mind's ear reconstructs Miss Davis's idiosyncratic tone and intonation and her particular regionless, nationless accent—all of which she deliberately acquired, in exchange for 'a high, tiny' voice and a 'Yankee accent', at John Murray Anderson's drama school on 58th Street (where Martha Graham taught her dancing). Interpreted via that unique method of expelling the words as though snubbing them, many of Miss Davis's phrases become pointed to the verge of wit. And in general she is as good an impressionist of wit as of beauty. Even her occasional illiteracies can be turned to witty account, like the malapropism in her retelling of the story of one of her films, in which a love affair has led to murder: the affair, Miss Davis says as aptly as incorrectly, 'is all *a priori* to the film which starts dramatically with the shooting'.

When it comes to a subject on which she is sardonic, Miss Davis's inversions can be lethally turned—for instance, 'those brothers Warner or my husbands four'. (The last are the subject on which she is supremely—superbly—sardonic.) She achieves a beautifully frosty distancing effect about her father—who in fact during her infancy distanced himself from his family, leaving the mother to bring up the two girls by working as a professional photographer, housekeeper or whatever other makeshift métier came her resourceful and optimistic way. Miss Davis's narrative regularly refers to her father, as nakedly as though he were a troika-named character in a Russian novel, as Harlow Morrell Davis. The trick seems to place him, frost-outlined, in the middle distance of a vast and empty Russian landscape. Bearing the Davis intonation in mind, one knows just what Miss Davis means (not to mention what *he* did) when she records, 'It was one of Mr Warner's irritations that I never called him anything but *Mr* Warner.' One not only knows but concurs in what she means by 'Joan of Crawford'.

For her fellow-stars, indeed, praise from Miss Davis must carry all the value that goes with discrimination; it is like praise from Leonardo, who of all his contemporaries mentions only Botticelli. To her honour, Miss Davis singles out Brando, Hepburn (K.), Simone Signoret in *Room at the Top*, and Magnani. After her first meeting with Magnani, Miss Davis's husband 'fell into a chair' remarking, 'The two of you! There was enough electricity in this room to light all of New York City.'

So inevitable was Miss Davis's stardom that she wasted no time having a vocation. Again the parallel is with St Teresa, who felt at first no inclination for the cloister or even an aversion from it. But where else — at that period — was a woman of St Teresa's commanding personality to exercise it? Where else — at her period — was a woman of Miss Davis's temperament (and lack of money) to exercise hers? With no single bent (as a child she was simply good at everything), without a creative or intellectual vocation that could be pursued in solitude, she was destined to express herself socially, through other people — which accounts for much of the restlessness and frustratedness of her personality. She didn't make up her mind to go but simply went into the theatre, and thence inevitably, despite a hatred of being photographed ('I had been Mother's model so often I had a phobia about it'), to Hollywood, since it historically happened that the rise of talkies was setting a premium on players trained and experienced in the theatre. It is true that as a girl Miss Davis had a crush on her Sunday School teacher, who was Lillian Gish's stand-in: but not only was that the last time Miss Davis had anything so weak as a crush on anyone (later on it was the objects of her love who were likely to get crushed); it was the only hint she ever shewed of being stage-struck. (She picked up film technique from watching Garbo films — but only *after* she had a Hollywood contract.) Her career had the inevitability of one of those marriages so ideally suitable that the participants never bother actually to fall in love. It was like Bernard Shaw's reply to 'When did you first feel inclined to write?' — 'I never felt inclined to write, any more than to breathe.'

Having placed Miss Davis under contract, Hollywood had no more idea what it had got hold of than the Church had when it consecrated Teresa a nun. Miss Davis's employers were as suspicious of her as St Teresa's superiors of her. Miss Davis infuriated them by knowing infinitely better than they what they ought to do with her. She fought — and lost — a tremendous liberating action to free herself from the tyranny of a standard contract. (The case was fought in England, because Miss Davis, the first of the stars to try to escape from Hollywood stereotyping to the European cinema, was intending to test the legality of making a film in Europe: she infuriated Sir Patrick Hastings into throwing his wig across the courtroom.) Even when Hollywood took her advice and put her, to its immense profit, into films that did suit her, she infuriated the camp-followers by not conforming to stereotype off screen. She describes a scene — it might come straight out of *All About Eve* — at the celebrations for her 1935 Oscar. 'During the evening I went to the ladies' room, where I was followed and attacked by a lady fan-magazine editor ... One would have thought that I had defiled the Academy or eaten her young. Slowly ... I was able to piece together the now spluttering syllables. "How could you? A print! You could be dressed for a family dinner." I was wearing', Miss Davis glozes the story, 'a navy-and-white checked dinner dress ... It was very simple and very expensive.'

The films which did suit Miss Davis were, of course, strong stuff — heavy drama. Perhaps her only film to be superlative as a film is *All About Eve*, and there, playing a star, Miss Davis is paradoxically least star and most actress. So good is the film that it could almost have done without Miss Davis. Most of her other films would have been nothing without her. Many of them were appalling. (Her plot summaries do nothing to dissuade one.) But that is not to say Miss Davis was unwise to play in them. Indeed, she presents, aesthetically, a paradox more stringent than the curate's egg: she is actually good in *bad* parts.

A predisposition to emotional meatiness shews itself in an episode Miss Davis records — knowing what she is doing — from her schooldays. She was the school Santa Claus, and the Christmas

tree candles set fire to her costume and beard. The other girls
wrapped her in a rug and put out the flames. 'When the rug was
taken off, I decided to keep my eyes closed. Ever an actress! I
would make believe I was blind. "Her eyes!" A shudder of delight
went through me. I was in complete command of the moment. I
had never known such power.'

That—as well as foreshadowing some of the plots Miss Davis
summarises—hints the resemblance between the great-actress (or
the saintly) personality and the hysterical personality. The essence
is not belief (which is merely and involuntarily mad) but make-
belief in the fantasy—to the extent of giving a great performance or
of having, as a deliberately cultivated act of will, a mystical experience. Miss Davis needed her bad scripts as sorely as they
needed her; they were what she needed to wrestle through in
pursuit of that 'truth' and 'realism' (her words) which to her are
'more than natural'. For in Miss Davis control is always chasing
after the fantasy, insight after melodrama; the chase creates, in her
autobiography as in St Teresa's, a wonderful spiral of intensity.

Miss Davis has immense insight. She recognises that she took
her father's place as breadwinner and paterfamilias, succumbing
to the charm and exasperatingness of her mother—whom Miss
Davis could never leave because she had been, so woundingly, left
already. She amusingly discloses a puritanism so extreme that,
asked to play a scene with a baby, she was concerned only with
whether it was a boy or a girl: when it proved a boy, she played
the scene crimson, which came out deep grey. (I could hardly
believe in such fanaticism of delicacy—any more than the people
on the set at the time, who could not understand what difference
the baby's sex could make—until, in a history of the novel, I came
on a parallel, in a female character who holds that a 'girl ought not
to set eyes on a baby that was not of the feminine gender'. The
date—which tells much about Miss Davis—is 1760.) Miss Davis
has insight into her puritanism, too. She knows it is a matter of
temperament, not conviction. 'Had I been a European, I would
have managed things differently.' As it was, the only way she
could contemplate taking out of a virginity which, maintained well
into adulthood and a successful career, seems to have troubled

everyone around her, was to marry. 'The deflowering of New England was unthinkable to this passionate Pilgrim.' So engrained was her virginity that she had to take this way out of it not once but four times. She recognises also as an aspect of her puritanism that unassuageable passion for work which is the great demonic quality she shares with St Teresa and which more than anything else made her unsuited to all her marriages. Perhaps the most characteristic of all her self-revelations is 'I wasn't in pictures for the fun of it.'

It may have been in pursuit of the reality beyond the fantasy that Miss Davis turned from fictional to historical characters—in whom, however bad the immediate script, there is bound to be a basis of literal truth. One of the many ways in which she knew better than Hollywood is that she was agitating to play Queen Elizabeth long before she (twice) did. (The first time she actually did, she knew better in the matter of costumes, too. She had two lots made, one to the director's taste and one to hers. She made the tests in the first and the film itself in the second.) The predicament of the inveterately virginal Miss Davis is in fact that of the Virgin Queen. She is unable (hence the loneliness of the title) to find a man to match her. Miss Davis, who has a predilection for the sixteenth century, describes herself as always looking for a Petruchio. (She hints that she found one, but fled him.) Again and again, she comes back to her affinity with Queen Elizabeth: 'Elizabeth Tudor was right. She ruled alone. I'm afraid I'm a Queen—with all the prerogatives of that station. All except one. With it, heads would have rolled ... Yes! A Queen I was. Ask any of my husbands.' So perfectly is she in the rôle that she catches the very accents of the great address to the troops at Tilbury when she magnificently details the contract she eventually won—'Three pictures annually and a Queen's ransom for each.'

Miss Davis's liking for the sixteenth century now could and should extend to another historical impersonation. For it she must come to Europe ('You are for us,' Magnani told her, ' ... Come to us'), because a Hollywood *A Nun's History* implies a taste too perverse to be very generally shared. It is perhaps under the direction of Bunuel that she should undertake the rôle of Queen Elizabeth's

Spanish-Jewish contemporary, a virgin who fantasised a bride-groom fit for herself out of no less material than God himself.

When those two restless, commanding, controlled personalities sat down each to write her autobiography—St Teresa in obedi-ence to her superiors, Miss Davis because, in the falling off of Hollywood, she had to do *something* ('I have never looked back before. I've never had the time ... ')—each produced a book that is in some sort a classic. In just *what* sort is harder to say. In both cases, the imagination is flaming but untutored. In neither case is the book a work of literary art. But the category of 'human interest' is sullied. Psychology comes to mind; what can the interest be if not psychological? Yet 'a classic of psychology' sug-gests 'a classic case'; and though both St Teresa and Miss Davis *are* (and Miss Davis *knows* she is) classical Oedipus cases, Miss Davis is perfectly right to insist she is much more. There is not only the beauty of a Freudian (in the sense of Euclidian) demon-stration: there is also a (in the best sense) picturesque effect. The clinical word 'case' implies the possibility or desirability of cure—which is not only an impertinence but a philistinism. I think the category must be literature after all: that most elastic of cate-gories, widest of safety nets, which catches up into immortality things which began as holy scriptures or, like St Teresa's *Life* of herself, works of devotion but which are now dropping out of belief. (Even the Hollywood myth is dropping out of belief now: it may not outlast the Christian faith.) Like all good works of literature, Miss Davis's autobiography brings out the existentialist in the reader. Her situation is moving: yet, so far from proffering a 'cure', one would change not the least item in it. Her ultimate star quality is to compel one to concur in her judgments. 'I do not regret the dust I've kicked up ... I'm larger than life. That's my problem ... At this point I wouldn't change a thing if I could.'

Henry Miller

Tropic of Cancer

by Henry Miller
[Calder, 1963]

London Magazine, June 1963

Henry Miller is a commonplace personality whom we have all
met several times. I am referring, by the way, to the hero and
first-person narrator of *Sexus* and the now published in England
Tropic of Cancer, who, by a Proustian device which makes a far
from Proustian effect, bears the same name as the author. I shall
distinguish between them by calling the character Henry Miller
and the author Mr Henry Miller.

I first saw Henry Miller when I was fourteen. It was in Kensing-
ton Gardens, and he was playing baseball for a United States
Army team. Whenever the ball was scooped up really high, Henry
Miller would run to where he thought it was going to descend,
stretch up his hands (he wore enormous gauntlets like a knight in
armour) and scream 'I got it, I got it, I got it'. The other players
cleared a holy circle round him. In the sky — that sharp blue wartime sky — the ball seemed to halt for solid minutes. Henry Miller
started screaming he had got it long before he could, let alone did,
have it, and he did not stop until it actually fell — sometimes wide
of him, sometimes plumb on his gauntlets. Not once, wherever it
fell, did he catch it. Not once was he abashed by the failure. It
seemed that in his mental world to assert he had the ball was as
good — was the same — as having it. With hindsight I suspect some

of the other players were deceived into inhabiting Henry Miller's world: after the game they remembered only his assertion, and forgot whether it tallied with the facts. Probably Henry Miller had a reputation for catching—perhaps even among men who themselves sometimes caught the ball.

Since the war I have seen him in many parts of Europe, usually in the evening and in a café. He is loud-mouthed, bodily coarse and dressed in ugly clothes designed visibly to mop up his sweat. He is drunk—on incredibly little alcohol, if you bother to check up—and may be going to vomit on the floor. He is boasting to the other Americans he is with (he is always with other Americans), and boasting inaccurately. He may be tipping them the wink about the places which are the real thing, where tourists don't go — in which case he is quite likely to name the Folies Bergère. He may be detailing, as being in the Uffizi, the pictures which are in fact in the Pitti. Evidently he does not know either museum is open to the public, since it has never crossed his mind the pictures have been seen by anyone else. As it gets darker and he gets drunker (not necessarily through taking in any more alcohol), he starts to grab at every female buttock that passes. Eventually he persuades a pair of them to sit in his lap. If it is a French prostitute he has got hold of, you can predict the evening will evaporate without any sexual event taking place, because there will be a stalemate between her meanness and his. The way Henry Miller demonstrates he is an habitué of Europe is to baulk at the price of everything, including sexual intercourse. In Italy he always gets hold of that sad girl of whom there is one in every Italian small town— half nymphomaniac, half half-wit; her conversation runs skittishly along just beside the point, and her shoulder strap straggles just below her sleeve; as she sits in Henry Miller's lap, she giggles, puts her hand affectedly up to her mouth, and reveals the thick black hair in her armpit. With her you can guess Henry Miller will end the evening in a ditch just outside the town. He will boast about her for months afterwards, getting her name slightly wrong: his ear is unattuned to Italian syllables and he has never grasped that girls' names in Italian are more likely to end —a than —o.

In other words, Henry Miller is THE (not the typical but the noticeable) American in Europe: quintessentially, the American in Paris. When he turns writer (the character called Henry Miller is a writer, too—the books in which he is a character are his work), he wants to epitomise his emotions towards Paris. His emotions can be described as warm, human and from the guts. He does not believe in the discipline of art but writes in a near-automatic state, as though taking down dictation from his guts. He is confident the results will be valuable, because he has a deep faith (the faith which persuaded him no one else had ever visited the Uffizi/Pitti) in his originality. In his creative trance, he rolls the paper into the machine and, convinced no one else has ever brought forth any such idea, types: '*Tropic of Cancer*, p. 209. Paris is like a whore.'

From well before p. 209, Henry Miller has been at his old game of asserting 'I got it, I got it, I got it'—in this case, genius. O, and a penis. We'll come back to the second, which he probably has got. Genius he has not. Like an amateur doing the crawl, he kicks up a terrific foam, but actually he has been hanging on to the rail all the time. He is exuberant, but lacks energy. His narrative, without direction and equally without form, potters from anecdote to anecdote. It neither creates an imaginary nor re-creates a real-life world. The Paris of *Tropic of Cancer* is indistinguishable from the America of *Sexus*, and almost as exclusively populated by Americans. For all his boasting how he loves it, Henry Miller has really only one thing to say about Paris—'Miller was here.' To chalk that and a few rude words on the walls of Paris is what *Tropic of Cancer* amounts to.

It is not the intensity of his inner life which makes Henry Miller a failure at reportage. His anecdotes are wholly concerned with externals: accounts of the acrobatics of copulation; accounts, leadenly told ('my fear turned my legs to lead'), of down-and-out life; rambling accounts of eccentric 'characters', in which the characterisation is many rungs below Saroyan ('He is big and tender, a man every inch of him, but with a woman's heart'). People who live without definite income and with an indefinite connection with the arts make Henry Miller palpitate like any Du Maurier or Murger. His are scenes from the vie de Bohême with more sex but less charm—and even scrappier. The only passages of inner life come when Henry Miller spills his warm, human guts at our feet. His guts turn out to consist of the rhetoric of Walt Whitman (whom he idolises), an unaimed invective perhaps inspired by Nietzsche, some of the more banal images of surrealism, plus Henry Miller's own persistent image of human excrement, which he relies on to shock and soil our minds at each repetitive encounter, quite as though he did not know it is a substance we all produce every day. (Perhaps he believes this, too, is an originality on his part.)

Now and then a phrase splashes up (in the sheer gush it could scarcely, on the law of averages, help it) which does lodge in the mind—or, rather, which would, if it were not unfeelingly pounded out again by the next noisy phrase. As a tactician with words, Henry Miller is so clumsy as repeatedly to get himself into a rhythm which serves no artistic purpose in the first place and which he then cannot get out of: ' ... the fumbling fingers, the fox-trotting fleas, the lie-a-bed lice, the scum on his tongue, the drop in his eye, the lump in his throat, the drink in his pottle, the itch in his palm, the wail of his wind ... ', ti tum ti ti tum, etc. etc. (I've quoted only about a third)—I've known a train be more subtle. There might be a childish point if Henry Miller were evoking a train. But he's not. Still, just as it's possible to be a famous catcher without being able to hold the ball, it's possible to make a reputation by writing like a train, provided you do it loudly enough. One of the Sunday critics actually said you can open any of Henry Miller's books at any page without finding a clumsily written sentence.

The monotony of his style and images extends to Henry Miller's behaviour. In *Sexus* he remarks to a friend (for once he is making his friends the receptacle of an apology instead of a boast) 'You can't fuck every woman you run into, can you?' But to do him justice he has a pretty good try. Or perhaps it's just that he doesn't notice the woman he runs into and doesn't fuck. Not that he really *notices* the ones he does. He becomes aware of their psychological characteristics at the moment when he is about to do something to them, but the idea of a woman as a personality by whose autonomous existence he might feel moved is beyond him. Curiously enough, so is the idea — the sexual idea — of the female body. Proclaiming that sex is everywhere, he seems insensitive to sexuality, so blunted that nothing less than a primary sex characteristic can force itself on his attention. He is no sensualist. He might have made a mechanical engineer. He sees the female body as an assembly of knobs, pipes and slots. The connecting passages of flesh mean nothing to him except as a containing wall, on which he might well chalk — he really feels no more about any woman than about that whore, Paris — 'Miller was here.' Monotonously, he records his monotonous behaviour. Lacking D. H. Lawrence's puritanism, he lacks the effect of literary fastidiousness which puritanism, perhaps by accident, lent to Lawrence. Henry Miller does not even understand that if you are going repeatedly to use 'fuck' in its proper meaning you will debase that meaning out of it if you also repeatedly use it as a swear-word. Henry Miller holds himself up to us to be admired on the grounds that he is for ever fucking: and yet the strongest diatribe he can fling at the world in general is that it's a fucking world.

When he is not boasting his untutored genius, Henry Miller is boasting the high cultivation of his knowledge and taste. With a snootiness Bloomsbury never touched, he tells us that his difficulty as an employee is to avoid the boss's intellectual envy: Henry Miller has to 'play' the moron and take care not to use polysyllabic words — but, even so, 'I knew too much. It leaked out now and then, despite all the precautions I took.' For verisimilitude's sake, it is a pity that Henry Miller's own style is often semi-literate (he prefers 'commence' to 'begin', and 'prior to' to 'before') or illiterate (he thinks 'effluvia' is a singular and gives the impression he thinks 'exhaustive' means 'tiring'). As for taste, his insight into art is almost as valueless as his attempts at it. He can be merely scatty — he insists at length there is a close similarity between Matisse and Proust; and he can descend to a banality truer than truism — he mentions Uccello and adds 'That fascinating world of perspectives!'

It might be that Mr Henry Miller had written vernacular novels which brilliantly caught Henry Miller the character, pretentiousness, bathetic performance, self-unawareness and all. But that is not supported by the real-life Mr Henry Miller who stated in an interview that his first-person novels are autobiographical and that his literary method was his salvation. Evidently Mr Henry Miller is not outside and seeing all round the character but right down in there with him: he seems to subscribe to Henry Miller's fantasy that shouting 'I got genius' is equivalent to having it. Mr Henry Miller does not claim it exactly for himself, because he subscribes also to Henry Miller's theory that writing is a matter of taking down dictation from another personality inside, but Mr Henry Miller does not hesitate to number the results of his own stenography among the great books. 'Listen,' he says, explaining and justifying the dictation-theory. 'Who writes the great books? It isn't we who sign our names.' The coincidence of Henry Miller and Mr Henry Miller is finally established by *The Colossus Of Maroussi*, in which the American in Europe reaches Greece. The 'I' of this book must be the real-life Mr Henry Miller — indeed, the book can hardly be fiction, since the other important character in it is Mr Lawrence Durrell who, I am told, is a real-life person, too. The sexual tone is here muted (which leaves nothing but boredom for the reader), but otherwise the author of *The Colossus Of Maroussi* has exactly the same literary manner as the character Henry Miller of the earlier books — even to the point ('Durrell, whom I could see now was caving in with fatigue ... ') of failing to distinguish between 'whom' and 'who'.

Mr Henry Miller has declared himself in favour of obscenity, which he calls 'forthright', and against pornography. This is just as well, because Henry Miller lacks the skill of the commercial pornographer. The sensibility which is blunt to the poetry of the erotic cannot exploit the erotic either. His descriptions of sexual intercourse do (though more in *Sexus* than in *Tropic of Cancer*) make an effect, as any tolerably graphic descriptions of it will; and it is a subject on which it is easy for an author to be graphic, since the reader usually meets him halfway. Perhaps the reader is inclined to be ungrateful afterwards, as he is to any book which depends wholly on excitement: as soon as the mystery is solved, one may turn contemptuous of the thriller which gripped one all afternoon. But Henry Miller cuts across any self-accusation on the reader's part. He will go on and *on*, over-earning the reader's gratitude by proffering after the reader is surfeited: 'forthright' indeed—to the point of garrulity. Almost the only claim of Henry Miller's which is justified is that he is honest about sex. No one could accuse him of making it falsely attractive to the reader for whose natural susceptibilities he shews so little consideration. To his credit, neither does he use sex to seduce the reader into sadism, such violence as he describes being of the legitimate, purely erotic kind which occurs between consenting—indeed craving—adults. It is not in writing about sex, it is sheerly in *writing*, that honesty proves an insufficient policy. All very well to be so literal-mindedly honest that you disdain to learn the skill necessary to making an artistic effect: but then your honest course is not to write. What makes Henry Miller not a mere neutral but an enemy of art is that he disdains the skill and yet screams unskilfully that he has succeeded in becoming a great writer without really trying.

It is almost always dangerous to state *one* of your opinions. If I say I think Coventry Cathedral ugly, I risk being congratulated by the circles which hold that all sacred building should be in suburbs gothic; and I can cause nothing but hurt feeling when I add that actually I like 'modern architecture' and don't consider churches sacred. Let me therefore be explicit. In my opinion, *Tropic of Cancer* is without literary value, but I do not mean anyone should be prosecuted for publishing it—or for publishing any book, even one whose intentions are purely pornographic and whose execution fulfils them. The notion that writing about sex is O.K. provided the sex is alloyed with a certain percentage of 'literary merit' is—as well as a philistine misprizing of art—one of the law's quaintest asininities. It is as absurd as it would be to require that any food which is not strictly nourishing should come in an 'artistic' packet. A taste for pornography is as legitimate as a sweet tooth, and none of the law's business. If people want to be corrupted and depraved, they have a perfect right to seek to be— though in point of fact I doubt if even the best executed porno-graphy is capable of doing it. If anything could deprave, it would

not be Henry Miller's bad language but his bad use of language:
but anyone with twenty-five shillings and a taste for either has a
perfect right to indulge it. Pornography is a false problem.
Obscenity is no problem at all. There are obscene actions, like
capital punishment, but no obscene words. Thought ceases if I
cannot refer to capital punishment, though it may be only to call
it obscene, without myself committing an obscenity. Certainly a
word cannot be *more* obscene than the thing it signifies. 'Shit'
chalked on a wall has exactly the same meaning as the paragraphs
of a laxative advertisement (and the literary advantage at least of
terseness). Of course advertiser and chalker have different intentions: the one wants to make money out of you, whereas the other
hopes to shock—that is to hurt—you. However, his assault is not
carried out in the real world. The word in itself can no more really
hurt or dirty you than the laxative advertisement which means
precisely the same thing. The chalker is only expressing his wish
to hurt; he is casting spells. To call upon the law to stop him is to
make an ass of the law and yourself. It implies you believe witchcraft works.

Dr Eissler's Leonardo

Leonarda da Vinci: Psycho-analytical Notes on the Enigma
by K. R. Eissler
[Hogarth, 1962]

Apollo, October 1962

Wrapped in the genteel green covers of the International Psycho-Analytical Library and quietly dropped into a specialist pool, Dr Eissler's book on Leonardo is one of those rare works of scholarship and research which deserve to make a general stir.

Leonardo's artistic personality, after baffling his contemporaries, passed into intellectual folklore as one of the standard enigmas. The ancient puzzles of Achilles' feminine pseudonym and what song the Sirens sang have been superseded by the *Marie Celeste* and the man in the iron mask; the ending of *Edwin Drood*; the real nature of Greta Garbo; and the meaning of Mona Lisa's smile.

A solution to the Leonardo enigma was propounded in 1910 by Freud, who applied psycho-analysis to the single memory — probably of a childish fantasy rather than a real event — which Leonardo recorded from his infancy: the story of the bird which, while he was still in his cradle, opened his mouth with its tail and struck his lips. Combining this transparent symbolism with the few known facts of Leonardo's early life, Freud conjectured that Leonardo felt himself to have two 'mothers': the real one, to whom he was an illegitimate child; and the woman who married

239

his father, into whose household Leonardo was received some time during his childhood. Freud reconstructed a child uncertain whether to expect good or bad from the idea *mother*; for fear of bad, directing his affections away from sensuous and towards intellectual experience—a direction continued by his adult tendency to renounce painting for investigation; developing, towards the ambiguous idea *mother*, an ambiguity in his own attitude, and presently extending this to the idea *women* in general, thus establishing the homosexual temperament which, whatever his acts may have been, seems indisputable in the adult Leonardo. The subject of this psychic biography was no longer present to corroborate or contradict it by giving his 'associations'. But his paintings were. The 'two mothers' reappeared in the anomalously coeval Virgin and St Anne of the Louvre picture, and the ambiguity of Mona Lisa's—and other Leonardo characters'—smile reflected the ambiguity of the painter himself towards the first image, the first 'sitter', to impress herself on his mind.

Freud's study was brief but cogent, and it comprehended the whole Leonardo. If it was right, it was an astounding vindication of the new science, in a field far from where psycho-analysis had started and a field where other scientific methods had achieved nothing—though intuitive understanding had carried Walter Pater a long way in the direction Freud was to take by ratiocination. To some people the reconstruction, even if (or especially if) it was right in point of fact, was wrong in point of taboo: human wishes have put almost as much energy into insisting that great artists must not *have* a psychology—any psychology—as into insisting that women must not have a physiology. But in any case, right or wrong, Freud's feat was one of the most dazzling acts of detection ever conceived by a human mind.

Then it turned out that Freud had made one of his rare factual errors. Relying on the German translation of Leonardo's note, he had taken the bird in the infantile memory for a vulture: the word really means *kite*. Freud had plausibly traced Leonardo's probable associations with the thought of vultures. Obviously, these must now be discounted. But, even with these gone, had enough been excised? Or had surgery continued to the point where the whole reconstruction must collapse? The vultures — or kites — gathered above the operating table.

Dr Eissler's excellent book begins by patiently considering and reasonably answering recent onslaughts on Freud's Leonardo. He refutes the *canard* that psycho-analysis is set on having things both ways. He exposes the argument that a 'simple' historical explanation, such as a classical prototype, is enough to account for those items in Leonardo's iconography which Freud found psychologically significant. As Dr Eissler points out, a renaissance painter may have had a hundred such precedents open to him; we must still ask why he chose to follow one rather than any of the equally classical others.

Dr Eissler entitles the first part of his book 'Polemics', but his tone is unbelligerent and his arguments rational and scientific. He is a truth-seeker, not a point-maker. With the help of sixty-four plates which closely follow his text and by virtue of his own clear and jargon-free prose, he has written in a calm manner a deeply exciting book. Dr Eissler's muscular use of reason — and some of his opponents' contortions — would make a grand acrobatic spectacle in themselves. But of course the book has a much higher importance: it is a test case for anyone who cares to examine the claims of psycho-analysis; and it is about a great man. In his second section Dr Eissler gives us freely, and with admirable scholarship, the 'notes' on Leonardo which came to him out of his work on the first part: notes on the Leda composition, on Leonardo's anatomical studies, on the sketches of a deluge. A Freud pupil, Dr Eissler paints us a finished picture of Leonardo — for which Freud did the cartoon.

Dr Eissler's discussion of the Leda composition finds against the version which shews two eggs — and two pairs of twins — on the grounds that this makes a needless and over-ornate reduplication in the composition. Yet Dr Eissler himself points out Leonardo's interest in Helen of Troy and traces it to the similarity between Helen's history and that of Leonardo's mother. Precisely this might have induced Leonardo to include the second egg in his composition, even at the risk of over-burdening the picture, since one of the twins hatched from this second of Leda's eggs was Helen herself. If the two little boys from the first egg echo the infant Christ and John the Baptist, the relationship of Leda to Helen echoes that of St Anne to the Virgin.

Nobody need feel a superstitious dread of disturbing Leonardo's psychic bones. Indefatigable investigator that he was, Leonardo would surely have practised psycho-analysis. Indeed, at moments he seems to be halfway there, as though this was yet another of the sciences he anticipated. It is endlessly interesting that, of the two great geniuses of the high renaissance to whom one may attribute a homosexual temperament, Michelangelo, with his preoccupation with male bodies, painted and sculpted the *results* of his homosexual situation, whereas Leonardo, the scientist, was drawn to the causes of it; again and again, both as painter and as embryologist, he fixes his attention on the theme of mother and child.

Freud and Dr Eissler between them have acceptably solved the Leonardo enigma. People who are ignorant of psycho-analysis and, I suspect, without much true love for art are given to complaining that psycho-analysis 'spoils' works of art. For once psycho-analysis need not stop short when it has denied the charge, but can advance a positive claim. We are well rid of an enigma that was hiding the true mystery inherent in great art. Psychoanalysis has demolished *Mona Lisa* as the most famous problem picture in the world and allows us, at last, to see the portrait.

Firbank

The New Rythum and other pieces
by Ronald Firbank
[Duckworth, 1962]

London Magazine, October 1962

The three greatest novels of the twentieth century are *The Golden Bowl*, *À La Recherche Du Temps Perdu* and *Concerning The Eccentricities of Cardinal Pirelli*.

It is possible that all three are by homosexuals.

It is certain that all three have mauve roots. Firbank's highest praiseword is 'artificial'. Proust's land- and seascapes are, like Elstir's own, washed on with the third or fourth rinse after impressionism. James (besides inventing Madame de Mauves) was a contributor to *The Yellow Book*. Obviously, nothing is so good for the prose as the habit of assuming a pose. Not only the styles but the mental attitudes of all three writers have been formed by the aesthete's practice of continual refinement. Both James and Proust, however, when they think of another stroke that would bring them yet closer to their precise meaning, *add* it — a method which makes, at the same time, for solidity. Only Firbank, perhaps the most ruthless, does not build up to strength but excises to it. Most elegant of dandies, he actually devours the suits he sloughs, and presents to us only his dazzling, exotic, snakeskin-tight slimness.

His sister, instead of devouring, stored. Of her cache, her discarded dresses have gone to the V. & A., and her brother's papers have been sold. The new Firbank volume prints the relevant bits

of the sale catalogue; two complete early Firbank pieces and
extracts from others; a facsimile glimpse at the notebooks (there
is another all over the dust jacket—repeated, sensibly, on the
binding); various photographs, including one of Firbank at
Cambridge, desperate in running shorts, and two taken, when he
was eighteen or nineteen, in Madrid, full of that *fade* charm of a
hideous epoch of which Madrid is still redolent, and shewing that
the young aesthete had a difficulty in keeping his mouth closed—
as well as, in general, a face there was no doing anything with;
and the seven chapters which are all he finished of his last novel—
which is a masterpiece.

The new volume has an excellent introduction by Alan Harris.
(Here it contrasts with the now incomplete *Complete Ronald Firbank*
of last year; the publishers would oblige Firbank-lovers if they
bound up some copies of that without the dreadful introduction
by Anthony Powell.) Mr Harris is mainly factual; where he comments, it is perceptively: for instance he likens Firbank to Wilde
inasmuch as each was both aesthete and wit. In Wilde, however,
the aesthete was a fake and therefore never dared meet the wit
face to face. Wilde's sense of humour failed to see through the
plasticine prettifications of his fairy-tales and the costume-
jewellery beautifications of *Salomé* because he had, simply, no
taste. He is at his most brilliant in the purely philistine world of
The Importance, horseplaying with cucumber sandwiches like the
Owl of the Remove; his aesthetic milieu was an extension of the
editorial office of *The Woman's World,* itself an annexe to Speranza's
appalling salon. Firbank, as Mr Harris remarks, was socially
observant before he became so aesthetically; but when the
aesthetic faculty did develop it grew straight and sharp. His novels
were admiring eighteenth-century houses while it was still fashionable to despise them; and well before most art historians or
connoisseurs would have dreamt of doing any such thing Firbank
hung a drawing-room in *Vainglory* with the 'blotches of rose and
celestial blue' of 'a sumptuous *Stations of the Cross*, by Tiepolo'.
(*Vainglory* is 1915; as late as 1941 a history of painting—still in print
—concluded with a handy chart of relative importance in which
Tiepolo is given a slot one third the size of Madox Brown's.)

The early Firbank pieces published or listed in the new volume confirm Firbank's triple devotion: to French ('LA PRINCESSE AUX SOLEILS, AUTOGRAPH MANUSCRIPT'), to his sister (second autograph of the same piece, inscribed 'A ma sœur adorée ... ') and to flowers. Like James and Wilde, Firbank seems to have virtually made himself French. All of them may have felt an impetus, practical or unconscious, to escape English law and convention, but there was also an overwhelming cultural motive fixing on France above all the rest of 'abroad', however much the rest might be plundered for its exotic value. Decadence is a rearguard revolutionary movement, and it was drawn to the soil on which THE revolution—with a traumatic effect on our culture which cannot be too much insisted on—failed.

To submit to tradition in French was in itself an act of anti-orthodoxy; in every other department Firbank was emotionally incapable of obeying the rules. He never properly distinguished the Italian from the Spanish language: in his own, his syntax is riddled; he punctuates, as he writes dialogue, by ear—a brilliantly accurate one; the notebooks shew that he spelled on the same principle, but less accurately. It is quite possible that *The New Rythum* is so spelt because Firbank supposed it *was*. In one of the novels he proves incapable of getting even the terminology of grammar right: when the king of Pisuerga, who usually calls himself 'we', lapses into 'I', Firbank says he has spoken in the singular *tense*.

Firbank's flower-cult (nicely exemplified in the new volume by an early, mild, Henry Harland-ish story where the aristocratic hero takes a job as a gardener—and a fellow gardener sits up all night with a sick orchid) is also partly French; among its ancestors are Baudelaire's *fleurs du mal*. But in Firbank flowers are not only particularly personal (so many of his society women own flower shops that he could hardly help it) but actually personified (in one of the flower shops the flowers, only just avoiding Maeterlinckism, talk—after the shop is shut for the night). The unpublished juvenilia shew that the personification began early: one manuscript is entitled 'THE ROSES WERE NEVER CALLED BEFORE SEVEN ... '. It also continued late: *Prancing Nigger* contains an orchid named Ronald Firbank. Perhaps the flower in *The Flower Beneath The Foot* is Ronald Firbank—or Heather Firbank: for no doubt two of Firbank's devotions fused on the point of his sister's floral name.

In Cardinal Pirelli Firbank achieved what James never quite did: a commanding male figure. Pirelli is Firbank's Charlus. But in the other mature novels Firbank's predilections take him in the Jamesian direction of self-identification with women. Here he achieves what Proust never quite did: women drawn from the inside. It is not difficult to guess that he was imaginatively living more and more through the personality of Heather Firbank. He even achieves what James attempted only in disguise and what Proust manifestly failed at: lesbians drawn from inside. In *The Flower Beneath The Foot*, which also contains that most poetically suspended (in a becalmed boat) of love affairs—between Mademoiselle Blumenghast and the Countess of Tolga (Olga and Vi)— the very nuns are in love with each other ('Perhaps I'll come back later: it's less noisy in my cell.' 'Now you're here, I shall ask you, I think, to whip me.' 'Oh, no ... ')

Eroticism plays over Firbank's surfaces like sunlight on a Watteau sleeve; and because it is so evanescent, resting for so brief a space on each facet, the effect, as with Watteau, is of tragedy. (It is because *The Flower Beneath The Foot* is, like *Pirelli*, a tragedy that one dare guess the personal identity of the flower.) The Firbank technique is that of mosaic in a glittering material. The more ruthless and masterly he became, the more spaces were left deliberately unfilled by anything except his immense power of suggesting whole characters *in absentia*. The later books are discoveries of fragmentary mosaic pavements, like the discovery of a Sappho fragment in *Vainglory*.

In his interstices lies Firbank's flexibility, which in the end encompassed not only tragedy and his unparalleled wit but farce (four lines in *The Flower Beneath The Foot* state virtually the whole of *Clochemerle*) and wisecracks which, for their combination of no meaning with double meaning, resemble only Groucho Marx's. The butterfly net Firbank dragged through exotic places captured also homely species in exile—like Mrs Montgomery, the British but h-dropping governess to the royal house of Pisuerga, and Mrs Bedley who saves her the best books in the long-exhausted lending library. One evening Mrs Montgomery's mail consists of 'only a picture postcard of a field mouse in a bonnet, from her old friend Mrs Bedley'. Fortunately, Mrs Montgomery is consoled by being wooed by Dr Babcock—'Bollinger, you naughty man'; and as they drink it, it is in accents of intensest jungle-Greene that 'for a solemn moment their thoughts went out in unison to the sea-girt land of their birth—Barker's, Selfridge's, Brighton Pier, the Zoological Gardens on a Sunday afternoon'.

Firbank is by no means a 'nineties author left over: he is a pioneer of twentieth-century art. One has only to snatch at this conversational fragment from *Inclinations* (1916)—'There's the Negress you called a *Gauguin*'—to recognise that by 1924 Firbank had produced, in *Prancing Nigger*, something which, in its tropically enervated vitality, simply *is* a Gauguin. Firbank's emergence from the aesthetic movement is parallel to Gauguin's from the mists of Puvis de Chavannes or Picasso's from the pretty but (like Firbank's) Maeterlinck-verging pathos of his rose and blue periods. It is all part of the characteristically twentieth-century fusion of 'nineties decadence with those primitive motifs from overseas which were among the last booty sent home by the empire builders: a fusion which amazingly, and almost overnight, turned mauve into *fauve*.

Unerring, Firbank adopted for his last book the new rhythm: jazz is also one of the twentieth century's fusions of decadent with primitive. To the Negro patois he had invented for *Prancing Nigger*, Firbank now adds a free fantasia on white American slang. The novel is set in New York, where Firbank had never been. So he gives it to one of his New Yorkers to confess 'Somehow I've no desire much to visit England. I seem to know what it's like', and himself goes boldly on to invent New York, spreading over it 'a sky like the darkest of cinerarias'. The Sappho fragment in *Vainglory* is outtopped by a Praxiteles Hercules ('the Herc') shipped to the new world ('Fingers five by three, phallus ten by eight; restored …'). The flagellant secrets of the convent have combined with the eternal Firbank roses and both open to a rather astonishing fullness

of bloom when Mrs Rosemerchant reads ('with nonchalance')
in her newspaper: 'New York's New Vice: Society Women
Birched With Roses ... Widow Of Defunct Senator Mandarin-
Dove Declares For *Gloire de Dijon* While Mrs Culling Browne Says
Dorothy Perkins Are Best.' And at the first climax of the
novel (beyond which it hardly continues) the flower-cult bears,
at last, marvellous fruit—in a strawberry-picking party in *indoor*
strawberry-beds.

Some reviewers have suggested that the proper reception to
accord *The New Rythum* is to be a little tired of Firbank. What *do*
they (to quote a thunderflash of dialogue from the *New Rythum*
notebook reproduced on the cover) mean? ... ?!

Miss J. Austen

Jane Austen's Literary Manuscripts
by B. C. Southam
[Oxford University Press, 1964]

New Statesman, December 1964

I had hoped it was collapsing of its own accord, but since a reviewer in the current *British Journal of Aesthetics* invites tenders for its demolition I must suppose there still is a cult of an early nineteenth-century novelist to whom her devotees attribute such qualities as 'gentle irony' and 'playful wit' and (presumably in a spirit of gentle irony or at least playful wit) the name Miss Austen.

This cult title evidently wants to emphasise its subject's spinster-ishness. The mock respect implies that, though she is a stickler for the prissier proprieties, her sternness, like the scratches of her wit, goes no more than skin-deep. The cumulative suggestion is of a rather dear village schoolmistress — a figure who has no connection whatever with the late-eighteenth-century novelist Jane Austen.

True believers in the autonomous imaginative worlds of great fiction resent literary cults, which they intuitively — with the very hairs on the nape of their necks — interpret as acts of crypto-philistinism, whose unconscious purpose is to distort the artist they consciously laud. The distortion is exactly symbolised in the coy, quaint fashion for speaking of Jane Austen as Miss Austen. By a beautiful malign irony, 'Miss Austen' is a howler. In English usage, only the eldest daughter of Mr and Mrs Smith is Miss

Smith, later-born daughters being Miss Mary Smith, Miss Emily Smith and so on. Jane Austen naturally followed this rule both as an author and as a real-life member of the upper middle class. Indeed she relied on it, or a shorthand version of it, to introduce and identify as sisters two of the characters in a fictitious letter (in the juvenilia), where the heroine records: 'Miss Greville laughed but I am sure Ellen felt for me.' In superscribing her own non-fiction letters, Jane Austen correctly reserves 'Miss Austen' for her elder sister Cassandra; conversely, when she tells John Murray where he may write to her, she specifies that he direct his letter 'to me (Miss J. Austen), Chawton, near Alton'.

Miss J. Austen is the opposite of the cult-figure. She would have made a lamentable schoolmistress. For one thing, and not such a tiny one as it seems because it may well be a symptom of anarchic forces in her temperament, she couldn't spell. (R. W. Chapman gallantly footnotes his edition of her Minor Works with the explanation that her spelling of 'Freindship' is 'not eccentric'. Yet though orthography was still fluid at the time there is a suspicious fatality whereby Jane Austen seems always to pick on the spelling —'peice', 'veiw', 'greif', even 'teizing'—which was *not* to become the correct one; and the point seems settled against her by her own inconsistency in 'Catharine', where she spells the heroine indifferently with an *ar* and an *er*.) She would not make a schoolmistress because she is in fact a grand, programmatic educationalist; and far from being rather a dear, she is the most sardonic person who ever set pen to paper.

The earliest scraps to which she set pen (and which she preserved in fair copies) shew that she was sardonic from further back in her history than any other writer whose history is known. She never had, like Gibbon, to deplore her adolescent enthusiasms; not even in childhood was her imagination costume-dramatic; its first literary act was to start straight in satirising other people's romances. Those who believe great literature to be the outcome of a meeting between sweetness and light are refuted by Jane Austen. It was by the apparently 'destructive' method of tearing to bits the nonsensical content and the inflexible epistolary technique of the novels she read that she brought off, in the ones she wrote, the tremendous creative feat of fashioning the classic conventions of the modern novel of morals.

This is the modern novel inasmuch as the form is still—immensely—alive and its moral subject matter datelessly the concern of all human beings who have to construct a morality for themselves instead of relying on a supernatural religion. The preoccupations out of which Jane Austen created the form were, however, those of the eighteenth century. She is an eighteenth-century writer in the sense that she is the novelist that century had been trying to produce all along. She is an educationalist in the same way as Rousseau or a hundred lesser propounders of ideal educations—as part of that supreme educational programme, the Enlightenment. Like every other eighteenth-century thinker from Pope to Sade, she confronts the problem that God, though he may be allowed to have created, is no longer held to intervene in Nature, and yet Nature, instead of prompting a morality, seems morally neutral. She argues, by satire, for Natural as opposed to Affected behaviour, yet has to oppose sense to the nonsense—or society to the selfishness—of perfectly natural passions. She puts her heroines in the love-and-duty dilemma of the typical eighteenth-century operatic heroine—*Persuasion* is one long, saddened and beautiful love-and-duty aria. Since she believes in neither magic nor miracles she can release her heroines only by bringing them out at the end of a rigorous moral education. A Jane Austen novel is what its sub-title calls *Così Fan Tutte* (that other masterpiece of anti-romantic satire)—a school for lovers.

The nexus of these moral educations is domestic, yet Jane Austen is slandered if she is called either a miniaturistic or a naturalistic novelist. Her books are domestic in the sense that the *Oedipus Rex* is domestic. Her moral dilemmas are often drawn in precisely oedipal terms: the end of *Northanger Abbey* explicitly questions whether the story's tendency 'be altogether to recommend parental tyranny or reward filial disobedience'. A childish nonsense piece discloses no less explicitly the matters on which her fantasy played, though the fantasy is turned to the pointed literary aim of sending up the vogue for first-person (Fanny, Moll etc.) confessions: 'I murdered my father at a very early period of my

Life, I have since murdered my Mother, and I am now going to murder my Sister.'

The metaphors of her adult work are less violent than Sophocles', but they cut as deep and are no less metaphors. For all their surface verisimilitude, her plots are too symmetrical for naturalism: her lovers emerge from her imbroglios paired as in high comedy or opera: her books are crystals, which she taps pitilessly apart with the precision instrument, developed in satire, of a remorselessly analytical intellect.

Though no naturalist, she is a realist and knows that remorse no more solves the real dilemmas imposed by Nature than trying not to disbelieve in fairies conjures fairies into being; and she is not so short of life herself that she has to lay on her intellect sparingly for fear of drying herself up. She harries her heroines to logical extremes, with the relentlessness of a great tragedian, though her flail is not sadness but irony. Her heroines are capable of two sorts of response, which may reflect a manic and a depressive aspect of her own artistic personality. The *joie de vivre* which is sketched in Elizabeth Bennet, but with such uncertainty of tone as to carry the book to the verge of vulgarity, comes to perfection, in *Emma*, in a sheer fountain of the Life Force which not even the author's just and unyielding realism could resist. But another group of her heroines can learn from their moral education only by sacrificing to it a part of their Ego. The sketch here is *Mansfield Park*, from which Fanny (or, indeed, Edmund) cannot emerge without turning into a prig; this depressive branch of her work culminates in the autumnal masterpiece of *Persuasion*, whose heroine grows not priggish but old. Perhaps in *Sanditon* Jane Austen was going to encompass both poles of her genius.

Tackling the same material, Jane Austen differs from her eighteenth-century predecessors only as Mozart differs from his: she was a better artist. She was not only intensely intellectual, as many eighteenth-century writers were; she was, as few of them thought it worthwhile to be, intensely literary. Mr B. C. Southam's study of her manuscripts as a clue to her methods brings out both her meticulous and versed craftsmanship and the primarily bookish inspiration of her childish writings. He proposes an earlier dating than usual for *Lady Susan* chiefly because he thinks, I am sure with justice, that it, too, has a bookish inspiration and that by the date usually accepted Jane Austen had developed away from the epistolary form. It seems possible, however, that even a late bookish inspiration might tempt her back if it persuaded her that the form was more flexible than she had supposed. I should like to think, though she might censure the wish as a romantic folly, that Jane Austen had (perhaps through her cousin, who became also her sister-in-law, the Comtesse de Feuillide) come on *Les Liaisons Dangereuses* and that it was Madame de Merteuil who inspired Lady Susan.

It is by a prejudice that we compliment painters and composers when we call them painterly or musicianly but insult a writer by calling him literary. By a still worse prejudice do we suppose that the 'domestic' experience of a spinster is too limited to produce great art. As a matter of fact, we are all domestic nowadays—the word is synonymous with 'civilised'; only in some Hemingway daydream is domesticity exclusive to women, while men wander as free as bandits in a landscape. And in any case, we have learnt nothing from psycho-analysis if we do not yet know that the emotional material of great art is experienced by everyone in the most incontrovertibly 'domestic' period of his life—before he is five; and we have learnt nothing from art if we have not noticed that all the adult experience in the world avails an artist nothing if he cannot relate it to and draw on the earlier deposits.

Mr Southam's scholarly book, which originated as a thesis, is sometimes written in subfusc, but in an appendix he lends cogency to his sentences as well as his arguments while he refutes the theory that Jane Austen took her plots and people by direct observation from events and people she knew. Far from character-drawing after the life, she anticipates life. In that wit and literate among clergymen, Henry Tilney, she invented, a decade or so *avant la lettre*, Sydney Smith. Mr Southam persuasively demonstrates what no one with an eye for a creative process could doubt: that she is essentially and to perfection an *imaginative* writer. Mr Southam (especially in his chapter in praise of *Sanditon*) makes a sound workman's contribution to the demolishing of the cult figure. The novelist whom the cult obscures is, I believe, the greatest of all time.

(*Note :* After this article was published, Mr Frank W. Bradbrook wrote to the *New Statesman* saying that he had suggested in *Notes and Queries* of February 1954 that *Les Liaisons Dangereuses* might have influenced *Lady Susan,* and that Mr John Sparrow had suggested in *The Times Literary Supplement* of July 2nd, 1954, that Henry Tilney was based on Sydney Smith.)

Katherine Mansfield*

London Magazine, December 1962

Once upon a time a sensitive soul was born in New Zealand, took the name Katherine Mansfield and came to Europe, where she wrote evocative fragments, loved delicately and died young — technically of pulmonary tuberculosis but really because life was too gross for her.

Fortunately, this banal person never existed. Katherine Mansfield was in the habit of running up spare personalities for herself: one evening she would wear the decadent sophisticate, the next the unfathomable Russian. The fragile stray from elfland was the least pleasing of her creations but the longest-lasting — because it had the backing of her second husband, John Middleton Murry; and not only did Murry represent her after her death but throughout their life together she was trying — to the point of falsifying her true personality — to capture his approval or even attention.

Her true personality, which includes the polymorphous poseuse, is at once more attractive, more cogent and more bitingly tragic. This did not become wholly accessible to the public until the 'fifties, when Murry published the uncut text of her journal and of her letters to him and when the biography by Antony Alpers told the full facts of her picaresque life: the inconsequential, almost surrealist first marriage; the two extramarital pregnancies, ending in a miscarriage and an abortion; the dash almost to the Front in 1915 for a few days' love affair with a literary French conscript. The life of the 'free woman' which is now being imposed on us as a postwar phenomenon — post *our* war — was being lived by Katherine Mansfield, and with incomparably more style, before women were properly out of long skirts.

* This and the piece on Colette which here follows it were construed by a few of my readers as attacks. I do not know whether the blame lies with the propensity I have observed some people have to assume that anything approaching analysis must be destructive or with myself for writing in a gruff tone of voice — through which I believed, perhaps wrongly, my affection for my subjects would shew. As a matter of fact, both Mansfield and Colette are literary personalities towards whom I feel nothing short of idolatry.

255

avenged the mother's voyage to Europe when it was the baby who was left behind. Three years before her death Katherine Mansfield did, quite consciously, achieve identification with her mother, but she was also quite conscious of the cost. 'I am become— Mother,' she wrote in her journal, and followed it immediately with 'I don't care a *rap* for people'.

If there is no constant writing personality, Katherine Mansfield did leave, over most of her work, fingerprints which would identify her anywhere—sticky ones. With Murry's encouragement, she tried to domesticate her fierceness under suburban cosiness and tweeness. One of the unseen presences at her Garden Party is undeniably a pottery gnome—with features very like Murry's. Murry, however, did not invent the stickiness she secreted under the stimulus of anything that might bear her own label of 'Something Childish but Very Natural'. At the unnatural age of fifteen she was already cooing 'Are you very fond of small children? They always will captivate me.' The difficulty of identification was redoubled when it was a question of the daughter's taking a motherly rôle herself. Her own mother's coldness probably left Katherine Mansfield psychologically incapable (Murry believed she eventually became physiologically incapable) of having a child: an incapacity she tried to overcome by swallowing a fantasy of motherhood—which could result only in children who ring false. Accurately as she observed or remembered her fictional children, there is a frightening mawkishness about them and their babytalk—and *her* babytalk: her dear little this's and thats, the nursery friezes of toddlers in E. H. Shepard smocks which decorate her letters, her whole tendency to curl up beneath toadstools. It goes beyond the pathetic into the pathological: beyond the merely uninformed fantasies of a woman who has never had children into the compensatory fantasies of a woman whose unconscious impulse is towards child-murder—of a woman who did, in fact, have an abortion rather than have a child. That her impulse towards the helpless and unprotected was not solely help and protection she revealed in *The Little Governess*, a story which owes more to Hans Andersen than the form of the title and the fact that the governess is never given a name. The imagination which devised it was

Neronic; and because she for once did not slobber over the ambiguity of her own feelings it is a masterpiece.

The ruthlessness which plays peep-bo behind her sentimentality is that of the unloved child towards its siblings. (Evidently she held herself unconsciously guilty of her brother's death in the war, since her reaction to it was to write in her journal a promise to join him.) If she could not bring herself to become a mother, it was because she could not forfeit the hope of belatedly becoming the loved child herself. Significantly, it was on hearing that her mother was coming to Europe that she decided to have the abortion. It is impossible not to wonder if the earlier miscarriage in Germany (which happened just after a meeting with her mother) was really or was wholly an accident. Immediately after it she performed an act not merely surrealist but dissociated. If it was not dictated by compulsive remorse towards the child she at least unconsciously believed herself to have murdered, it was a moral monstrosity. She simply—she Neronically—sent to a friend in England demanding a child: any child. A small boy was found near Welbeck Street and despatched to her. He spent some weeks with her (knowing her by yet another pseudonym, Sally). She brought back to England the satires she had written on her fellow-guests in the German pension, and the boy was returned to Welbeck Street. Even Zeus gave Ganymede a permanent position at court. Katherine Mansfield, after satisfying a different but no less overweening lust, seems never to have given the boy another thought— except in the one way that is unforgivable: for, according to Alpers, the living little boy from Welbeck Street was the chief model for the dead little boy in *Life Of Ma Parker*, which of all Katherine Mansfield's stories teeters on the most perilous brink between the unbearably maudlin and the unbearably moving.

Her ambivalence was one legacy from her mother; another was Murry. It might seem the figure of Katherine Mansfield's father (brash, bearded, decisive, insensitive—everything that is called, to the slander of the male sex, typically masculine) which pointed to her choosing, for her only permanent lover, a man who was the opposite. Murry was eminently a man who had to be chosen. It was she who proposed herself for his mistress (he at first resisted);

she who chose to stick to him despite their incompatibility and his supineness in the whole affair. He was too supine to leave her, as he was too supine to love her. He was ethereal, delicate in mind and body, and passive. With the terseness of literary genius, she summed him up in two syllables when she nicknamed him Betsy. However, it was not, fundamentally, the contrast with her father which made Betsy attractive. Her crucial frustration had occurred before her father entered her emotional world at all, and he left no impression in his own right on her imagination. Her accusation that he grudged her money only echoed the deeper accusation that her mother grudged her love and nurture. In one of her stories (others sketch the same situation) a father tries to offer love to his children by giving them a present. (Characteristically, it is some- thing to eat; symbolically, it is a fruit.) The gift is frustrated by the mother. It was Katherine Mansfield's mother who fore- doomed her to Murry: in relation to him she re-lived her infantile agony. She could no more wring love — or even hatred — from him than she could have wrung milk.

Yet Murry did publish her private writings, including her sar- donic insights into him. (He was exhausted after a minor expedi- tion: she noted down 'He was dying, Egypt, dying'.) He even gave himself away in his editorial comments, which read like one of those first-person stories — like her own 'Je ne parle pas français' — where the narrator exposes more than he knows of his own awfulness. It is the private writings which express both her genius and her personality at their most incisive, engaged not only with Murry's half-love but with the moving true-love extended to her by the woman who appears in them as L.M. Unlike the original mother, L.M. grudged nothing. She subjected her personality to Katherine Mansfield as generously as her name: 'L.M.' (= 'Lesley Moore') was itself a pseudonym foisted on her by Katherine Mans- field, and presently she even submitted to being called 'Jones'. (She was so often the companion of Katherine Mansfield's un- comfortable journeys to the continent in the hope of health that I think this name must be a reference to Wordsworth's 'Jones! as from Calais southward you and I ... '). Katherine Mansfield made use of L.M. emotionally, financially and for getting the chores done, admitted eventually that she had been a perfect friend but never stopped despatching at her her sharpest and most Jane Austen ironies.

These are often couched in the favourite metaphor. The journal satirises L.M.'s way with bananas: 'But she eats them so slowly, so terribly slowly. And they know it ... I have seen bananas turn absolutely livid with terror on her plate.' Discerning in L.M. a false delicacy at table, Katherine Mansfield was perhaps reminded of her own false delicacy over the cradle and her own indifference to adopted waifs (it was, of course, L.M. whom she had commissioned to obtain the child from Welbeck Street): ' "Does anyone want that piece of bread and butter?" says L.M. You would really think from her tone that she was saving the poor little darling from the river or worse, willing to adopt it as her own child and bring it up so that it never should know it was once unwanted.' The metaphor became openly cannibal when L.M. fussed over Katherine Mansfield's health and was told it was 'as though you took a piece of my flesh and gnawed it'.

Katherine Mansfield had, indeed, a cannibal imagination. Her *aperçus* are of the world glimpsed by an assassin. A 'darling baby' in a French café 'is drowning her brioche in a cup of weak coffee'. An English tourist cuts a Dundee cake 'so tenderly that it almost seemed an act of cannibalism'. The French maid is 'throttling, strangling by the throat, a helpless, exhausted little black silk bag'. Even when it had taken up every conceivable pretext in the outside world, her imagination still crackled with free aggression: her fantasy-life ran to inventing the receipt of unwanted or insulting gifts, so that she might flay the giver in imaginary thank-you letters in her journal.

She was, of course, far too intelligent to suppose that the murderousness of her world really resided in L.M. or French maids or anywhere other than in herself. For all her rage, she was wholly rational. She could no more submit to God than lose herself in elfland, though she tried briefly to do both. Even her final decision to put herself in the hands of Gurdjieff's quasi-mystical clinic merely expressed in the only terms available to her a truth nowadays known even to the medical profession, that in tuberculosis the

mind counts as much as the body. ('Do I believe in medicine
alone? No, never ... It seems to me childish and ridiculous to suppose one can be cured like a cow *if one is not a cow*.') Her greatest
literary gift was a beautifully illuminating and devastating intelligence, which led first to aggressive farce, then to wit and finally to
the more than Stendhalian self-comedy with which she recorded
her own tragedy. She could turn against herself even her propensity for dear little this's and thats ('I must take some of my
dear money out of the Bank'), and even her favourite metaphor:
the marvellous mood-piece in her journal which begins 'What is
the matter with today? It is thin, white, as lace curtains are white,
full of ugly noises' enumerates nine of the day's gritty enormities
and culminates in '10. The tea was not hot. I meant *not* to eat the
bun but I ate it.'

As everyone said, her illness exacerbated her anger. But her
anger had been there first; it was probably one of the precipitators
of her illness. (I think her inkling of its psychosomatic nature gave
her a false feeling of being in control of her tuberculosis and that
this may be why she was convinced she would not die of it. 'I feel
today' — three years before she did die of it — 'that I shall die soon
and suddenly: but not of my lungs.') At fifteen she had described
how she 'felt *ill* with anger'. At thirty-one, she *was*, in a sense, ill
with anger; but she knew herself with total honesty. On the subject
of honesty, she said in her journal, she would like 'to write a *long,
long* story': and in honesty she added 'And another on the subject
of HATE.'

Terrified by her passion of hatred, warned by not mere rages
but cold-blooded daydreams in which she wished L.M. dead,
Katherine Mansfield resolved her crisis by diverting her aggression
from the outside world to herself. Perhaps the logical conclusion of
identifying herself with her mother and coming thereby to the
knowledge that her mother would have preferred not to give her
birth was to acquiesce in the mother's preference: she arranged,
as it were, for her mother to have a postdated abortion. When
Katherine Mansfield refused to undertake a proper cure for her
illness, she was acting out what she had written years before as a
healthy but wrought-up adolescent: 'I shall end — of course — by

killing myself.' The disease through which she did kill herself was consumption (this was the name she regularly used for it) — the cannibal disease which *consumes* its victim. Seeing life as a choice between eating and being eaten, she came to the conclusion that the honest course was to be consumed. To eat the bun — or the friend — when you had meant not to was sham; honesty lay in starving. Three months before dying she wrote in her journal 'I feel a bit of a sham ... And so I am. One of the K.M.s is so sorry. But of course she is. She has to die. *Don't* feed her.' (Her mother *hadn't* fed her.)

Katherine Mansfield died in 1923 at the age of thirty-four. She was buried at Fontainebleau, her epitaph the epigraph of *Bliss*: ' ... but I tell you, my lord fool, out of this nettle danger, we pluck this flower, safety'. In her journal she had left her 'Last Words to Life' — the title of the long, long story she would have liked to write, whose theme would have been: 'Honesty (why?) is the only thing one seems to prize beyond life, love, death, everything. It alone remaineth.'

Call Me Madame Colette

The Blue Lantern
by Colette
translated by Roger Senhouse
[Secker & Warburg, 1963]

New Statesman, August 1963

'And my dearest friend put a circlet of gold round my wrist — my favourite metal whether it comes in the shape of a bracelet, a medal or the links of a chain.' Gold (no doubt there were sound reasons in the state of the market for preferring it to diamonds) was an old girl's best friend (and her 'dearest friend' in fact her third husband). The occasion was Colette's seventy-fifth birthday.

The Blue Lantern is a book of, and about, Colette's old age, describing the visitors, letters and memories which came to her, arthritis-bound, in the Palais Royal, and trips which she made, by car and chair, to witness the manufacture of scent at Grasse and of wine in the Beaujolais region. I would say that this — discontinuous, non-fiction — was not the book for Colette tiros to start on, were it not for the unanswerability of Which is? From the first — that is, from Claudine — she shirked developing a narrative and, whenever plausible, told her stories through a disjointed journal. From the first she made precious little distinction between fiction and autobiography. All very well to claim afterwards that Willy forced her to write in the scandalous bits of the Claudine novels (which as *Livre de Poche* paperbacks still appear as by 'Willy et Colette': appended to the second name is the anachronistic and incongruously respectable 'de l'Académie Goncourt'). But she was out of Willy's power—married, indeed, to someone else—and the scandal twenty years out of date when she herself brought it up again and, by pinning the name of Claudine to her straight autobiographical memories of childhood, publicly affirmed that Colette *was*, scandal and all, Claudine. There is in fact no one book where readers ought to begin and by which Colette must be judged. There is only the creation of a single character, Claudine-Renée Néré-Colette. Perhaps all three persons are co-equally autobiographical ('I have been able', this book says, 'to tell only of what I know'). More probably, they are all equally fictitious.

The Blue Lantern takes its title (*Le Fanal Bleu*) from the reading lamp for which Colette rigged up a shade out of the blue paper she wrote on. By its light the character Colette rigged up for herself (likewise, one might say, out of the paper she wrote on) is still vigorously at all its old devices and vices. Here is the usual talk about animals—for which all honour to her, especially in so anti-animal a society as France: but there is also the usual talk *by* animals. Colette is still name-dropping: Cocteau, of course, and, if Cocteau, then naturally Jean Marais. (It is Marais's dog, who, asked what he is looking for, replies 'A bidet, to drink from.') Sadly, some of Colette's names have themselves dropped out of circulation. What can be conjured now with Francis Carco? (Only, perhaps, that he was Katherine Mansfield's lover in 1915. Mansfield herself, incidentally, entered in her Journal in 1914, 'Colette Willy is in my thoughts tonight.') A section about her long relationship with Marguerite Moreno gives Colette a pretext to bring up her favourite scandalous subject—and then withdraw it, as teasingly as she once flirted her naked body behind a sheet on the stage: she takes care to sound, even if she isn't, disingenuous, with her 'We were young enough ... for our friendship to develop into the sort of schoolgirl crush which young ladies at boarding-schools find so intoxicating.'

It is all—to the last, calculated o là là about fly buttons—professionally French. Not that that means for export. It is the English who possess national characteristics only by contradistinction from wogs and fuzziwuzzies and, now that their empire has shrunk (fewer deserts in which to dress for dinner), suffer a doubt

about their national identity for lack of anything to be contradis-
tinguished from. The French hardly bother to *be* French if the
audience is less than French. Only one of Colette's trips in this
book takes her outside France, and then not outside its language.
In Geneva just after the war she gluttonises professionally over the
abundant food, pointing out with shock that in Paris milk is
rationed 'even for the old'; she discovers presently that even in
Switzerland some foods are short—and explodes her deepest, and
most French, outrage at finding there is simply no black market on
which to buy them.

   Yet, as a writer, Colette is against the French grain. She, rather,
has a grain: whereas the *génie français* has, since Racine, flowed
classically without one. Where the whole tendency of French
literature is, magnificently or banally, to substitute an abstract for
a concrete and an intellectual antithesis for a tangible gesture,
Colette's prose is forever bringing you up against whorls and knots
—not merely substantives, but particular, even peculiar, substantives. Page after page in the Claudine books is footnoted with
explanations of words 'en patois du Fresnoy'. In *The Blue Lantern*
she lists (and Mr Senhouse resourcefully translates) the varieties
and nuances of needle and thread; goes into horticultural minu-
tiae; expounds the rustic method of gathering and her own
method of eating (while her friends watch 'with incredulity and
circumspection') water-caltrops. The personality this implies may
be fake all through. I could believe she never set foot in the
countryside, that she hired someone to coach her in her Burgundian accent, got her botany out of books, could not tell tulip
from turnip, dog from cat or man from woman, and ate the revolt-
ing water-caltrops solely to provoke her friends' incredulity. (The
peasant grunt with which, in that film they made about her, she
bites into a raw onion has always sounded to me more like pain
than relish.) What is authentic is the literary power which evokes
these things in more than *trompe-l'œil*—in *trompe-la-langue* and
trompe-le-nez—actuality. Impatiently, one might ask by virtue of
what, except Colette's opportunist eye for publicity, one instantly
recognises 'Pauline' as Colette's housekeeper, or what on earth it
can matter whether Colette was or wasn't lesbian. The answer is

that it matters for the same reason as it does about Albertine: that one knows Pauline in the sense one knows Françoise.

Colette's perseverance in the truly Proustian creation she carried out in life as well as on blue paper measures her narcissism. Almost auto-erotically she played with her own name (she even got as far as 'Willette Collie'); and by the same symptom she revealed that her sexual ambiguity went back to an indecision about whether to identify herself with her mother or her father. She inclined first towards the father. To call herself simply by her (and his) surname, Colette, shorn of female first names, was as blatant a claim to masculinity as the shorn hair which she adopted soon after. (Claudine herself is named for her father—his Christian name is Claude.) Maturity and fame made Colette into 'Madame Colette'—which was, of course, what her mother was. Colette's reconciliation and identification with her mother shewed itself not only in the open mother-worship she put (safely after her mother's death) into *Sido* but also in her ability to incarnate herself in the disreputable mother-figures of the novels: Chéri's mistress old enough to be his mother; the grandmother who, with an acute eye to an erotic detail, grooms Gigi's body for prostitution. And the object who is cherished, groomed? Colette again. (She confesses in *The Blue Lantern* that the only flower she did not like was the narcissus. It must have come too near the bone.) Colette is Gigi, lovingly groomed to receive a stranger's money and love, just as she had been Claudine, groomed by Willy for Willy. Colette is all those admired cats—especially the one she greeted in America as at last someone who spoke French. She is even (how imperceptive of the journalists to keep asking what *man* modelled for him) Chéri. The transposition of sex was of course nothing to her. (Even Gigi can be a man's name in Italian.) And as a matter of fact Colette had been in name both 'pussy' and 'Chéri' since her childhood—when her mother used to call her 'Minet-Chéri'.

The appreciating eye, the pampered body: both are Colette's. If she never actually went to bed with a woman, it was probably because she could not bear another woman to be the object of sexual admiration. (Her best novel is the one where Claudine actually does; but it may be good through its truth to Colette's fantasy life rather than to her life.) Oscar Wilde, whose epigrams in so many flashes anticipate psycho-analysis, had perhaps picked out the homosexuality in narcissism when he had Lord Goring say (just before looking in a mirror) that to love oneself is the beginning of a lifelong romance. But Wilde, with his generous propensity for falling in love with others—to the point of destroying himself—could not match Colette for fidelity to that romance. In the over-circumstantially furnished nineteenth-century-baroque brothel which was Colette's imagination, Colette was the tart (seventy-five-year-old heart not of but set on gold), the madame and even the establishment cat. Indeed, she was even the client. *The Blue Lantern* records that it was in Marguerite Moreno's company that she first, from the box of a music hall, saw Polaire; and it is in the tone of one old roué connoisseur to another that Moreno tells Colette before the curtain rises: 'You're going to see the strangest little creature.' Colette in fact loved both actresses—and in them herself: Polaire played Claudine on the stage; years later, Moreno played Chéri's mother, when Colette played his mistress.

The Dijon museum contains a Burgundian statue—old, battered, beautiful—of St Colette. In the pantheon-without-walls of literature, where there is none of that literal-minded insistence on belief which raised such a rumpus about Colette's funeral and where myths are prized not for their supposed factual content but for their authenticity as fictions, pilgrimage will always be made to the Blue Lantern district of the Palais Royal. *Sainte* Colette— holy fraud—pray for us.

Françoise Sagan and the
Art of the Beau Geste

London Magazine, February 1963;
Texas Quarterly

—Est-ce que ce n'est pas assez faux chic, assez snob
à côté, ces Sagan? dit-il d'un air sarcastique.
—Mais pas du tout ...

Le Côté de Guermantes, II

When Françoise Quoirez chose herself a pseudonym out of Proust,
she picked on the name of a princess; and Françoise Sagan,
whom she thereby created, has lived ever after inside a dry little
fairy-tale about a poor little rich princess.

Quoirez had been well-to-do by birth; Sagan became rich by
writing—rich, and admirably famous. Writing quickly, without
self-torture and often, she was able to follow up the stir she had
created as an eighteen-year-old by writing *Bonjour Tristesse*
virtually between exam papers, and settled into a mature habit
of being news. Nothing (except love, of course—which was publicised, too) would go wrong. Financially she could afford fast cars,
morally the clothes of a Sorbonne student on a rainy day, and in
every way to be photographed in both. Even when she crashed
the fast car, it was not really an impediment to the progress; the
crash was followed by further publicity and her recovery. When
she gave birth to a child, it was good for a comment (though not,
for once, a very funny one) from the *Canard Enchaîné.* Her fifth
novel recently provoked *L'Express* to a double page re-telling the
novel in the form of a strip cartoon drawn by Siné and a half-page
photograph of Sagan working in bed (record player open on the
bedside table, TinTin book halfway down the covers; but the

problem of how to prop the pillow she has solved no more comfortably than the poor and less leisured).

The glass coach rolls on: more and more crowds turn out to stare: more and more the face on the other side seems to be uttering the howl of a Francis Bacon face in its rigid Perspex cage or show-case.

No more urgent intimation that something is wrong has been conveyed by a publicised face to its public since Katharine Hepburn launched her appeal to the chivalry of cinema and theatre audiences to deliver her from whatever angels or Erinyes it was (part of the trouble was that we couldn't see them) which came between her personality and us. Of course, Hepburn's *was*, in a sense, the dumb cry of a Bacon character: actors make the appeal of half-dumb creatures, because they are gifted with speech only to the extent that the author has given them lines.

Yet it is not only as actress differs from author that a Hepburn differs from a Sagan. There is a period difference as well. Hepburn's appeal, though it is an appeal for *help*, is unavoidably addressed *de haut en bas*, from high glamour to groundlings. Sociologically, it belongs to an age when people wanted—when they paid—to be stunned. The cry is floated to the audience on the stunning beauty of Hepburn's face. Unavoidably, the audience *can't* help, because she is not one of them.

The photographed face of Françoise Sagan, on the other hand, is unbeautiful. (It is not ugly: it is just—rather like a lemon.) This makes it immediately re-assuring and up-to-date in a generation suspicious of formal beauty (in art as well as faces) along with formal clothes and formal manners. Chic, breeding and glamour are all dismissed as pretentious. (Two of them were, but the third was sometimes a matter of creating that willing suspension of disbelief which is essential to art.) The legend of the political Leader and the legend of the public-school leader of men are out—carrying with them the legends of Prince Charming and the *princesse lointaine*, because those, too, might be putting something over on you. Safer the material glamour of the fast car and the record player, which cannot lie because their prices can be exactly ascertained; safer the fairy tale which is only me, raised, in day-dream, to a higher income.

To the *jeunes gens* of this generation Sagan is instantly assimil-able. She wears their kind of clothes; she works for her living (doubly sympathetic of her if she doesn't need to); though rich, she is not unimaginably so—it might happen to you, if you won a pool, in which case you'd go on working, too, though you didn't need to. She is probably better placed as a writer (no nimbus surrounds that; everyone knows how it's done) than she could have been in any other profession—unless she had been a pop singer: but then, though she might have made a still earlier start, she would hardly have lasted so long. Wearing their kind of clothes, she is, perhaps, a sort of French, female James Dean (himself the last of the stars to possess the real glamour, and the first to cast it aside for jeans) ... a James Dean who survived the crash—bearing witness not only to the proverbial toughness of little girls as compared with little boys but also to a perhaps genuine greater resistance to the death wish in creative than in executive artists. For Sagan writes her own lines.

Bacon's scream pictures exploit the fact that paintings don't squeal. The horror of standing in front of his personages is that we shall never hear the inarticulate noise they utter. The film star is articulate but caged in his author and sound-track. (James Dean half broke out between his lines—by the mutterings and hesita-tions which made him seem incapable of delivering them; you were half deluded into believing that if you sat the film round again he might escape from the sound-track and get the words out better next time.) Bacon's Perspex cage loses horror but is sharpened in irony when the person inside is literary and literate. (Sagan is literate to her fingertips, which hold a pen saturated in French literature.) The irony now is that we *can* hear—every word; and every word is precisely articulated and justly placed. As the glass coach rolls by with Sagan inside, we are auditors of a series of low-toned but fluent and exactly calculated mono-logues ...

What has escaped most people's ears is that they are works of art.

You can't really blame the intellectual nobs (2¾ cheers for them: I'm 7/8ths one myself) or dismiss them as intellectual snobs if they assume in the intellectual world what Bloch did about her namesake in the grand world, that Sagan is a touch *faux chic*. In general, it is quite a workable rule of thumb that writers who sell as grossly as Sagan aren't very good. But some thumbs sometimes have to get broken.

Good or bad, Sagan can't be ignored, a salience which seems so to irritate the intellectual that, being obliged to deal with her, he deals carelessly. Even the *Express* strip cartoon which recounts the story of *Les Merveilleux Nuages* recounts it inaccurately round the edges of the letterpress. (This was compiled, I think, by sub-editors in the depths of the night. The name of one of Sagan's minor characters, Laura Dort, seems to have been so suggestive as to lull them into actual somnambulism: it is with the near-wit one expects of dreams that she appears in the strip cartoon telescoped into Dora.)

The authors of the *Paris Review* interview with Sagan (one of that series published as a book under the title *Writers At Work*), though presumably awake throughout the interview, substitute for the glass coach of the Sagan fairy-tale a tangled little cage, a rococo farce, every strand of which is wrought of their own mis-understanding. The introductory piece (whether it is by the interviewers or by the editor of the volume I do not know; I shall call its author *they* in sheer vengeance) starts off by saying that the Sagan pseudonym is derived 'from Proust's favourite author, the Princesse de Sagan' (Saint-Simon, is it, they have in mind?— the author, do they suppose, of *La Princesse de Clèves*? And they can do this to a writer who is literate to—the tips of her *toes*.) They go on not merely to mis-spell but to mis-syllabify the name of Sagan's publisher. But it is when they get to the interview itself that the thing becomes (in the finely ironical simile the heroine of *Les Merveilleux Nuages* applies to her marriage) 'comique et triste à la fois, comme une erreur judiciaire':—

INTERVIEWERS: Did you find it difficult to switch from the first person of *Bonjour tristesse* to the third-person narrative of *Un certain sourire*?

SAGAN: Yes, it is harder, more limiting and disciplining.
Both *Bonjour Tristesse* and *Un Certain Sourire* are in the first person.

To step, through the publicity cage and the meshes of critical
misunderstanding, into the novels themselves is like stepping
into the spaces of a still life—a Braque, perhaps, in its classical
structure, but naturalistic. Low-toned, distinct, plausible by the
test of everyday appearances, the elements of the composition are
perfectly disposed at the very points where they will do the most
work and carry the most fabric.

In this case the elements are not, of course, the bric-à-Braque
of a still life, but characters. As a matter of fact—and not by
accident—Sagan's world contains hardly any objects. Never was
a writer more free from the tyranny of the thing in itself (or in its
associations or its symbolic value). There is weather, but scarcely
vegetation—only the few trees necessary to be *agités* or *figés*,
according to season, *by* the weather. The telephone exists (though
implied by the most abstract possible phrasing) only for the
conversation, alcohol only for the effects of one character's
drunkenness on another. The thing in itself is all but suppressed—
expunged, almost, from the very metaphors—in favour of the
character in his relationships.

Even the characters are not quite there in their own right,
apart from the structure they support and which supports them.
They are slightly more caryatids than people. The author takes
three, four or six of them, sets them down in well-thought-out
positions and orders them to spin a roof over their heads. They
do: the fabric of the book. It is neat, logical and pleasing. And
thus each of the characters *does* stand up, but only thanks to his
inter-relationships with the others.

If the purpose were to bring the fabric of the book gradually
closing in on the characters, push them to breaking point, and
force them to snap and shew their essences, the elements Sagan
chooses would often seem too banal. (In *Aimez-vous Brahms ...* ,
where they are middle-aged man and mistress and young lover,
they would definitely *be* too banal.) Nothing startling can be
revealed by obliging a caryatid to shew what is inside it. But in

fact that is not the purpose at all. Sagan's architecture is of the kind where the fabric—which is limited to the economical minimum consistent with logic—is only there to define the space enclosed. Short as they are, these books make the effect not at all of tours-de-force. They are neither condensed nor intense. They are empty. In these human still lives it is not the spatial relationships which matter—they are only there to give you the scale: it is the spaces.

Sagan is a relentless writer, but not a relentless expositor of human relationships. Towards those she is merely ruthless, in the cursoriness with which she will treat them. As relentlessly as Simenon evokes physical atmospheres to fill his books, as relentlessly as Firbank harps on the erotic, so relentlessly does Sagan harp on a single emotional mood and empty her books in order to accommodate it: for the mood *is* emptiness.

Inside the book one is still—one is even more—trapped in a Perspex cage. Part of the horror of Bacon's cage is that it is *not* oppressively small: it is a good bit roomier than a coffin: that is why its horror is so much more psychological than Poe's. Sagan creates the same horror of vacuum—or, rather, vacuum of horror —round her characters precisely by *not* oppressing them too closely with the plot and their inter-relationships. The ceiling is *not* descending on them. The fabric she creates is exactly one which leaves her characters room to turn round: to turn round *and* round: to notice how, though related to others, they are not interwoven to the last point of being compelled. Tour-de-force novels swaddle the character in a situation which in the end makes it imperative to commit that crime, leave this husband, go to bed with that mistress. Sagan, who sets her characters socially free from compulsions by making them rich and leisured, sets them free of emotional compulsions, too. In love, they are obsessed by the awareness that their love is not quite obsessive. Every act, even every sexual act, is performed in the emptiness where the actors can ask both, and equally, 'Why should I?' and 'Why shouldn't I?' They are all in the situation of Josée in *Les Merveilleux Nuages*: 'Elle était libre. Ce n'était pas désagréable, ce n'était pas exaltant.'

Autobiographical in nothing else, all Sagan's novels are autobiographies of mood. The characters exist in order that they may all dwell in a prolongation of one of those days when the earth looks flat. Most of the time we conjure up interesting mountains in our path: not merely our marital arrangements, but our very arrangements with the laundry and the grocer seem momentous and suspenseful enough to keep us alive in order to find out what happens next: only on the flat days does one contemplate vast events—very well, I shall emigrate to Australia, I shall divorce, I shall have a child—and return oneself no comment except 'So what?' Sagan's is the art of 'So what?' Her pessimistic realism insists that it is only one's deluded narcissism which sees momentousness. She is too realistically ironical to allow her characters the delusion that the plot and the situation are pressing upon them, compelling them in certain directions. She keeps the Perspex walls of their world a little apart from them, a little disdainfully—they can never complain they were ill-treated. The fabric of life must remain ambiguous—is it one's cage or one's shelter? By the same token she forbids her own narrative manner to impinge on or oppress the characters. They make no extravagant gestures; she flowers into no poetic improbabilities. The effulgence of a metaphor rarely crosses her pure style. Her very irony is kept to the sub-epigrammatic. 'Il préférait avoir été malheureux pour une bonne raison qu'heureux pour une mauvaise.' Her wit and observation are allowed to shoot no more than a shimmer of amusement across the surface. 'Ils dansèrent. Il la tenait solidement, traversant la piste d'un bout à l'autre sans aucun rythme, l'air très content de lui-même. Elle était très heureuse.'

Sagan's realism is the quintessence of the Realpolitik which has been beaten-in to the very pavements of Paris and yet rises to fly back at you in the form of a grit in the eye. It was an old-fashioned Frenchman who replied, to 'Il faut que je vive', 'Je n'en vois pas la nécessité'—old-fashioned in the elegant, the uneconomical, turn of the answer. Nowadays the answer is just—and not even spoken —'So what?' Announce that you want or feel compelled to anything, in Paris—I want to live, I want to buy a ticket to Châtelet— and 'So what?' is the reply: 'Et après?' Perhaps it is the joylessness of French childhoods which beats the narcissistic delusions out and the cynicism in: every incipient want or claim to necessity slugged (like an incipient Sagan metaphor) by 'Do you think your parents are made of money?'—even, one imagines, when they *are*. Sagan's own lemon face resembles those old child-faces— faces which have sucked too many lemons too young and actually acquired the pitted, the slightly shrunk-into-itself skin of a lemon —which were photographed in *Les Quatre Cent Coups*. Significantly, Sagan, who seldom explores her characters' past and rarely endows them even with parents or siblings, more than once allows an important character a reminiscence of a moment's unsurpassable happiness experienced in childhood or youth (and usually during the holidays): the happiness has passed, it has often been remembered subsequently, and in the end the memory itself has come to resemble 'à celui d'une promesse mal tenue'.

In the flat world where the past is broken promises, the present without compulsion and the future without suspense, actions are hardly worth doing. Sagan's characters droop, in their unaired cages, with fatigue and ennui (a word which presagingly occurs in the first line of her first book). The plot of *Aimez-vous Brahms* ... unrolls in terms of progressive tiredness. On page 36 the middle-aged man is 'étendu sur le canapé du salon ... épuisé de fatigue'. Page 90 and his mistress is 'lasse, ce matin'. Meanwhile, page 95, the other man, the young one, 's'allongea sur le tapis'. By page 101 this young man is suddenly 'las à mourir'. It is in this moment that the heroine falls in love with him—naturally enough: she has suddenly seen him as 'semblable à elle'. By page 132 he has spent the night with her and has next morning 'l'air d'un somnambule'. Twenty pages on, the middle-aged lover is telling her 'Tu as l'air très fatigué.' On page 163 she tells her young lover 'Pas ce soir ... je suis lasse.' He plans a holiday with her, but she 'se sentait trop fatiguée, même pour prendre un train'. Finally, when she is beginning to break with her young lover, she refuses to sleep with him 'alléguant une fatigue qu'elle ne ressentait pas'. Strange that at this stage she really doesn't feel it: but it must have made the most plausible of excuses.

Occasionally the author herself seems invaded by this fatigue, and writing a novel becomes one of the actions that is hardly worth doing. Taking, for *Dans un Mois, dans un An*, a larger cast than usual, she seems exhausted by placing them in position for the quadrille; what follows is merely the synopsis of a novel. (But the promise was in a sense redeemed when she took up two of these characters, a little further along their life history, for *Les Merveilleux Nuages*.) In *Aimez-vous Brahms* ... , she adumbrates a couple of incidents but is too tired to realise the scenes themselves when she comes to them. Simon is going to a dinner party which he fears will be provincial. When he gets there, all we are shewn (it is through his consciousness) is that 'Ses prévisions se confirmèrent.' One would scarcely notice the economy were it not that, a mere dozen pages later, Roger, too, attends a dinner which he has feared will be boring; and again we are told 'Le dîner se passa comme il l'avait prévu.'

All the same, it would be silly to bear puritanically hard on Sagan's occasional sketchiness, like an employer insisting the employee put in the stipulated office hours. Art is, above all, piece work. One pays an author to imagine the things one cannot imagine for oneself. Everyone's imagination is competent to fill in a provincial dinner party. Readers of the average English decently-selling library novel, beside which Sagan's look so brief, seldom realise to what extent they are cheated by the bulky package: forty out of the eight thousand words are ones the reader could have put equally well to himself. Besides, there is often, in art, a psychological connection between economy of line and getting the analytical structure right. The intellectually brilliant building *is* the one where each prop does the work of two. Laziness (or, in energetic people, impatience) is at the service of intellectual penetration. One day it will be recognised that many great and fundamental principles have been discerned *because* one principle saves the mind the trudge through a hundred examples.

If Sagan's narrative manner sometimes verges on insolence by being too tired to be vivid, her first incursion into drama actually crossed into insolence—but from the opposite direction. Where the characters in the novels had been too fatigued to make extravagant gestures, those in the play had reached the point of fatigue which is called feverish and made nothing else—indeed, *were* nothing else; they existed only as gestures. Before, there had been only rare and muted effulgences: here was a whole creeping-growth of luminous efflorescence—but lightweight, without roots, fungoid: unconsidered truffles in the shape of witticisms (genuine), farcical twists (genuinely funny) and theatrical *coups de foudre* which genuinely detonated but were aimed at nothing. The most insolently extravagant gesture of all was the author's own. It *was* a farcical *coup de foudre* for Sagan to write a play by Anouilh.

That would have been all (except that it is rather entertaining) that need be said about *Château en Suède* were it not for Sagan's fifth novel, *Les Merveilleux Nuages*. The play now turns out to have been a practice exercise in the use of gestures, a preparation for introducing into the world of the novels just that modicum of volition which makes Josée capable of—not of extravagant gestures, certainly, not of any flamboyance, but of one or two calculated, deadpan acts of defiance against the mood of 'So what?' which are allowed to make their full report and even echo briefly before dying out.

Les Merveilleux Nuages is not *better* than the earlier novels: its relation to them is that of after a Japanese flower has gone into the water to before. There is no under-realisation this time. If the American scene is not evoked, American weather is (perhaps Sagan could not rely, in this case, on her readers' filling it in for themselves); and the cage which circumscribes the heroine is detailed in terms of external circumstance as well as mood—or, at least, circumstance is shewn first seeming to enclose her, though it is mood which is still the inner wall.

The circumstance is Josée's American husband, Alan. In him Sagan almost rises to a character with an obsession. He is, in the way of the American way of life, almost addicted to alcohol and almost fixated on his mother; above all, he is all but obsessively jealous of Josée. But not quite. Sagan's own literary concentration perhaps lacks the stamina to draw obsession. That is just as well, because it would not be to her purpose: or, rather, of course, her purpose is tailored to her limitations. Her real concern is with Josée, who wants to leave Alan but is detained first because she seems indispensable to him, presently on the grounds that she may really love him, alternatively on the grounds that she may be in thrall to him sexually, then because, although she may take a lover, she can feel no urgent reason to run off with the lover, and ultimately, of course, at the heart of it all, because while she can ask 'Why shouldn't I leave Alan?' she can also ask 'Why should I?'

Unlike the earlier Sagan heroines (or heroes), Josée has enough resources in herself to throw a bottle of ink at the Perspex walls round her. She improvises her first gesture when she contrives at the last moment to go on a fishing trip alone with the professional boatman and ('Why shouldn't I?') makes love with him. When she comes back, there is dinner in a restaurant for the four people who by the original plan would have constituted the fishing party: Josée, Alan and the married couple who are their only American friends. At dinner, Alan

buvait beaucoup.

—Voici le dessert, dit tout à coup Josée et elle pâlit.

Le garçon arrivait avec un gâteau rond surmonté d'une bougie. Il le posa sur la table.

—Une bougie, dit Josée. C'est la première fois que je te trompe.

Later, when she has returned to France (where Alan follows her), Josée employs *ad hoc* promiscuous sexual intercourse at slightly bizarre moments as an *acte gratuit*. In the end she does break with Alan and becomes free; but only in the sense of stepping into the vacuum which has actually surrounded her all along.

For although the character can now protest against the cage, the distance between character and cage is not diminished. As before, the walls do not impinge on the character; and neither can the character, though she is now trying to, impinge on them. Josée can throw; she can hit; but she cannot bring the walls down about her head. The gesture of the candle does not fall flat; but it sets nothing on fire. The candle flame simply burns, isolated, at the centre of the cage. It is merely using up the oxygen.

Sagan's novels continue a tradition which passes through *La Princesse de Clèves* and *Adolphe* and is usually said to be peculiarly and untranslateably French. She writes—beautifully—the classic French prose which French people always warn English people against over-estimating; it can, they say, be written by any French person who has been to a lycée. (Then why do so few of them take the trouble to write it?—apart, of course, from those who write an acceptable or more acceptable alternative. But surely Sartre and Beauvoir were *at* a lycée?) No doubt Sagan is difficult to translate with justice. (She would not have been in 1800; but since then English, unlike French, has failed to keep its classical manner in working order.) Fortunately, the classic lucidity which makes the translator's task hard also makes it unnecessary. (The English-speaker who is assuring the English-speaking world of this is that world's worst linguist.) Racine (out of favour with the *jeunes gens* but not with Sagan, who—she *is* literate to her fingertips—borrowed the title of *Dans un Mois, dans un An* from him) is likewise untranslateable and likewise perfectly, pleasurably, comprehensible, both in sense and in tone, to foreigners. The reason, as with Sagan, is that an abstract is always easier than a concrete. The object-less world of Sagan is the novel's equivalent of the handkerchief-less high drama of Racine. Sagan will never trip her English readers up on the furniture or, as Colette so regularly does, on the exotic word which turns out to be the Burgundian patois for 'forget-me-not' but which looked, until you had got up and fetched the dictionary, as though it carried the whole weight and emotional point of the story (probably because the dear old affected creature, writing away in her gardening gloves in the Palais Royal, was at the time pretending it *did*).

All the same, Sagan, crystal-clear though she is to foreigners, is professionally French. (Foreigners who assume this to mean oo-là-là will find only oo-las-las. An author too tired to evoke a dinner party cannot be expected to evoke the ambience of sexual intercourse. She merely states that it has taken place. No doubt it, too, fulfils the *prévisions* of the participants.) Sagan is a stick of rock stamped 'Paris, France' all the way through. One of the best of her sub-epigrams displays in passing the true Parisian self-regarding-

ness: Paule, in *Aimez-vous Brahms* ... , is advised by all her friends
(it is another of her moments of looking tired) 'de changer d'air,
et elle songeait, tristement, qu'elle allait simplement changer
d'amant: moins dérangeant, plus parisien, tellement fréquent — '

English literary chauvinism (He was back, back with it all — the
white flannels in the sun, the thud of the ball ... By God, he
thought suddenly, I'd die for it. His hand had to visit his eye
before he could go in to tea. Ten years later just such young
men as he *were* dying for it) has the fumblingness of an auto-erotic
act. French chauvinism has gone the whole hog into group
narcissism. Perhaps its strength comes from the individual's being
so devastatingly realistic about his private Ego. It is, more than a
simple belief in one's own language and tradition, a failure to
bring any conviction whatever to the belief that other ones exist.
Colette was right when she greeted that cat in America as at last
someone who spoke French: French civilisation can no more
wonder if it is being just a touch xenophobic than a cat can ask
itself if it is being just a touch selfish.

Such nods as Sagan concedes to other cultures are more likely
to be, in the French fashion, across the Atlantic (no hard feelings
— I am delighted her characters have seen *All About Eve*) than
across the Channel. Yet one of her characters does read 'un livre
anglais, une étrange histoire au sujet d'une femme transformée en
renard'. Against all the hazards of French education (a not very
old edition of the *Larousse de Poche* mis-spells his name) Shakespeare
has lodged in the consciousness of the heroine of *Un Certain Sourire.*
And yet: I do not think you would find an English or a German
author quoting Racine in English or German. Sagan's heroine
tells us that 'Une phrase m'obsédait sans que je susse pourquoi';
and Sagan does not scruple to tell us that the phrase is 'Il y a
quelque chose de corrompu dans le royaume de Danemark.'

Sagan's Frenchness is at its peak in the one absolutely non-
endearing and infuriating characteristic of the French: their
willingness to do anything whatever to music except listen to it.
Sagan's characters, who live by 'le pick-up' and the car radio,
fully display the philistine belief that background music makes
driving, daydreaming or talking a more spiritual activity: but

Sagan herself is capable of the telling and discerningly phrased episode which closes *Un Certain Sourire* and justifies its title, with the heroine's listening to 'une musique dans la cour, diffusée par la radio généreuse d'un voisin. C'était un bel andante de Mozart, évoquant comme toujours l'aube, la mort, un certain sourire.' Perhaps it would be unfair, in a passage so deliberately and indeed crisply vague, to ask Sagan *what* andante. But when, in *Aimez-vous Brahms* ... , Paule (who has evidently had the record in the house for some time without trying it) puts on her pick-up 'un concerto de Brahms qu'elle n'avait jamais écouté', one does feel entitled to ask *her* What concerto? Was it, at least, violin or piano? She really might look at the label. But as a matter of fact (Sagan is not unironical about the national characteristic), having put the record on, Paule 'en trouva le début romantique et oublia d'écouter jusqu'au bout'.

The question 'Aimez-vous Brahms?' is what Simon asks Paule when he proposes taking her to a concert. At the concert, there is again *a* concerto — 'un concerto que Simon pensait reconnaître'. Again one thinks he might have looked at the programme. Instead, he closes his eyes. Paule reflects, 'en voyant son expression, qu'il devait être vraiment mélomane'. However, the art of Sagan is realistic, avoiding the extravagant and improbable. Soon 'une main tremblante chercha la sienne'.

I do not believe the current catchphrase about writing being communication. Incredible as it seems that it could be so, I believe it is all based on an elementary semantic mistake. The idea of communications was much in the air at the rise of television, when it became fashionable to talk about radio and television as modern media of communication. Writing thereupon seemed to be one of the older ones. So it is: but 'writing' in the sense of having and using an alphabet. Alphabets can be employed, of course, for sending a message, just as morse can. But to suppose that writing a work of literature is equivalent to communicating a message is to make a fundamental error about the psychology of creation. Creating a novel is no more an act of communication than having a baby is.

We are psychologically on much more accurate ground with the older metaphor (*vide* Shakespeare's Sonnets, *passim*) whereby the work of art is the artist's child. It is a projection of the artist's personality — at least of that specialised bit which constitutes his artistic personality; and, as Freud explained about the love of parents for their children, the artist-parent lavishes on the projection his own narcissism. The most urgent compulsion towards making the projection is to circumvent the mortal enemy of one's own individual narcissism, death. The work of art (*vide* Shakespeare again) is potentially immortal, just as your children's children are. ('Il ne devait pas être supportable', Josée suddenly thinks in *Les Merveilleux Nuages*, 'de perdre un enfant.') The artist's primary desire is that the progeny should come into existence and continue to exist. It is not, as it is when you send a telegram, a question of wanting the message to be received and understood (and then torn up). If one bothers about its reception by others at all, one's wish for the work of art is not that it should be understood but that it should be loved. But the fundamental wish is that it should be made beautiful (that is, simply, lovable) enough to attract and hold one's own self-love. Just as it is more lasting, so it is more beautiful than one's own original self. It is a receptacle for one's own narcissism, which is often so ill served by one's proper Ego, and not a radio beam in search of a receiving set.

Therefore, while it is useful shorthand to speak of a novelist's having something to say, it is truer to speak of his having something to *do*. (It is secondary that he can only *do* by using words. Declaring war, getting married and standing for Parliament are actions which can only be done in words, too.) To make these projections of the artistic self, novels, endowed with a miniature Life as a baby is with a miniature life, is, above all, a *gesture*. An artist of the desperate honesty of a Sagan is elegant, restrained and classical for fear not of making false statements but of making false gestures — those that have no true roots in the artistic personality. One can, so to speak, give one's brain-child the wrong father. (Anouilh was the wrong father for *Château en Suède*.) The urgent impression Sagan makes of something's being, if not rotten, uneasily wrong in the state of Denmark is not an appeal to an audience to receive a message from inside the cage but a gesture *at* and in the cage, at and in life itself. Josée's gesture at dinner is an analogue to art itself: the artist hopes this day to have lit such a candle as by someone's—life's, perhaps—grace shall never be put out.

To say that Sagan's books are concerned with nothing less elemental than life is not to say that she makes statements about life. Indeed, it would be fatal to her art to do so. Art is declaration, not statement. Sagan is making, creating, artistic gestures in the face of life, and elegance is of the essence of a gesture. Her elegance is vital to her artistic integrity. She could no more afford metaphysics in her thought than woolliness in her style. She perfectly understands that to be a philosopher is merely to be earnest, whereas to be an artist is to be serious.

Of Sagan the artist one can say what she says of Josée: 'Les gens qui parlaient d'absolu la dégoûtaient encore plus que ceux qui n'y pensaient pas.'

Simone de Beauvoir

Force of Circumstance

by Simone de Beauvoir*
translated by Richard Howard
[G. P. Putnam's Sons, 1965]

New York Times Book Review, April 1965;
Books and Bookmen

'Since her conversation makes its point by way of ellipses, allusions, implications and unfinished sentences, I always felt it would be pedantic of me to finish mine, but I just couldn't get used to breaking them off halfway through, and always wound up unable to think of anything to say.'

Thus Simone de Beauvoir describes her 'rare meetings' with Françoise Sagan and incidentally defines the difference between her own and Sagan's literary personality. To my mind Sagan is the most under- and Mlle de Beauvoir the most over-estimated presence in postwar French writing. Both misestimates are the result, I believe, of a fundamental misesteem of art. Our age has been bullied into the misconception that the clumsy and laborious must somehow be *worthier* than intellectual penetration achieved by economy and with elegance. Only in such a climate could critical opinion have put the carthorse before the racehorse.

The more I read of Mlle de Beauvoir, the more I have the impression that I met her, under various manifestations, during my schooldays. No doubt there is one in every educational establishment. She was the one in the front row of the class whose high marks led you to hope for an original intelligence. Dis-

* English edition published by André Deutsch and Weidenfeld and Nicolson, 1965.

appointed (quickly) of that, you still looked for a reliable academic mind. It turned out to be a mind capable of missing entire points, and incapable both of the precision of an artist and of the accuracy of a scholar. Not inspired enough to be slapdash, it was often slipshod. In the end, you were obliged to admit that the high marks reflected nothing but obedient work; that what seemed to be intellectual passion was only a sense of duty—plus, it might be, a devotion to the professor; that you were up against, in short, a plodder.

Mlle de Beauvoir is a plodder *par excellence* and even, I almost suspect, by wanton and perverse choice. Her first novel, *L'Invitée*, ill articulated as it was, did generate an intensity of moral atmosphere. It was a thunderous afternoon from which something might have flashed. Since then Mlle de Beauvoir has made it plain that in her judgment the flash of wit, irony or poetry is no better than the flashy. Neither the strategy nor the tactics of her writing will have any truck with metaphor. She disdains—or does not command—those moments of thought or language which simultaneously fuse two images and illuminate or sear the reader. Not for her the masterstroke which cuts a long story short; she opts every time for the Long March—the long plod.

Whereas her essay on Sade approached the brink of insights (though it promptly looked away from them into an undergrowth of irrelevant, and perhaps actually factitious, metaphysical problems), *The Second Sex* revealed her as a compiler of trees rather than a discerner of woods. The section she boldly called 'The Psycho-analytic Point of View' betrayed that, incredible as it seems, Mlle de Beauvoir had simply missed the point of Freud. Moreover, unless the English edition belies her utterly, she was not to be depended on even as a reporter. She could refer without explanation to Freud's 'later calling the feminine form of the [oedipal] process the Electra complex'. (What makes me think an explanation necessary is Freud's remark, of 1920, 'I do not see any ... advantage in the introduction of the term "Electra-complex", and do not advocate its use.') Indeed, she could not tell chalk from cheese—that is, in this case, Jungian from psycho-analytical terminology; she could speak of psycho-analysis doing something or other 'in the name of the "collective unconscious" '.

The third and latest volume of her autobiography is Mlle de Beauvoir's most pedestrian plod yet. It covers the years — 1944 to 1962 — in which she was pretty much top of the class, thanks partly, it seems fair to guess, to her devotion to the professor but thanks also to the prevailing mystical belief that the tedious must be profound. Her method here is simply to amass: 'Since June, my sister and her husband had been living in Casablanca ... Sartre's thought, as I have said, was gradually stripping itself of all idealism; but he did not reject the existential postulates and continued to demand, within the realm of *praxis*, a synthesis ... Sartre also had personal troubles.' Précis of the newspapers is piled on her and Sartre's (separate) love affairs; friends' names ring no more intimate or vivid than politicians'; recording her love affair in the United States, Mlle de Beauvoir jots down the population of Cincinnati.

It is a sheer heap. (*La Force des Choses*, the French title is; should it not have been the *weight* of things?) In it, intellectual analysis and atmosphere are alike suffocated. The political vision is as banal as a leader-writer's: there are two power blocs in the world, and it is hard for a European intellectual to choose between them. Mlle de Beauvoir's account of her trip from a still austere France to the luxuries of Switzerland is less evocative than one stylish nail-paring from Colette's aged and arthritic hand — the baroque paean of gluttony, for instance, which (in *Le Fanal Bleu*) Colette made of *her* postwar visit to Geneva.

Mlle de Beauvoir compiles away. *Les Temps Modernes* is founded (who would have guessed its name alludes to Charlie Chaplin?); Sartre encourages her to work at and a friend thinks up the title for *The Second Sex* (a title which seems inept to the point she was trying to make about women when one remembers that in eighteenth-century idiom women were 'the sex'); she becomes famous. She complains that people take *The Mandarins* for a *roman à clé*, even while her very defence ('I described as happening between 1945 and 1947 events, problems and crises that actually took place later') and such remarks as 'My first days in Chicago were very much like those Anne spent with Lewis in *The*

Sartre

The Words

by Jean-Paul Sartre
translated by Bernard Frechtman
[George Braziller, 1964]

New York Herald Tribune Book Week, October 1964

Charmingly unexpected, and unexpectedly charming, *The Words* is Sartre's autobiography up to the age of ten.

At moments you might think he *wrote* it at ten, instead of fifty-nine. He seriously confesses that 'even now' he reads thrillers 'more readily than I do Wittgenstein'. If you retorted 'Don't we all?' you would shatter a genuine innocence. Sartre still really believes that other people are 'the grown-ups'.

However, Sartre is no mere *naïf*. He has a *talent* for *naïveté*. If he is ignorant of one or two things which everyone else knows, he says several which everyone knows but no one else has pointed out. 'I was a fake child,' he writes — 'J'étais un faux enfant.' Only now that he's said it about his own childhood does one recognise that of course all children are fakes; indeed, to be a child is to be in a false position. *The Words* performs a tremendous feat. It exposes the pretentiousness of childhood.

An only child whose father died before he was weaned, Sartre was brought up in his mother's family, the Schweitzers. (Sartre is second cousin to Albert Schweitzer.) His mother's love for him was strong but her personality faint. She was, like all the adults in the family (and like Sartre's book), dominated by Sartre's grandfather, a hearty, bilingual Alsatian whose Christian name Sartre gives indifferently as Charles and Karl. The grandfather, however, chose to be dominated by his infant grandson.

The difficulty was that a child cannot dominate; it has no positive personality to impose. The only response the child could make to his grandfather's infatuation was to play the part of a child. He also played the beauty, at least till his curls were cut off. (Even the grandfather, Sartre sardonically reports, was disconcerted by having taken a 'little wonder' to the barber's and bringing home 'a toad'.) He played the infant prodigy – and there is a passage of lovely buffoonery in which he is briefly sent to school and withdrawn because the teachers fail to see his prodigiousness. Occasionally, he plays not a rôle so much as the droll: he reads *Madame Bovary* and, to his mother's objection 'But if my little darling reads books of that kind at his age, what will he do when he grows up?', brings out the *enfant terrible* reply 'I'll live them!' Eventually he accepts the rôle of genius elect, the boy predestined to be a famous man of letters.

And in fact the whole story is told through Sartre's relation to literature. The excellent translation (by Bernard Frechtman, the brilliant translator of Genet's *Our Lady of the Flowers*) contains only one exceptionable word, and that may well not be Mr Frechtman's responsibility – the definite article in the title. By '*Les Mots*' Sartre obviously means just 'words'.* His account of his infantile relation to them is divided into two parts, *Reading* and *Writing*. In the first, he pretends to read before he can – and thereby accidentally teaches himself to; he stage-manages little dramas in which the adults come on him devouring Corneille; his true but surreptitious literary diet, furtively supplied by his mother, consists of garish weekly instalments of blood-and-thunder. In the second part he becomes a prolific novelist. His novels merely re-arrange his favourite reading: 'I ... had not the slightest difficulty in re-inventing ... the exciting adventures that I read in *Cri-Cri* ... I loved plagiarism, out of pretentiousness.'

The Words might have been designed to be flung in the face of those nobly-meaning educationalists who seek to discover what

* And the English edition of the same translation of his book was published (by Hamish Hamilton) under the title *Words*.

children 'really' enjoy reading, and try to free children's writing from grammar and syntax so that the children may be 'true to themselves'. The truth is that children do not particularly like — or even, unless it oppresses them to the point of bodily pain, particularly dislike — anything. A truthful child cannot tell you whether it likes or dislikes spinach, but only that spinach has a 'very strong' taste. It is the foods, not the eater, which have tastes. No more can a child write something true to a self which is not yet formed. The child is in a false position because he is not yet responsible for the effect of his acts on the outside world. His destiny is to wait until he is. He can fill in the time (time passed by children is always boring) only by play-acting various adult rôles, for none of which has he any marked predilection.

It is the nullity of childhood which Sartre evokes with, I think, more exactitude and concentration than any writer before. He speaks of 'the insipid happiness of my early years' (how could it be other than insipid since a child *has* no tastes?) and of his self, his very Ego, as '*nothing*: an ineffaceable transparency'. Had there been siblings or a father — someone to be irritated with him for his monstrousness or even his mere existence — he might have been so occupied in replying to their impingement, in *producing* those reactions whereby a child's personality is eventually formed, as never to catch himself in the act of having no personality. As things were, Sartre was 'idolized by all, rejected by each'. His circumstances were a warm and loving nest which nonetheless did not pack him tightly. There was a layer of vacuum between him and them, a space into which everyone invited him to expand and express himself — the space in which he had room to realise that he had nothing to express and that he was a vacuum himself.

Having caught himself being a child, Sartre deep-froze the perception at the point of catch. He discloses that what he did with his childhood between finishing it and starting his auto-biography was to forget it. 'When I was thirty, friends were surprised: "One would think you didn't have parents. Or a childhood." ' Presumably it is the deep-freeze which accounts for the clarity with which he perceived at the time. It may also account for some of his *naïveté*, and for one inestimable literary advantage. The *naïveté* is simply a matter of Sartre's having no standard of comparison. Every now and then he treats as idiosyncratic what is really a common childish experience; he was virtually without other children to compare himself with at the time — and later on, if those surprised friends recounted their childhoods to Sartre, Sartre (even supposing he listened) clearly did not bring up his own into direct comparison.

It is just this which is the literary advantage. Sartre is not in a position to write about 'childhood'. (I can't help feeling that if he could he would.) He *has* to concentrate on the particulars of the unique Sartre childhood. The result is that *The Words* is in a different artistic category from all the words previously written by Sartre — all those words that have made him the writer of some of the most interesting books of our century but never one of our century's most interesting writers. Up to now, even in that almost tightly open-and-shut classic case *Huis Clos*, there has always been some faltering of Sartre's faith in the power of an artistic structure to stand up on its own. Fiction, since it escaped from the duty of pointing a moral, has been autonomous (existentialist, if you like); there is no *point* to *Madame Bovary*. Fictions are elaborate metaphors from which the other half of the equation has been stealthily removed; they are still metaphors, but not metaphors *of* anything. Sartre has always seemed to me a novelist and playwright who (no doubt working against Sartre the philosopher) is stealthily trying to put the other half of the equation back — to make the situations of his particular heroes *mean* something in terms of a universal human situation.

The felicity of *The Words* is that, as it is not fiction, Sartre is not called on to feel faith, and that he cannot refer to a universal child situation. There *is* a sounding-board to which his particular hero is continually referred, but it is another particular — the adult and, especially, the literary Sartre. Sartre traces the influence of his early reading on his later writing: sometimes explicitly — he says the blood-and-thunder conventions explain why Oreste, in *Les Mouches*, is so quick to take decisions; sometimes implicitly — when he says 'I was afraid of ... crabs', he presumably has the hero of *Les Séquestrés d'Altona* in mind; once without knowing what he

is doing — only in the light of his 'I had an epic mind' can I explain
Sartre's indeed epic blunder in applying the word 'epic' (*anything*
would have fitted better — 'limerick' would have fitted better) to
Genet's baroque masterpiece *Notre-Dame des Fleurs*.

By interleaving the adult and the child writer in himself, Sartre
seems to be working through — and reshaping — his acceptance of
his literary vocation. 'Like all dreamers,' he says, 'I confused
disenchantment with truth.' Did he make the same mistake about
his own talent? Knowing that his grandfather foisted the rôle on
him, and that he accepted it pretentiously, did he conclude that
his literary vocation was itself false? He almost persuades you that
it was. His 'One speaks in one's own language, one writes in a
foreign language' is the remark of a born teacher, not a born
writer. And yet: Sartre knows what only a writer can, the secret
of *why* writers write (a secret impenetrable even to Freud): he
wrote, he says, 'in order to be forgiven for my existence'.

Nowhere is Sartre's distrust of art (or of himself as artist) more
plainly figured than in the texture of his prose. As he correctly
says in *The Words*, 'I'm not a gifted writer ... I've been called
laboured.' But even in the labouring of his prose I've always
suspected an imposture. Sartre has been like a man with a flair
for dressing well who (confusing disenchantment with truth)
insists on wearing stained tweeds on the assumption that dandyism
must be false or frivolous. In his autobiography, however, he
makes a use of the French language which convinces me that in
recounting his relation to words he is reforming it. In sheer haste,
which may be inspired by sheer distaste for his child self, he beats
out a terse manner that is almost epigrammatic; he lets a few
aphorisms flower, providing they are quick-flowering; his sardonic
tone sometimes raises itself to an elegant irony. It is still a hurried,
perhaps shamed, dandyism — that of a man who would not like
to be seen lingering long enough at the mirror to get his bow-tie
straight: all the same, it *is* a bow-tie; the new Sartre style *is* a style.
And after all, as he points out, if he rejected the original terms of
his vocation, he went on writing. As one of his sub-epigrams puts
it, 'I've given up the office, but not the frock: I still write. What
else can I do?'

I suspect Sartre of being on the verge of realising that that is not the proper question: it should read 'Can I do it well?' The reason I suspect him of being about to get the question right is that he has already got the answer right. He can indeed write well—witness this charming fairy-tale whose hero is a little boy with a talent for *naïveté*. (In Sartre's version of the fairy-tale, what the little boy points out and what no one else has dared to say is that the *little boy* has no clothes on.)

Genet

Our Lady of the Flowers

by Jean Genet
translated by Bernard Frechtman
Introduction by Jean-Paul Sartre
[Anthony Blond, 1964]

London Magazine, June 1964

J'entends déjà tomber avec des chocs
    funèbres
Le bois retentissant sur le pavé des
    cours.

Thus Baudelaire: and the *retentissement*, having reverberated down a century, was caught up and reissued by the opening line of Jean Genet's long poem, 'Le Condamné à Mort':

Le vent qui roule un cœur sur le
    pavé des cours.

The first thing to realise (and Sartre, it seems, *doesn't* realise the first thing—or most of those that come after) is that Genet virtually *is* Baudelaire. Not that he's—except in the deliberate re-reverberations—an imitator. *Being* Baudelaire means being as original as Baudelaire. Genet is, however, a Baudelaire of the twentieth century, with the result that he writes finer poetry in prose than in verse. 'Le Condamné' is tinged with Reading Gaolery. It is the prose of 'Notre-Dame des Fleurs' which defines and realises the most cogent mythology of poetic images since Baudelaire's.

Our present disesteem of writing (or, more probably, our insensitivity to it) is bitterly shewn up by the fact that the English reviewers, approaching Genet as philosopher or sociologist, have scarcely noticed that he is a *writer*. This must be quite personally bitter to Mr Bernard Frechtman, who has made a brilliant translation into American: clever when need be—when Genet, seemingly defying translation, writes of himself as 'exilé aux confins de l'immonde (qui est du non-monde)', Mr Frechtman ingeniously comes up with ' ... the confines of the obscene (which is the off-scene of the world)'—but rising above cleverness to positive inspiration as constructions and paragraphs pursue and come excellently close to Genet's very cadences. The tiny points where one demurs are probably the fault of one or other of the languages concerned. That 'amours' comes out as 'carnal pleasures' must be blamed either on French for not possessing a separate word for sex or on the United States for not possessing the English middle-class tradition that everyone has at least boarding-school French, a tradition with some horrible implications but which would in this case have permitted 'amours' to stand untranslated except into italics—and would also have left the character called Mignon as Genet christened him, instead of which he is translated, and slightly watered-down, into Darling.

The fashion for scarcely noticing Genet's imagery is set by Sartre, who stands sentinel over this edition in a long introduction (consisting, in fact, of the relevant chapter from *Saint Genet*). True, Sartre has a section headed 'The Images'; but he turns out to mean things like Genet's 'will-to-unify', his desire to '*verify* his *conceptualism*' and his Platonism—which 'one would think ... at times' is 'a kind of Aristotelianism'. He is noble and grotesque, this impresario who, apparently blind and deaf to the talents of his prodigy, nonetheless intuitively—and generously—feels there is *something* in him, and goes stumbling round and round while he tries to think what on earth it can be. (Brilliance of metaphor, melody of language—you can shout the answers; but he only turns in another muddled circle, trying with good will to catch what you're saying.) There he stands, the gangling and admirable professor, goggling through his global spectacles, making lunges with his butterfly net—and above him swoops, sombre and solid, dazzling in smoothed black-and-white marble, a vast, wing-spread, baroque angel of death.

Genet's images are all of death: to be more precise, all of funerals. His is the imagery of the *chapelle ardente*. It is in seductively beautiful bad taste. The book starts with a shrine of faces torn from the illustrated papers, photographs Genet has stuck to the wall of his prison cell and whom he takes as his imaginary lovers when he masturbates on his 'straw mattress, which has already been stained by more than a hundred prisoners'. The faces make a 'merveilleuse éclosion de belles et sombres fleurs'—funeral flowers. All these handsome young men are murderers who have been executed. The heads, cut off in the photographs, have in fact been cut off by the guillotine. For 'the most purely criminal' of them Genet has made frames—'using the same beads with which the prisoners next door make funeral wreaths'. The form of the book is the stringing together of images into a funeral wreath. It is part meditation, part memory, part masturbation. The whole book is, according to Sartre, 'the epic of masturbation', but epic it is not: it is *not* a story, though it includes episodes of masterly narrative; and it is about sainthood, not heroism.

It was not Sartre who invented Saint Genet but Genet himself—in this book, where he is identified with the character named Divine: 'it is my own destiny ... that I am draping (at times a rag, at times a court robe) on Divine's shoulders.' 'Tantôt haillon, tantôt manteau de cour' ... but always female. Divine is an 'il' always referred to by Genet, and almost always by her own thoughts, as 'elle'. Only when the narrative goes back to her country childhood does Divine become for sustained passages 'il', the boy Lou Culafroy; once she has come to Paris, where she lives as a prostitute, sharing her attic with a succession, an attic frieze, of handsome 'macs', Divine is in permanent travesty: literally so in a phosphorescent night-scene at a drag party, and always so in imagination. On the very evening of her arrival in Paris, she rises from a café table 'wriggling in a spray of flowers and strewing swishes and spangles with an invisible furbelow'. Having estab-lished that Divine is himself, Genet goes on 'I want to strip her of every vestige of happiness so as to make a saint of her' — to make, in other words, Saint Genet, a saint in drag, like a doll-madonna in a lacy skirt.

Calling the book an epic, Sartre has ignored the information Genet gives: 'I raised egoistic masturbation to the dignity of a cult.' The whole nature of the book is stated in the *cult*. Genet does everything, strings his entire wreath, with—in the Catholic sense—an intention. His opening sequence is strung from a clutch of queers with flowering, frocked or girlish names—'Mimosa I, Mimosa II, Mimosa mi-IV, Première Communion, Angela, Monseigneur, Castagnette, Régine': a 'long litany', he calls them, 'of creatures who are glittering names'. These he threads (they themselves are carrying 'wreaths of glass beads, the very kind I make in my cell') into a black funeral cortège in the rain. (The priest leading it becomes lost in an erotic fantasy.) The funeral is of Divine herself. The book begins and ends with the death of Divine: in between, she has betrayed herself to the police for a minor crime, and a murderer has betrayed himself and been executed. Genet is having a masturbation fantasy, but he is also dedicating an altar. As he tells us at the start, meditating before his shrine of assassins, 'c'est en l'honneur de leurs crimes que j'écris mon livre.'

Noticing the insistence on hosts and masses, and the tributary garland of the title itself (in fact Notre-Dame des Fleurs is the name of the handsomest young murderer), Sartre mistakes the psychology of religious observance for religious faith, leaps at the notion of the ages of faith and hammers in his introduction at the idea of a medieval Genet. It is a ghastly howler, of the sort liable to be made by the tone-deaf. Anyone with an ear for a style—any antique dealer or auctioneer—could have told Sartre Genet is baroque. His essence is that he's post-Counter-Reformation. (It can even be demonstrated scholastically. Divine's death-blood is 'revealed with dramatic insistence, as does a Jesus the gilded chancre where gleams His flaming Sacred Heart'. The cult of the Sacred Heart was not observed before 1648.) Like the 'litanies' and the 'ex-voto dans le goût espagnol' of Baudelaire's vocabulary, Genet's is the overblown, peony-sized language of devotional flowers that did not come into existence until faith had been

challenged from outside. It is necessary, precisely, to *counter* the
Reformation: you must screw your eyes tight shut and *exclude* the
outside world — that is, you must *induce* the images.

As it happens, faith has been emptied out from this tight-shut
imaginary world. The idiom of rites and cults is employed to
induce a state not of grace but of mind. Genet says nothing about
religion, either way. It is his literature, not his faith, that is
Catholic. Linguistically and psychologically, the idiom of the
erotic and the idiom of the religious are the same; therefore the
two are wholly the same for Genet, who is utterly a psychological
linguist. When Notre-Dame des Fleurs is — 'la bouche ouverte en
o' — penetrated by Mignon ('sa queue lourde et lisse, aussi polie
et chaude qu'une colonne au soleil' — the cult practised by Genet's
imagination is a phallic cult), he is Bernini's St Teresa pierced to
the heart of ecstasy by an angelic spear. Indeed, one of Divine's
lovers is a soldier named Gabriel, whom Divine addresses as
'Archange'. And Genet is an ecstatic — 'mon âme de cambrioleur
extatique'. The *cambrioleur* is interchangeable with the saint. The
confessional is interchangeable with the outdoor lavatory in the
country (in both places 'the most secret part of human beings
came to reveal itself'), where the boy Culafroy 'roosts' ('juché
sur le siège de bois'), listening to the rain on the zinc roof and
aggravating his 'bien-être triste' by half-opening the door and
letting himself be desolated by the sight of 'the wet garden and the
pelted vegetables'. An invocation may in psychological fact be
offered interchangeably to a divinity or a lover. (We all pray
when we are in love — to the person we are in love with.) When
Divine is arrested on the boulevard, she is singing the *Veni, Creator*,
of which the essential item is the *Veni*, the inducing of a presence.
For Genet, the essential item throughout is that rites are performed with an intention, gestures are, like masses, offered — whom
or what for is not the point. First, induce the images. When they
exist to be dedicated, you can offer them to whom you will, just
as the 'thou' of a sonnet can be equated with whatever initials you
care to write at the top.

Sartre is for once construing Genet right when he traces to
masturbation fantasies the peculiar technique of Genet's story-

telling, whereby he admits to making up his characters as he goes along, dithers visibly about what form to make them up in, signals in advance that such a one will presently enter the book and sometimes leaves the reader free to imagine the dialogue two of them have on meeting. He is a resurrectionist, treating his characters like zombies. Even Divine, who is Genet, has to be led by the hand by Genet—to sainthood: 'Et moi, plus doux qu'un mauvais ange, par la main je la conduis.'

The technique of ushering his characters into the book permits Genet to create effects of baroque theatrically, as if he were seeing them onto the stage down a *trompe l'œil* avenue. Thus 'Our Lady of the Flowers here makes his solemn entrance through the door of crime, a secret door, that opens on to a dark but elegant stairway.' This is *trompe l'œil* indeed, for having effected Notre-Dame's entrance into the book Genet continues 'Our Lady mounts the stairway ... He is sixteen when he reaches the landing'—and at this point the narrative merges into actuality; the character is on a real landing, about to knock and go into a room and murder an old man.

The rhythm, whether of masturbation or of Genet's prose, is designed to induce the images to take on enough solidity and durability to be dwelt on. And it is interesting that Divine's sex life is lived almost wholly in the imagination. It is not only that most of the narrative is the product of Genet's masturbatory fantasy: even when the narrative steps wholly inside the play-within-a-play, the sexual acts with partners do not replace masturbation, on which Divine still depends to 'finish off'. The acts with others do not advance Divine towards direct sexual satisfaction; they serve to consolidate and sharpen the contrast on the images—so that in the end the images almost take off into a detached sex life, coupling and enjoying the process on their own.

Indeed, it is the images rather than the characters that Genet animates, which is why he is more poet than novelist. The independent life he charges them with is so erotic that it is no surprise to find them combining; they themselves are the population of a gallant and promiscuous society. Since the images combine, Genet's mythology is metamorphotic. (This is a point Sartre half-takes; he keeps using the word 'metamorphosis', but without much direction.) In two sentences heavy with nineteenth-century —with Second Empire—baroque, Genet includes and surpasses all the fusions of image and the evocations of décor attempted so pretentiously by *Marienbad*. Genet writes: 'For low masses are said at the end of the halls of big hotels, where the mahogany and marble light and blow out candles. A mingled burial service and marriage takes place there in secret from one end of the year to the other.'

That is the conjurer's *trompe l'œil* of the author who speaks of 'my taste for imposture, my taste for the sham, which could very well make me write on my visiting cards: "Jean Genet, bogus Count of Tillancourt".'

The furniture actually lights and blows out candles by one of Genet's most poignant devices, a fusion of images in the melting-moment of a syntactical plus semantic paradox. When Divine and her men leave the all-night drag party, 'the dawn was tight, a little tight, not very sure of itself, on the point of falling and vomiting'. And when the boy Culafroy waits in the moonlit country garden, among the washing, hoping the man he loves will come, 'La lune sonna dix heures.'

Indeed, the entire language of *Notre Dame des Fleurs* is built up from the grammatical metamorphosis of 'il' into 'elle'. From this flowers the queer *argot*—which is used only by 'male' queers; for Divine to use it would be as unseemly as 'whistling with her tongue and teeth ... or putting her hands in her trousers pockets and keeping them there'. Even so, the metamorphosis is never fixed. It is a film Genet can run backwards at will—and which he does, when, with the meticulous and dispassionate love of an early watercolourist recording exotic fauna, he describes that bizarre change of life that comes to queers at thirty, the moment when a beloved crosses over and becomes a lover. Suddenly Divine does whistle, does put her hands in her pockets—until she discovers that after all she 'had not become virile; she had aged. An adolescent now excited her ... '

I feel tolerably sure that this particular metamorphosis has a reflection in Genet's own name. (Is it his real one? He seems to

hint not by calling his boy-self Culafroy. Accident or assumption
as it may be, Genet is not the man to have failed to contemplate —
to make a cult of — his own name.) Take him straight and he is
un genet, a jennet, a Spanish horse — an image, to his mind, as
another of his transformation scenes demonstrates, of virility: but
put, as surely his own imagination often does put, a circumflex on
the second *e*, and he becomes some kind of flowering gorse or furze
— a companion to all those secondary characters named Mimosa
who weave a decorative and feminine garland through the book.

Genet plays paradoxes and transformations not only with
words and single images but with myths: Christian (Mignon goes
to church to pray 'Our Mother Which art in heaven ... ') or
pagan (Genet is *so* queer that for him it is the sailors who charm
the Sirens) or both (were Genet making Divine not in his own but
in the image of the men who command his love, he would make
her 'with flat and polished cheeks, heavy eyelids, pagan knees so
lovely that they reflected the desperate intelligence of the faces of
the mystics'). In describing Divine's love-making with Gabriel, he
starts from one metamorphosis — 'One night, the Archangel
turned faun' — and is led, by an associative chain, into a sustained
conceit in which he breath-takingly performs another: ' ... Gabriel
avait acquis une telle virtuosité qu'il pouvait, tout en restant
immobile lui-même, donner à sa verge un frémissement comparable à celui d'un cheval qui s'indigne. Il força avec sa rage
habituelle et ressentit si intensément sa puissance qu'il — avec sa
gorge et son nez — hennit de victoire, si impétueusement que
Divine crut que Gabriel de tout son corps de centaure la pénétrait ;
elle s'évanouit d'amour comme une nymphe dans l'arbre.'

The most astounding metamorphosis of all is the one which
transforms the images that activate Genet's personal erotic tastes
(which few do and some cannot even expect to share) into poetry,
poetry being, precisely, a universal imagery of eroticism, which
provokes the imagination to an intangible but all the same completely sensual erection — a universal love-language which is,
however, in fact understood by fewer readers than French and
practised by fewer devotees than the most esoteric sexual per-
version.

Personal

My Mother

Sunday Telegraph, August 1964

Whenever I see a reference to that most poetically named of operas 'The Lady Macbeth of Mtsensk',* I think of my mother. My mother is the Lady Macbeth of (at the moment) sw5 — a woman born to utter 'Infirm of purpose! Give me the daggers.'

Not that she is likely to commit murder, which is against her principles. But if she did she would carry it through resolutely, and get away with it. Judge and jury would, in one of her own favourite expressions, eat out of her hand. (Her fondness for the expression may reflect the remarkable way she has with cats, who will eat out of my mother's hand melon, grapes, pineapple or whatever she happens to be eating herself while they are on her lap — I am not speaking of those cats whose idiosyncrasy it is to like fruit, but of cats who would not ordinarily dream of eating any such thing but who take it from my mother for the sheer pleasure of sharing her diet.)

Neither would she stand for any insubordination from her own conscience. Shakespeare's Lady Macbeth was by comparison weak and conventional-minded. I cannot imagine my mother losing two minutes' repose in remorseful sleep-walking. If she had done murder she would come straight out and avow the *fact*: but that does not mean she would for an instant consider herself *guilty*. My mother has given so much of her life to good deeds that she no longer distinguishes whether she does the deeds because they are good or whether they are good because done by her. If she murdered, it is the moral standing of murder which would have to be modified, not the moral standing of my mother, who is so used to being on the side of the angels that, were she now suddenly to change sides, she would expect the angels — like customers following the under-hairdresser when he sets up on his own — to cross over with her.

When, as a schoolgirl or an undergraduate, I took friends home,

* Sometimes now played under a less poetic title.

I was often asked for an advance account of my mother. I would give the brief facts: she has been headmistress, amateur hospital nurse and prison visitor (chairman, until serious illness stopped her, of the 'Lady Visitors' at Holloway); she goes indefatigably to church, especially at the least convenient times of day and week; no one has ever defeated her over a biblical quotation or a Latin declension; she eats nothing that contains sugar during Advent and Lent; she was one of the bravest Air Raid Wardens in London; and her combination of physical courage with impatience is such that she usually tells the dentist not to bother with the injection before he pulls out the tooth.

On this basis my friends prepared themselves to meet that common English character, the battleaxe. Impossible to warn them how much rarer and keener a blade my mother is. When they met her they were mown down in their hundreds by her charm.

Whereas the battleaxe shouts and looks even larger than she is because she is always mentally on a horse, my mother, who is often mentally on a trampoline, bounces so perpetually up and down that she looks smaller than the middle height she is, and courteously adapts her voice to her interlocutor's comfort. She has a pretty little figure and the legs of a pin-up, dresses well and has a flair for scent and for hats — which she buys for about 10s each in department stores in Paris and wears not quite so much provocatively as evocatively: behind an eye-veil her shapeless small nose and curry-coloured irises turn into delicate smudges, and she achieves, like some French period films, a ravishing pastiche of Impressionism. It was at her most Impressionist, at once crisp and melting, that she came, one high summer day, to visit me when I was up at Oxford. I remember that she spent the afternoon rolling down the slope of the college lawn — calling challenges to undergraduates, quite a lot of whom had collected to watch, to come and race her.

Antecedents do not explain my mother. Her background is interesting less for what it made her into than for what she made of it. She comes from a milieu which is now losing its solidity — or at least its self-importance — and ceasing to have the courage of its eccentricities: the provincial professional classes. Her father, son of a parson, was an architect who emigrated to Chicago in the hope of finding work in the rebuilding after the big fire, taking with him his Scottish wife. (It may be the Anglo-Scots combination or it may be the finesse of her own ear and her own innocence of class consciousness which resulted in my mother's speaking the purest English I have ever heard.) My mother was born, just before the start of this century, in Chicago, thereby acquiring dual nationality. However, when she was three, the family returned to England. Indirectly, the return was caused by my mother's mother, who belonged to a sect called by the outside world the Irvingites and by itself the Catholic Apostolic Church. To this she had converted her husband and she was, according to my mother, a touch piqued when presently her convert outdid her by being ordained a minister of what was after all *her* religion. He gave up architecture and America and became the Irvingite bishop (or, in the charming Irvingite terminology, Angel) of Liverpool.

There, although the Angel was much poorer than his parishioners (the Irvingites inclined towards a rich membership), his children led the conventional life of the time and place — nanny, nursery tea, the key to the gardens in the square — touched into eccentricity by the names their father gave them. An infatuated and autodidact Greek scholar, he not so much gave them Greek names as emptied the Greek vocabulary over them. My mother alone got a name — Charis — which can be, although it seldom is, a name in classical Greek; the others' names are mere common nouns. The eldest, a boy, was called the Greek for 'gift'. The youngest, another boy, is more noncommittally called the Greek for 'male'. The two girls are perhaps lucky to have been christened in Greek instead of English since their names mean 'Grace' and 'Violet'.

My mother rebelled against the snobbery of her home and its anti-feminism. For the boys there was Greek and Oxford. My mother had to make do with Latin and — after she had served in France as a Waac and amateur pierrot — Liverpool University, where she met my father, an Irishman of at that time poetic temperament, luminous purity and Sinn Fein politics.

She never rebelled against her religion. When she asked me to teach her Greek, it was so that she might read the New Testament. Much of my childhood was spent with my mother in Gordon Square (my parents settled in London a little before I was born) in the excellent Gothic Revival church the Irvingites had built there in 1854, where I was hypnotised by a liturgy composed — less felicitously — in Gothic Revival prose.

The Irvingites took their popular name (which I was never told — I came on it, when I was grown-up, in a magazine article) from Edward Irving, a Scot who became a star preacher in London during the 1820s and '30s. His sect had, if it is not a contradiction in terms, an oecumenical intention, and compiled its liturgy from the Orthodox, Catholic and Anglican rites. The services were so long that they might have consisted of the three rites tacked together in their entirety, and they could be prolonged further still because everything was held up if one of the congregation felt moved to 'prophesy'. A deacon took down the prophet's words in shorthand as they were spoken, and a committee afterwards sat in judgment on them; if they were found to be inspired by the Holy Ghost they were roneoed and circulated. All the prophesying I heard consisted of patchwork quotations from the Bible — perhaps on the theory that the committee would find it hard to deny the inspiration of those.

I record these memories because so far as I know no one will ever attend a full-dress Irvingite service again. The movement had built into it an idea which is characteristic of the early nineteenth-century romanticism to which it belongs. It was so far 'half in love with easeful Death' as to intend its own extinction. Its founders called themselves Apostles, and they alone could ordain priests. In default of the Second Coming, which was literally expected, the clergy was destined to die out and the congregations to return to the several communions from which they had come. The Gordon Square church has now been given to London University.

Since I grew up I have differed from my mother on every fundamental issue and agreed with her on every practical one (except that she wins my admiration by being so much more practical than I am). We differ about religion (I am a rationalist) and about art. My mother is naturally sensitive to most arts and takes a favouring, indeed a protective, attitude towards them. Sometimes she goes so far as to imply that she is the only champion the poor things have in the world, and does not scruple to imply that everyone else is a philistine with a hatchet in his hand. She once silenced my husband, who is a Deputy Keeper at the National Gallery and a person not easily silenced, by pleading with him 'But, Michael darling, don't you think *some* of the pictures in the National Gallery are beautiful?'

My mother's artistic crime is her determination to think *all* pictures, anywhere, together with all poems, novels and pieces of music, beautiful. In other words, she does not take art seriously. She will not recognise that universal charity towards works of art makes nonsense of art; that a person without discrimination is without appreciation; that in art destruction is implicit in creation. 'You see,' she says gently, ignoring these arguments and implying that anyone who advances them is a thug, 'I prefer construction to destruction.' If you put it to her that great art can be constructed only by the artist's ruthless weeding out of those of his ideas which are not artistically fit to live, you can read on her face that such weeding out is tantamount to infanticide.

It is perhaps hard on my mother that both her husband and her only child should have been professional writers. As a matter of fact, it would be difficult to name two writers more different than my father and myself. We never agreed what *is* good art or bad art, yet we were at one in our preoccupation with the problem, and we were together distinguished by temperament from my mother, whose theological beliefs pervade her whole life, and who cannot get it into her head that, although the artist has borrowed the moralist's terms, he gives a quite different meaning to the word 'good'.

My father's temperament my mother accepted whole, out of her immense love and admiration for him. In me she swallows it by a conscious and honourable—and loving—exercise of tolerance, which she has extended to me since I came of age. Even when I was a churchgoer, she suspected me of artistic idolatry—that I chose my church for its architecture or its singing. She asked me once if I would like to contribute to a fund for repairing the roof of what is undoubtedly (I make this sweeping claim in full knowledge of what I am saying) the most hideous church in the entire suburbs of London. I said that I would gladly give to a fund for pulling the church down but could not in conscience give a penny towards patching it up. My mother found this amusing, laughed and continued to hold out her hand for my donation towards the roof. When no donation came she said 'You don't mean you *meant* that funny remark?' I replied 'You didn't suppose I didn't?' We were both shocked.

My mother finds it hard to believe that I actually *act* on my artistic or rational perceptions: she herself acts only on promptings she holds to be beyond both art and reason. Sometimes it is a matter of God's will, sometimes of her own. She finds it hard to believe I mean what I say, because what she herself says often expresses her perception not of a fact but of her or God's will. If she knows Tim and Tom hate one another, she is likely to take Tim aside and tell him Tom thinks him a dear fellow, and vice versa. She is expressing her absolute conviction that they *ought* to think one another dear fellows. Likewise, when she says it has stopped raining, she is expressing her absolute determination to go for a picnic. When you get outside and remark that it is still raining, my mother says it is slackening off. You point out that on the contrary it is just turning into a real downpour. 'Well what does it matter anyway?' my mother says. 'Are you so soft you can't stand a drop of rain?'

Her immeasurable will is the source of the immeasurable good my mother does for the poor, the sick and, particularly, the imprisoned, whose sufferings are all the more bitter because they are deliberately inflicted on them by other human beings — acting at the behest of our vindictively materialistic law. When it comes to making good their loss by theft, the law places a curiously high value on material objects — so high that it cannot be calculated in money but has to be reckoned up in time taken out of the thief's life. To put a person in prison for ten years is nothing less than to shorten his life by ten years, because, as anyone who has visited a prison knows, life 'inside' is not life, the prisoner being deprived of

surprise, suspense and having to choose between alternatives—
which are the very medium in which human life is carried on. We
no longer crop our thieves' ears, but we still crop their years: to
imprison a man for a decade is exactly equivalent to, and exactly
as cruel as, performing on him some mutilation which would
shorten by a decade his life expectation.

On these matters my mother and I, for our different reasons,
quite agree. Similarly, we are both egalitarians, I because I have
noticed the power of privilege and detest its injustice, she because
snobberies and titles are to her absurd affectations which she
can't, as she says, 'be doing with'—to the extent that she can't be
bothered to get them right. I have heard her, as a hostess making
the introductions, introduce a married couple as 'Sir John and
Mrs X'—and give, of course, not the least offence in the world.
Sometimes I think she regards even one's proper name as an
absurd affectation. She uses the name of my six-year-old daughter,
Kate, interchangeably with my own. 'Brigid', she told a friend
recently, 'is getting on quite well with her writing.' The friend
nodded. 'And', my mother continued, 'she can read even quite
hard words now.'

Off duty, so to speak, my mother's inexhaustible will makes her
life an unending competition. She has engaged in every sport that
does not involve atrocity, and nowadays engages herself
emotionally when she watches sport on television. If anything in
me disappoints my mother more than my reasonableness, it is that
I am almost pathologically non-competitive. I decline to enter
any competition I cannot be sure of losing. Luckily, my daughter is
more spirited; and when she incites my mother by claiming she
can twist, my mother hauls her skirts above her nice knees and
twists better. My mother will make a competition out of anything:
dispute the derivation of a word with her, and she will cry 'Bet
you sixpence' over her shoulder as she goes to fetch the dictionary.

There is no expertise she does not believe she can practise better
than the expert. (Soon after marrying a novelist she wrote and
published a novel herself.) She relies not on skill but on will. Not
only does she think the law exaggerates the value of material
objects; she thinks anyone craven who concedes anything, even

respect, to the properties of material objects. Faced with a tin of sardines, she *defies* it to keep her out; she forces objects, too, to compete with her. It is true she will never take over the dagger from an irresolute murderer, but with the substitution of any other implement Lady Macbeth's speech is forever on my mother's lips: Infirm of purpose! Give *me* the tin-opener, the hockey-stick, the map, the bedpan, the steering wheel … I am interpreting for her. What she really says is 'Give me the thingummy'—for, of course, if in her eyes it is slightly pretentious of a *person* to have a name of his own, it is ridiculous of an inert object to lay claim to one. Other people say 'thingummy' abjectly, as a weak prop for a confessedly lame memory. From my mother it comes with force, as an expression of her scorn for objects that impede her will—with such force, indeed, that I cannot think how Shakespeare created his Lady Macbeth, or how his vocabulary ever passed for rich, without recourse to the word.

Am I An Irishwoman?

New Statesman, November 1965

Ever since Mr Bernard Levin demanded of himself in the *New Statesman* 'Am I A Jew?', I have been hearing a small voice which from time to time asks me 'Are you an Irishwoman?'

To ascribe this voice to a leprechaun would come easily to me, since leprechauns seem to run in — or, more precisely, run after — my family. My father once committed an infinitesimal misdemeanour on the island of Achill and was pursued down a quite empty, fuchsia-hedged lane by a voice asking 'Sean, Sean, what have you done?' Even at the time (I was six), I was interested, when my father recounted this to me, in the leprechaun's acumen. To reproach my father in English was no more than politic of it, since my father had little Gaelic, yet it made an appeal to his patriotism by translating his name — which was in fact not Sean at all but John. My fantasy, in which this story has been lodged ever since, could now go very fluently on to a hypothesis that there is a whole family of *them* devoted to pursuing with nagging questions the family of *us*. What's more, I'll bet I know where they come from: a small place just about in the middle of Ireland, called (the existence of this place is probably not widely known, so I make a free gift of it to any readers who, exasperated by my Irish rationality, may have been searching for the apt adjective to prefix to my name) Ballybrophy.

However, the voice of that rationality within me knows very well how to answer the voice that nags me. The correct reply is 'Nonsense, you're no leprechaun and I'm no Irishwoman.' By nativity, schooling and economics I am English. I speak the usual modified cockney of a Paulina. Only on the telephone, whose tricks there is no accounting for anyway, is my intonation sometimes taken for Irish. Apart from the rationality I have mentioned, which occasionally irritates people in England (a country where 'reasonable' is not a word of praise when applied to thoughts or arguments but only when applied to prices), I possess none of the standard Irish characteristics. My pen may have the gift of the gab but my tongue hasn't. I am fond but frightened of horses in the horseflesh and bored by them as mathematical prospects to gamble on. It's true I go quite often to Dublin but only because it's a beautiful city and my cousins there are dears. I *can* (I've tested it) assume Irish speech well enough to pass for a native, but so can many an English raconteur of supposedly funny stories, and anything I gain on the spoken I lose on the written word. Ireland deprives me of my very literacy. I've naturally mastered the more elementary ones like Dun Laoghaire and Cobh, but I can't feel anything other than a foreigner in a land most of whose geography and history I have not the smallest idea how to pronounce.

And yet. The geography and history of Ireland hold my imagination in a melancholy magic spell. Dublin and Limerick are cities beautiful to me not only with some of the most superb and most neglected architecture in Europe but with a compelling litany, a whole folklore, of tragic and heroic associations. At an Abbey Theatre performance when I was in Dublin earlier this year I discovered I cannot sit through *Cathleen ni Houlihan* without crying. Still, I don't believe this is because I am, if I am, Irish. There are some reasons for it in my personal and family history, but I think it is chiefly for the simple reason that the history of Ireland is unbearably sad.

To the voice which urges that I am mainly Irish by blood, I make the round reply that, nonsense, my blood is entirely Group O. I don't believe in 'blood' in that sense any more than I believe in leprechauns. But it is true that my exact sociological situation is too complex to allow me to make the simple assertion that I am English. I reject what has sometimes presented itself to me as an Irish fatality in my personal life, whereby, set loose in an English environment, I seem to have made more Irish choices than chance would warrant: the dearest to me of my contemporary fellow-writers is Irish; and were I superstitious I would certainly make something of the curious fact that I chose to marry an Irishman without even knowing that he was one—and thereby ensured that, whereas neither he nor I is Irish on both sides of our ancestry, our child is more Irish than either of her parents. I rigorously refuse to read this as a compulsion in the blood, but I suspect it may reflect a community and affinity of temperament among people brought up between two nationalities—and they, of course, include (as other personal choices of mine symptomise) wandering Jews and wanderers between the continents or the social classes.

Though in one pleasing respect I'm not treated as a foreigner in Ireland (it's the only place on earth where people spell my name correctly), I feel a foreigner there: but I feel a foreigner in England, too. I was brought up to do so. I belong by upbringing to a highly specialised class (though I wouldn't be surprised if numerically it's larger than the population of Eire): those who are reared *as Irish* in England. The Anglo-Irish come from English who went over, intermarried and grew into the Ascendancy. We're representatives of the opposite process. It is from a Descendancy in Ireland that we Irish-English originate. We were squeezed out from the bottom layer of the country by poverty and English oppression, and came to England to take advantage there of the affluence and tolerance the English never exported to Ireland. In England we remain, generation after generation, as immigrants. We are as unassimilable as the Jews—who have only their religion to set them apart from the rest of the community, whereas the Irish are set apart from the rest by the fact that their fierce religious divisions set them apart even one from another.

People of the Irish-English class have, of course, distinguishing marks of speech and thought. They are without social snobbery, and preserve an ancestral dread and detestation of the poverty which is the disease of Ireland. Not only do they wear shamrocks on Saint Patrick's Day; they are intensely pedantic about the word *shamrocks*, some of them insisting, as I was brought up to do, that it is a word which occurs only in the plural and others, of course, insisting the opposite. Indeed, they are more than average pedants in general ('Shaw is the greatest pedant alive,' he wrote in one of his third-person accounts of himself, but the least of us could say the same) and are most particularly pedantic about the names of Irish things, where, now that I think of it, the point of the pedantry quite often* turns on that question of singular or plural: heaven help you if you speak of the Custom House in Dublin as the Customs House (though you will get away very easily with not noticing that it's one of the handsomest buildings on earth).

Their other speech tricks result simply from perpetuating a literal translation of a language they have long forgotten in a language they continue to speak with the clumsiness of a foreigner. Ignoring the fact that English *does* possess the handy words 'Yes' and 'No', they, like characters in the New Testament, reply to questions by the cumbersome formula of repeating the words of the question re-arranged as a negative or affirmative statement. Since, as foreigners, they manipulate English logically instead of idiomatically, when it's their turn to ask a question they say 'amn't I?' instead of 'aren't I?' (This usage made me much laughed-at as a child in England, but though it's still the one that comes naturally to my lips I notice I have scarcely any occasion to use it now; one's schooldays must have been much fuller than adulthood is of rhetorical contexts requiring the final, self-vindicating 'amn't I?') And above all, of course, they entertain the vision of a Promised Land. Ireland inevitably figures to them as a terrestrial paradise which it is their life's quest to regain, because they all spent, as I did at six, the long, nostalgia-bearing holidays of childhood among its fuchsias and leprechauns.

But if this makes them all romantics, it should also make them all disillusioned romantics and thus give them at least the pre-requisites for turning into rational people. The Irish-English, touched with two nationalities but belonging to none, should know, if anyone does, that the worst thing an oppressor imposes, when it holds down a nation, is nationalism; the ultimate wickedness committed by England was to drive Ireland into a nationalistic act of cutting off its nose to spite its face — whereupon it is not the nose but the now independent national face that withers. Likewise, they, if anyone, should know the bitter folly of religious intolerance. In Ireland, there are three permissible answers,

---

* Another instance: where the English and the Americans shout 'O boy', some of the Irish shout 'O boys'.

Catholic, Protestant and Jewish, to the eternal question 'What is your religion?' I, who have to answer 'None', am in Ireland neither a foreigner nor an Irishwoman but an invisible woman; and my husband and I, an ex-Catholic and an ex-Protestant united in happy rationalism (which is the dreadful state each side has feared all along the other would lead to), are the invisible married couple with an invisible child whom it would be, I surmise, virtually impossible for us to educate in Ireland. For this or a hundred other reasons, the Promised Land of the Irish-English class is one which most of them can't return to. The last and most ironic tragedy of Irish history is that though Ireland freed itself from the English it did not acquire English freedom. A year or two ago I stood, an invisible woman (and author of banned books) in one of the finest bookshops in Dublin and copied down the notice pinned to one of the bookcases: 'There are over 8,000 books banned in Ireland. If by chance we have one on display, please inform us, and it will be DESTROYED.'

I am not English, but I am a British citizen, grateful for the tolerance which has given refuge to unassimilable, unrepatriable and sometimes awkwardly rational third-generation immigrants like me. And almost as soon as I have finished setting out the love and disillusion I bear Ireland, my husband and I will be setting out for Wexford, there to hear a performance of *La Finta Giardiniera* or, as it will very likely be billed, *La Feinta Giaoirdieniairaigh* or some such. We shall, of course, be taking our more Irish than ourselves daughter with us for the first Irish holiday of her childhood.